Oracle® DBA

INTERACTIVE WORKBOOK

D1289159

ISBN 0-13-015742-2

90000

9 780130 157423

PRENTICE HALL PTR ORACLE INTERACTIVE WORKBOOKS SERIES

- Baman Motivala
  Oracle Forms Interactive Workbook
  0-13-015808-9

- Benjamin Rosenzweig & Elena Silvestrova
  Oracle PL/SQL Interactive Workbook
  0-13-015743-0

- Alex Morrison & Alice Rischert
  Oracle SQL Interactive Workbook
  0-13-015745-7

- Melanie Caffrey & Douglas Scherer
  Oracle DBA Interactive Workbook
  0-13-015742-2

Oracle® DBA

INTERACTIVE WORKBOOK

MELANIE CAFFREY

DOUGLAS SCHERER

Prentice Hall PTR
Upper Saddle River, NJ 07458
www.phptr.com

Production Supervisor: Wil Mara
Acquisitions Editor: Tim Moore
Technical Editors: Allen Riberdy & Carol Brennan
Editorial Assistant: Allyson Kloss
Marketing Manager: Debby van Dijk
Buyer: Maura Zaldivar
Manufacturing Manager: Alexis Heydt
Cover Designer: Nina Scuderi
Cover Design Direction: Jerry Votta
Series Interior Design: Meryl Poweski
Art Director: Gail Cocker-Bogusz
Composition: Pine Tree Composition

© 2001 Prentice Hall PTR
Prentice-Hall, Inc.
Upper Saddle River, NJ 07458

The publisher offers discounts on this book when ordered in bulk quantities. For more information contact: Corporate Sales Department, Prentice Hall PTR, One Lake Street, Upper Saddle River, NJ 07458. Phone: 800-382-3419; FAX: 201-236-7141; E-mail: corpsales@prenhall.com

Printed in the United States of America

10 9 8 7 6 5 4 3 2

ISBN 0-13-015742-2

Prentice-Hall International (UK) Limited, *London*
Prentice-Hall of Australia Pty. Limited, *Sydney*
Prentice-Hall Canada Inc., *Toronto*
Prentice-Hall Hispanoamericana, S.A., *Mexico*
Prentice-Hall of India Private Limited, *New Delhi*
Prentice-Hall of Japan, Inc., *Tokyo*
Pearson Education Asia Pte. Ltd.
Editora Prentice-Hall do Brasil, Ltda., *Rio de Janeiro*

To my parents, Frances and Donald
Melanie Caffrey

To my parents, Helene and Bernie
Douglas Scherer

FROM THE EDITOR

Prentice Hall's Interactive Workbooks are designed to get you up and running fast, with just the information you need, when you need it.

We are certain that you will find our unique approach to learning simple and straightforward. Every chapter of every Interactive Workbook begins with a list of clearly defined Learning Objectives. A series of labs make up the heart of each chapter. Each lab is designed to teach you specific skills in the form of exercises. You perform these exercises at your computer and answer pointed questions about what you observe. Your answers will lead to further discussion and exploration. Each lab then ends with multiple-choice Self-Review Questions, to reinforce what you've learned. Finally, we have included Test Your Thinking projects at the end of each chapter. These projects challenge you to synthesize all of the skills you've acquired in the chapter.

Our goal is to make learning engaging, and to make you a more productive learner.

And you are not alone. Each book is integrated with its own "Companion Website." The website is a place where you can find more detailed information about the concepts discussed in the Workbook, additional Self-Review Questions to further refine your understanding of the material, and perhaps most importantly, where you can find a community of other Interactive Workbook users working to acquire the same set of skills that you are.

All of the Companion Websites for our Interactive Workbooks can be found at `http://www.phptr.com/phptrinteractive`.

Timothy C. Moore
V. P., Executive Editor
Prentice Hall PTR

CONTENTS

ABOUT THE AUTHORS   *xiii*

FOREWORD   *xv*

ACKNOWLEDGMENTS   *xvii*

INTRODUCTION   *xxi*

CHAPTER 1 THE DATABASE ADMINISTRATOR'S JOB   *1*

    LAB 1.1 The Role of the Oracle DBA   *2*

        1.1.1 Understand About Becoming a DBA   *3*

        1.1.2 Understand the Role of the DBA   *3*

    LAB 1.2 Sources for Oracle DBA Help   *6*

        1.2.1 Prepare for Tasks   *8*

        1.2.2 Find Oracle Help   *9*

    CHAPTER 1 Test Your Thinking   *13*

CHAPTER 2 CREATING YOUR DATABASE   *15*

    LAB 2.1 OFA Basics   *16*

        2.1.1 Identify your ORACLE_BASE Location   *17*

        2.1.2 Identify your ORACLE_HOME Directory   *18*

        2.1.3 Identify and Configure your Admin Directory   *19*

        2.1.4 Identify the Location for your Database Files *20*

    **LAB 2.2 Creating and Configuring
an Oracle Database**   *25*

        2.2.1 Edit the Instance Configuration File   *28*

        2.2.2 Write Scripts to Create the Database   *34*

        2.2.3 Create the Database Using the Create Scripts *39*

        2.2.4 Test Database Viability   *44*

        2.2.5 Set the ROLLBACK_SEGMENTS Parameter   *46*

2.2.6 Review the Scripts That Create the Data Dictionary   47

CHAPTER 2 Test Your Thinking   56

**CHAPTER 3 ORACLE NETWORKING: CONFIGURING BASIC
NET8/SQL*NET COMPONENTS**   57

LAB 3.1 Setting up Network Configuration Files   58
3.1.1 Manually Configure the tnsnames.ora File   58
3.1.2 Manually Configure the listener.ora File   62

LAB 3.2 Managing the Oracle Listener   67
3.2.1 Start and Stop the Listener   68
3.2.2 Issue Other Listener Commands   70
3.2.3 Perform a Loopback Test   71

LAB 3.3 Configuring the Multi-Threaded Server   76
3.3.1 Configure and View Information about
the MTS Environment   76

CHAPTER 3 Test Your Thinking   81

CHAPTER 4 TABLESPACES   83

LAB 4.1 Tablespaces: Logical Areas of Storage   85
4.1.1 What a Tablespace is   87
4.1.2 What a Tablespace is Used For   87

**LAB 4.2 How Tablespaces Relate to the Oracle
Database and How to Manipulate Them**   91
4.2.1 Understand The Relationship of Tablespaces
to Physical Files   93
4.2.2 Create a Tablespace   94
4.2.3 Delete a Tablespace   95

CHAPTER 4 Test Your Thinking   102

CHAPTER 5 SEGMENTS AND EXTENTS   103

LAB 5.1 Segments   104
5.1.1 Define a Segment   104
5.1.2 Identify Common Segment Types   105

LAB 5.2 Extents   111
5.2.1 Define an Extent   111
5.2.2 Understand Segment and Extent Parameters   113

5.2.3 Understand Free Space   115
CHAPTER 5 Test Your Thinking   127

CHAPTER 6 DATA BLOCKS   129
LAB 6.1 Units of Storage Called Data Blocks   130
6.1.1 Define a Block   130
6.1.2 Understand the Makeup of a Block   134
6.1.3 Recognize the Physical Record Format   135
LAB 6.2 Block-Level Storage Parameters   145
6.2.1 Understand Block-Level Storage Parameters   145
6.2.2 Understand Row Migration and Row Chaining   149
6.2.3 Understand Free Lists   151
CHAPTER 6 Test Your Thinking   156

CHAPTER 7 REDO LOGS   157
LAB 7.1 Redo Logs   158
7.1.1 Understand Why Redo Logs Are Important   158
7.1.2 Understand How LGWR Writes To Redo Logs   161
LAB 7.2 Recovering Data with Redo Logs   170
7.2.1 Understand How Redo Logs Are Used
      In Recovering Lost Data   170
CHAPTER 7 Test Your Thinking   178

CHAPTER 8 DATAFILES   179
LAB 8.1 Datafiles   180
8.1.1 Understand Datafiles   180
8.1.2 Understand the Relationship between Datafiles
      and an Instance   182
LAB 8.2 Manipulating Your Datafiles   189
8.2.1 Create, Manipulate, and Delete a Datafile   189
CHAPTER 8 Test Your Thinking   199

CHAPTER 9 USER CREATION   201
LAB 9.1 Creating and Manipulating Users   202
9.1.1 Create and Manipulate Users   202
CHAPTER 9 Test Your Thinking   215

CHAPTER 10 PRIVILEGE AND RESOURCE GROUPS   *217*

LAB 10.1 Creating and Manipulating Privileges   *218*
    10.1.1 Create and Manipulate Privileges   *218*

LAB 10.2 Creating and Manipulating Roles   *230*
    10.2.1 Create and Manipulate Roles   *230*

LAB 10.3 Creating and Manipulating Profiles   *237*
    10.3.1 Create and Manipulate Profiles   *237*

CHAPTER 10 Test Your Thinking   *249*

CHAPTER 11 AUDITING   *251*

LAB 11.1 Auditing Sessions, Auditing Database Actions, and Auditing Objects   *252*
    11.1.1 Audit Sessions, Audit Database Actions, and Audit Objects   *252*

CHAPTER 11 Test Your Thinking   *269*

CHAPTER 12 ROLLBACK SEGMENTS   *271*

LAB 12.1 Rollback Segment Management   *272*
    12.1.1 Configure and Maintain Rollback Segments   *272*

CHAPTER 12 Test Your Thinking   *294*

CHAPTER 13 LOCKING   *295*

LAB 13.1 Locking and Data Consistency and Concurrency   *296*
    13.1.1 Create, Review, and Eliminate Locks   *296*

CHAPTER 13 Test Your Thinking   *310*

CHAPTER 14 LOGICAL BACKUP AND RECOVERY   *311*

LAB 14.1 Backup and Recovery Using the Import and Export Utilities   *312*
    14.1.1 Perform a Logical Backup Using the Export Utility   *312*
    14.1.2 Perform a Logical Recovery Using the Import Utility   *315*

CHAPTER 14 Test Your Thinking   *325*

CHAPTER 15 PHYSICAL BACKUP AND RECOVERY   *327*

   LAB 15.1 Backup and Recovery Using Archivelog Mode   *328*

      15.1.1 Perform a Physical Backup and Perform Different Types of Archiving   *328*

      15.1.2 Simulate a Media Failure   *338*

      15.1.3 Perform a Complete Offline Recovery   *341*

      15.1.4 Perform a Complete Online Recovery   *344*

   CHAPTER 15 Test Your Thinking   *364*

CHAPTER 16 APPLICATION AND SQL OPTIMIZATION   *365*

   LAB 16.1 Using the AUTOTRACE Command and TKPROF Utility   *366*

      16.1.1 Set up SQL*Plus's AUTOTRACE Utility   *373*

      16.1.2 Determine the Optimizer Mode   *374*

      16.1.3 Analyze Tables and Indexes   *375*

      16.1.4 Interpret the Output of the Execution Plan   *376*

      16.1.5 Use the TKPROF Utility   *377*

   CHAPTER 16 Test Your Thinking   *401*

CHAPTER 17 DATABASE TUNING AND OPTIMIZATION   *403*

   LAB 17.1 Optimizing the Use of Memory and Disk Resources   *404*

      17.1.1 Gather Performance Statistics   *404*

      17.1.2 Monitor and Enhance Memory Usage   *407*

      17.1.3 Determine I/O Distribution and Level of Contention   *413*

      17.1.4 Analyze Performance Statistics   *414*

   CHAPTER 17 Test Your Thinking   *425*

APPENDIX A ANSWERS TO SELF-REVIEW QUESTIONS   *427*

APPENDIX B RECOMMENDED READING LIST   *439*

APPENDIX C RAID SYNOPSIS   *441*

APPENDIX D ENVIRONMENT SETTINGS TO REMEMBER   *443*

INDEX   *449*

ABOUT THE AUTHORS

MELANIE CAFFREY

Before entering the world of Oracle and database technology in general, Melanie Caffrey was a researcher, first for the academic world in Colorado, then for the corporate world in New York. The desire to explore a new career path led her to Columbia University's Computer Technology and Applications (CTA) Program, which ultimately changed her life. Shortly before finishing at Columbia, she began developing applications using SAP technology with an Oracle database. Additionally, she enjoys spending a semester or two, here and there, teaching the class that is the foundation for this book and, occasionally, introductory courses in SQL and the Oracle Server, to the students at Columbia University's CTA program.

DOUGLAS SCHERER

Douglas Scherer (Chauncey and OCP certified) is president of Core Paradigm (www.coreparadigm.com), providing consulting, guidance, and formal training solutions primarily to Oracle users. He is a frequent speaker at conferences and user group meetings internationally and has appeared in *Visions of the New Millennium*, a series seen on PBS and its affiliates. Mr. Scherer's 12 years of IT and database experience has spanned analysis, design, implementation, database management, and project management. He is lead author of *Oracle 8i Tips & Techniques*, contributing editor to the *Oracle Designer Handbook*, second edition, both published by Osborne/McGraw-Hill (Oracle Press), and has articles in *Oracle Magazine*. Mr. Scherer is an instructor in Columbia University's CTA program and for three years held the position of Chair of the Database Track.

FOREWORD

As we move into the new millennium, the reality of the impact of technology on our everyday lives is never more apparent. As this impact grows, so too has the number of adults and professionals that attempt to dip their minds into the field of technology. As educators we see the need to help our students challenge themselves in order to transform them into more critical and reflective people. Indeed, to help people transform is to teach them how to learn and apply what they have learned.

Information technology and education together form an interesting challenge, for we see the "mountaintop" as the awakening of a student who understands logical concepts and how to apply them in a workplace environment. While theory provides the construct for critical thinking, "applied" learning presents so many of us with an interesting dilemma: how do we know that what we teach is effectively used by our students? Furthermore, true workplace success goes beyond just technical knowledge. With technology affecting every facet of business, even the protected "techies" of the past need to be able to connect with consumers, operations, and management. When we decide to write a book, we go even deeper into this dilemma. How do we construct a one-way dialogue with the reader and still accomplish our goals of transformation and connective learning?

The answer, of course, is to anticipate what we think students will have trouble understanding, and to provide them with preventative content that answers their probable questions. It's like creating a vaccine for a virus; there is no way to cure it once you have it—better to ensure it never occurs. Such then is the challenge that we have as authors, and these challenges become even more difficult when we need to convey technical content and describe how to use it.

Successful technical books today must be connective, in that they not only seek to provide facts, they cultivate the reader so that the facts can be better applied. Examples must be designed to reflect real-world problems. This helps ensure a transformation from technical information to successful implementation. *CIO Magazine* recently published an article in which they identified that about 74% of data processing projects fail to complete on-time and on-budget. Indeed, 22% never get done! Although I am not advocating a book as a solution, I am concerned that the educational process of producing capable technology professionals is failing us. The Gartner Group is consistent with *CIO Magazine* in that they are predicting that 75% of e-Commerce projects will fail.

The use of databases continues to be widespread. Indeed, the Internet has created an even more valuable facet of how stored data will affect our daily lives. Not too far away is a world where virtually every piece of text data we see on the Internet will be convertible to usable analysis information via powerful database products like Oracle. Thus, the study of good database design and how to interface databases with Web applications is critical. We are only seeing the beginnings of how e-Commerce will impact database design and development. There are many challenges to the linking of back-end legacy databases with the Web-enabled technology that drives e-Commerce business operations. The common driver of all systems, legacy, client/server, and e-Commerce, will continue to be databases. The challenge then is to find capable workers that not only understand database technology, but how to use and integrate it with all types of systems.

The Oracle DBA Interactive Workbook is a work that addresses many of the education issues I have discussed above. It presents the technical content in a manner that simulates classroom interaction, while providing real-world examples that readers can correlate to their workplace experiences.

It is not often that an educator has the opportunity to have students go on to professionally and academically contribute to the field in which they have been taught. I have always felt that teachers who have followed this path have had an advantage—they have been on the other side and know what can be helpful in a book that teaches product technologies.

Douglas Scherer and Melanie Caffrey are not only my past students, they are also accomplished professionals. They have combined to create a work that avoids the many technical book pitfalls that I have outlined above and is instead an understandable, practical, and technically sound approach that anticipates the learner's questions.

Dr. Arthur M. Langer
Chair, Faculty and Curricular Development, Technology Programs
Columbia University

ACKNOWLEDGMENTS

There were several people who were very instrumental in the writing of this book. None so instrumental, however, as my co-author, Douglas Scherer. I am incredibly indebted to Douglas, not only for giving me the opportunity to be his co-author in the first place, but for his literary and educational wisdom and his technical expertise, not to mention his constant words of encouragement and advice, without which my contribution to this book might never have taken place. I am also fortunate that he had the vision to take his Introduction to Oracle Database Administration course that is very popular (so much so that it remains one of the most difficult courses to gain enrollment in) and decide to make it available, through this book, to everyone else wanting to get their feet wet with Oracle database administration. I obtained invaluable experience as his student at Columbia University and am honored to have worked with and befriended this talented and well-respected database professional.

Several other key players who aided in the book's fruition include Alice Rischert, who wrote Chapter 16, "Application and SQL Optimization," and is one of the co-authors of the *Oracle SQL Interactive Workbook* in the Prentice Hall Oracle Interactive Workbook series. Meticulous edits and suggestions came from our two highly experienced technical editors, Allen Riberdy and Carol Brennan, who patiently and diligently provided painstakingly attentive detail to every aspect of every chapter and provided invaluable insight and advice. Finally, the RAID technology addition would not have been possible without the generous contribution of Josh Burns.

Thanks to the advice and editorial suggestions of respected colleagues Sudheer Marisetti, Susan Hesse, and Anne Hilliard Johnson, who allowed us to take advantage of them when we asked if they'd be interested in "having a look at a few chapters for us . . .". Thanks are also due to all of the editors at Prentice Hall: Tim Moore, Ralph Moore, Russ Hall, Miles Williams, and Wil Mara, among others, who provided vigilant assistance and guidance through every step of the writing process.

To the other authors in the Oracle Interactive Workbook series, I extend my deepest appreciation and gratitude. Without their expertise, hard work, and good humor, this collaboration would never have taken place.

I would like to thank my colleagues and co-students at Columbia University who provided me with the opportunity to work with and learn from what I consider to be some of the most knowledgeable and altruistic (not to mention, extremely hard-working) individuals I've ever met. Dr. Arthur M. Langer was my first instructor in the Computer Technology and Applications (CTA) program, and due to his wisdom and incredible gift for teaching, I remained in the CTA program. With his guidance, along with that of Dennis Green, Alice Rischert, Alex Morrison, Gnana Supramaniam, Nina Vorobyeva, Douglas Scherer, Baman Motivala, Ben Rosenzweig, and Mary Lett, and the modest, behind-the-scenes, but ever-critical assistance of Mohammed Islam, Matthew Kirkpatrick, Carl Niedzielski, and Peter Jamieson, I decided that working with database technology was and still is definitely what I want to be doing.

I would certainly be remiss if I didn't thank the students at Columbia University who I have been fortunate enough to teach and, in so doing, learn a tremendous amount from.

Special thanks are due to Martin Fellner, David Ricciardi, et al. at Proximo Consulting Services, Inc. for allowing us the use of their facility and resources (freeing us from collaborative efforts at the nearby Manhattan diner), where we were provided a quiet place to write.

Last but certainly not least, I would especially like to thank my parents, Frances and Donald, and brothers, Matthew and Michael, and friends, Lori, Aleida, and Cynthia (to name a few), who understood when I took six months to return a phone call and without whose unwavering encouragement, optimism, and enthusiasm I would never have even attempted the effort.

Melanie Caffrey
New York, NY

Have you ever had one of those dreams in which a monster was after you? You run as fast as you can, yet you don't seem to move at all. If you have, you can picture what it was like to write this book. When I accepted this project, I had just begun writing another book. Other authors warned me, "Don't take on two book projects at once." I was naïve and resolute, and did not listen. Yet, in spite of the various crises that were placed before us, we were still able to take the exercises from the Introduction to Database Administration course that I had created at Columbia University's Computer Technology and Applications (CTA) program, and turn them into this book.

I use the pronoun "we" in the previous sentence because this book was not a solo effort. It would not exist without the dedication and technical input from my co-author, Melanie Caffrey. She kept the pace going and took up the slack when, about halfway through the writing schedule, my writing time was unexpectedly and severely limited. I cannot thank her enough for the time and expertise she invested. If there was a monster running after me, Melanie jumped into the picture and slew it. I was proud several years ago to call her a student, and am lucky now to call her a co-author and friend.

Melanie and I had lots of help. The most critical came from our technical editors, Carol Brennan and Allen Riberdy. With full schedules of their own, they still agreed to participate in the project. They diligently and expertly read through the chapters, adding their experience, technical savvy, and clarity to the material. With their input, we were able to avoid some hidden disasters, and with their comments, were able to keep our direction clear.

We were lucky to have two development editors at Prentice Hall. First, Ralph Moore provided insight and direction in the Interactive Workbook series pedagogy. When Ralph was offered a promotion, Russ Hall took over and stayed with the project to its completion. We did not always agree, but Russ stuck with the project and turned phrases for us that added clarity to the material, and made sure that we stayed on track with the goal, given our slippery schedule.

Some of our students and colleagues pitched in and gave some of the chapters an additional reading—weeding out those pesky errors that seem to hide and persist no matter how many times the material is reviewed. They are: Carol Caine, Susan Hesse, Anne Hilliard Johnson, Sudheer Marisetti, Craig Rapley, and Jane Zhou. Jane and Sudheer took special effort to read through several chapters on a deeper technical level, providing us with additional insight.

Alice Rischert (co-author of the *Oracle SQL Interactive Workbook*) recently took over as the Database Track Chair when I stepped down this year. In spite of that new and time-consuming responsibility, she still agreed to help us by writing the entire chapter on SQL tuning. I give many thanks to her for taking on that chapter, and for her diligent review of the scripts that create the STUDENT schema for the Oracle Interactive Workbook series.

Many thanks also to Josh Burns, the best systems administrator I've met, for contributing the piece on RAID technology in Appendix C.

The authors in the Oracle Interactive Workbook series worked as a team to create a cohesive set of exercises across four volumes. Alex Morrison, Baman Motivala, Alice Rischert, Benjamin Rosenzweig, and Elena Silvestrova are an extraordinary group of people who, through work on this series, were taken to the limits of their patience. They have withstood the test and deserve a great deal of thanks for their interest and participation on the project. Luckily, I don't think that they knew what they were in for when they agreed to be authors.

Both Melanie and I are alumni of the CTA program at Columbia University. My first two teachers at CTA were Peter Koletzke and Dr. Arthur M. Langer. I consider their classes to be the most important that I've taken in this field. Their approach to all systems work evolves from thoughtful analysis, technical expertise, and the drive to perform with excellence. Their patient and stimulating teaching style contributed greatly to my success in this field, and I emulate it in my own teaching and working style. I thank Dr. Langer also for writing this book's foreword.

During nine years (and counting) of involvement with the CTA program, there are some people who played a significant role as colleagues and friends: Titus Bocseri, Thomas Bryant, Fritz Cloninger, Amanda Douglas, Martin Fellner, Kathe Frantz, Dennis Green, Mohammed Islam, Matthew Kirkpatrick, Judy Lapore, Norma Lau, Arthur Lopatin, Isabel Lopatin, Mike Marra, Chris McKeon, Jay Miller, Robert Montay, Potter Palmer, and Norman Starr. To them and the hundreds of CTA instructors, teaching assistants, and students who have passed my way and shared their enthusiasm in this topic and in the learning process, thank you.

Martin Fellner and his partner David Ricciardi at Proximo Consulting Services, Inc. deserve special thanks for providing a site in their New York office, where Melanie and I wrote and tested the book's exercises.

While completing my Master's Degree at Columbia University, I was fortunate to interact with these co-students, superiors, friends, and instructors—all of them mentors—who added their special influence to my career and skill set: Peter Caleb, Barbara Cangiano, Elizabeth Davis, Marsha Genensky, Jessica Gordon, Li-Chen Hwang, Marty Morell, Tom Osuga, Phyllis Stephens, and Patrick Thompson.

The Oracle DBA community is one where people enjoy sharing helpful information. Rachel Carmichael and Marlene Theriault contribute immensely to this community in their writing and presentations. They share their knowledge openly and enthusiastically on the Oracle listservs and at the Oracle conferences, and dedicate their time to assisting DBAs and developers. If you are just entering the field of database administration, you will learn—as have all other Oracle DBAs—that they are owed a great deal of thanks.

For my parents, Helene and Bernie, and the rest of my family, Jackie, Bob, and Renee, I hope that this work makes them proud. It's one small gift I can give to repay them for their support during the maturation years.

The ultimate thanks is reserved for my girlfriend, Nélida. She continued to give me her support, sometimes in subtle ways, even when the project seemed endless. As I start to reappear from the void, I hope that she remembers me.

Douglas Scherer
New York, NY

INTRODUCTION

The *Oracle DBA Interactive Workbook* presents an introduction to Oracle database administration in a unique and highly effective format. It is organized more like a teaching aid than a reference manual in that to learn basic administration techniques, you are challenged to work through a set of guided tasks rather than to read through descriptions. There is a list of additional reading material in Appendix B that you can reference if you wish to delve deeper into any of the topics covered in this book.

This book is intended for beginners in the world of Oracle database administration. It will take you through a set of tasks, starting with creating a database to using some of the Oracle database tuning, and backup and recovery utilities. Those experienced with Oracle databases will recognize that a workbook covering the topic of database administration will be an extremely useful introduction for the beginner, but it cannot be used as a deep study of the Oracle database environment. After working through this book, you will have been launched into the exciting and interesting (sometimes nerve-racking) world of database administration, but it will take years of experience to become a senior database administrator.

WHO THIS BOOK IS FOR

This book is intended for anyone who needs a quick and detailed introduction to Oracle database administration tasks. It is not the intention of this book to provide an in-depth study of the Oracle database server. The foundation for this book was developed to supplement the Introduction to Oracle Database Administration class in the Database Track at Columbia University's Computer Technology and Applications (CTA) program in New York City. The book's sidebars and answers often reflect questions that students have asked in class.

The student body entering the CTA program range from those who have years of experience in the IT field but no experience with Oracle, to those with absolutely no experience in IT and even no experience with PCs. The Introduction to Oracle Database Administration class is offered as an elective in the fourth and final term of the CTA program's curriculum. So, while it is geared for beginners with little or no previous experience with Oracle database administration, it is expected that the reader will have some experience working with an Oracle database. The reader should be comfortable with relational database concepts as well as SQL. If you are unfamiliar with any of these subjects, refer to the *Oracle SQL Interactive Workbook* in the Prentice Hall Oracle Interactive Workbook series.

WHAT YOU'LL NEED

There are software as well as knowledge requirements necessary to complete the exercise sections of the workbook.

SOFTWARE

- Oracle 7.3.4, 8.0, or 8i.
- Access to the WWW.

Note that prior to beginning the workbook labs, you should already have installed the Oracle Server software (it will make it easier to get through the labs if you do not install the default database, however) and the Net8 or SQL*Net components. Since the instructions vary greatly depending on the platform, you should consult your Oracle documentation (*Installation Guide* and *Getting Started*) for installation information.

ORACLE 7.3.4, 8.0, OR 8i

You can use either Oracle Standard Edition or Oracle Enterprise Edition. Since you will be performing actions that may affect other databases, **you should not work through the tasks in this book in an environment where there are critical data, programs, etc.!**

Since Oracle frequently improves and changes its products, new versions are released all the time. However, the concepts covered in this book are fundamental to the Oracle RDBMS (hereafter called the Oracle Server) and are unlikely to change significantly in the near future. Even if your version of the database is slightly different than the one listed here, you should still be able to make use of this book.

The tasks and descriptions represent core issues of Oracle Server architecture and are therefore universal to all three versions of the Oracle Server. There are occasional notes to point out a specific issue regarding a specific version.

Additionally, you should be familiar with SQL*Plus, the tool supplied with the database to interact with it in a command-line fashion.

ACCESS TO THE WWW

You will need access to the Internet and the WWW so that you can access the companion Web site for this book through—

http://www.phptr.com/phptrinteractive

Here you will find the files that are necessary for completing the exercises.

KNOWLEDGE

To complete the exercises, you should be familiar with relational database concepts and understand what an Entity Relationship Diagram is. You should also be comfortable using SQL to access and manipulate database objects such as tables, constraints, sequences, and so on.

If you are not familiar or comfortable with these subjects, then it is recommended that you refer to the *Oracle SQL Interactive Workbook* in the Prentice Hall Oracle Interactive Workbook series.

You should also feel comfortable working in your operating system's command-line environment.

HOW THIS BOOK IS ORGANIZED

The intent of this workbook is to teach you about Oracle database administration by presenting you with a series of tasks and challenges, followed by detailed solutions to those challenges. At times, an individual task acts as a complete unit of work, while other tasks are developed through a series of simple actions. Each chapter has a series of labs that introduce topics. The labs are composed of tasks, which are typical to the daily work of a database administrator. Beyond the labs, topics are further explored through questions and answers. What follows is the common layout of the chapters:

Chapter Objectives	A list of subjects the chapter will cover.
Chapter Text	An overview of chapter subjects.
Lab Objectives	A list of subjects the lab will cover.
Lab Text	An introduction to the lab subject, occasionally including steps that prepare the Oracle Server for the exercises.
Exercises	Questions that require hands-on interaction with the Oracle Server. The exercises will guide you through learning the subject introduced in the lab text.
Exercise Answers	Answers and discussion of the exercise subject.
Self-Review Questions	Multiple-choice questions to review lab material.
Test Your Thinking	Project questions to supplement the lab material.

Depending on the breadth of the subject, a given chapter may have more than one lab, and a given lab may have more than one set of exercises.

The exercises are not meant to be closed-book quizzes to test your knowledge. On the contrary, they are intended to act as your guide and walk you through a task.

You are encouraged to flip back and forth from the question section to the answer section so that, if need be, you can read the discussions as you go along.

The chapters and their exercises must be completed in sequence as the material in later chapters builds on what is presented earlier.

Chapter 1, "The Database Administrator's Job," introduces you to the world of database administration.

Chapter 2, "Creating Your Database," walks you through the steps of manually creating your own database.

Chapter 3, "Oracle Networking: Configuring Basic Net8/SQL*Net Components," guides you through setting up the components necessary for remote users to connect to your database over a network.

Chapter 4, "Tablespaces," teaches you how to create and manipulate tablespaces, and introduces you to logical storage constructs.

Chapter 5, "Segments and Extents," provides a more in-depth look at these higher level logical storage constructs, which were introduced in Chapter 4.

Chapter 6, "Data Blocks," examines data blocks, the smallest unit of Oracle storage.

Chapter 7, "Redo Logs," teaches you the basics of how redo logs operate and how they are written to.

Chapter 8, "Datafiles," describes how to view information about and manipulate datafiles.

Chapter 9, "User Creation," teaches you how to create and alter user accounts.

Chapter 10, "Privilege and Resource Groups," introduces you to the concepts and effects of privileges, roles, and resource limits and shows you how to assign them to user accounts.

Chapter 11, "Auditing," examines Oracle's mechanism for recording different types of database activity for purposes of maintaining database security and/or keeping records of billable activity.

Chapter 12, "Rollback Segments," presents a study of the use and operation of rollback segments and how they provide an Oracle database with read-consistency and "undo" information.

Chapter 13, "Locking," guides you through exercises that demonstrate the importance of Oracle locking mechanisms and introduces you to the concepts of data "consistency" and "concurrency."

Chapter 14, "Logical Backup and Recovery," covers logical data backups and recoveries using the Oracle-provided import (IMP) and export (EXP) utilities.

Chapter 15, "Physical Backup and Recovery," teaches you about different types of database failures, walks you through a simulation of a physical database failure and recovery, and explains the importance of archiving your redo log files.

Chapter 16, "Application and SQL Optimization," provides a look at optimizing standalone and application SQL code through Oracle-provided facilities such as AUTOTRACE, SQLTRACE, and TKPROF.

Chapter 17, "Database Tuning and Optimization," presents an introductory look at the other side of tuning an Oracle database by showing you how to gather information about and, if necessary, tune your memory and disk I/O through the use of the Oracle-provided utilities, UTLBTAT.SQL and UTLESTAT.SQL.

ABOUT THE COMPANION WEB SITE

The companion Web site is located at

http://www.phptr.com/phptrinteractive

Here you will find two very important items:

1. Files you will download for specific tasks in the workbook.
2. Answers to the Test Your Thinking questions.

Also, check the Web site for periodically updated information about the book.

CONVENTIONS USED IN THIS BOOK

There are several conventions used in this book to make your learning experience easier. These are explained here.

 This icon denotes advice and useful information about a particular topic or concept from the authors to you, the reader.

This icon flags tips that are especially helpful tricks that will save you time or trouble, for instance, a shortcut for performing a particular task or a method that the authors have found useful.

Computers are delicate creatures and can be easily damaged. Likewise, they can be dangerous to work on if you're not careful. This icon flags information and precautions that not only save you headaches in the long run, but may even save you or your computer from harm.

Passages referring to the book's companion Web site are flagged with this icon. The companion Web site once again is located through—

`http://www.phptr.com/phptrinteractive`

IMPORTANT NOTES ABOUT COMPLETING THE EXERCISES

- Complete the chapters and exercises in the order they're given. If the labs, exercises, and steps are not done in their proper sequence, you may have to start from the first chapter and work your way back into the material. This is similar to performing these tasks in a real-world environment. Database administration is less forgiving than application coding. In database administration, you cannot simply recompile your code and try the application again. If you leave out a step, you may lose a portion of the database in a way that is unrecoverable—losing your work. The only exception to this is Chapter 3, "Oracle Networking: Configuring Basic Net8/SQL*Net Components," which can be completed after all of the other chapters.

  In Chapter 2, you will learn about the command SHUTDOWN IMMEDIATE. After successfully completing Chapter 2, you should, from then on perform a SHUTDOWN IMMEDIATE on your database before rebooting or shutting down your computer.

- For Chapters 2, 3, 13, 15, and 17, you should allocate enough time to finish from beginning to end. It can take from 45 minutes to a couple of hours to complete the exercises in each chapter. The other chapters will flow better if you complete them in one sitting, but it is not as critical to your database if you are unable to do so.

- Check off the steps as you complete them. The most frequent error students make in the CTA course is not following each step, no matter how insignificant it seems. Learn to walk before you run. If you think there's a better way to accomplish an activity, don't try it out until you've completed the entire *Oracle DBA Interactive Workbook*. Some of the steps are in the text and some are explicitly in the exercises. If you check off each step as you go along, you will be more inclined to perform each task, and will have a way to trace whether you've missed a step if you run into trouble.

- The questions require you to think like an Oracle DBA. For example, you may be asked to look into an Oracle-provided script and report what you think it will do based on the information in the script. In another example, you may perform an exercise to make the database freeze. You're then asked to figure out what the problem is and what the next step should be to fix the problem, based on the knowledge that you've gained by that point in the book. Of course, the solution is given to you, but do your best to consider the problem before reading the provided answer. In either case, make your solution to the problem fall within the scope of the problem set in the chapter. This will be good practice for your work as a DBA, when you will be required to stay focused under pressure.

- For those completing the tasks in Windows, you should have administrative rights to the machine where the database is located.

C H A P T E R 1

THE DATABASE ADMINISTRATOR'S JOB

CHAPTER OBJECTIVES

In this chapter, you will learn about:

✔ The Role of the Oracle DBA   Page 2

✔ Sources for Oracle DBA Help   Page 6

In learning Oracle Database Administration, you will need to know your role as a database administrator, and where you can find help when you need it. With these two pieces of information, you will be able to organize any task you're given.

No matter how experienced and intelligent you are, you will always need some kind of help with your work. This is especially true in the world of the Oracle Server and associated products because the server and its tools are always undergoing modifications and improvements. The following labs and chapters will help introduce you to the basic functionality of the Oracle Server.

L A B   1 . 1

THE ROLE OF THE
ORACLE DBA

LAB OBJECTIVES

After this Lab, you will:

✔ Understand about Becoming a DBA
✔ Understand the Role of the DBA

Within each organization, your role as a Database Administrator (DBA) may differ. The path you take to becoming a DBA may help determine the focus of your work. Some businesses may be large enough to require the support of an exclusive DBA group, while others may need your assistance with front-end development in addition to maintaining the database. Depending on your level of expertise and experience, your first time as a DBA may be the outcome of a strategic career move or possibly the result of forced volunteerism. Some DBAs focus on procedural work, such as writing stored PL/SQL code and triggers. They are often called procedural DBAs. Other DBAs focus their skills strictly on supporting and organizing the database engine, its physical layout, and data security. In this lab's exercises, you will begin thinking about what tasks might be associated with the role of the DBA.

In this book, the word database (with a lowercase "d") will be used as a general term, as in the phrase, "I lost my password and can't connect to the database." The word Database (with a capital "D") will refer to the set of files that the Oracle Server uses to store and maintain data. These files will be described more fully in later chapters.

LAB 1.1 EXERCISES

1.1.1 UNDERSTAND ABOUT BECOMING A DBA

a) What is your current job title (or, if you're a student, what is your major)?

_____

_____

 You may not necessarily get the exact answers to the remaining questions in this lab's exercises, but the objective here is to get you thinking about the role of a DBA.

b) What are some of the paths that might lead you from your current work or study focus to the role of DBA?

_____

_____

1.1.2 UNDERSTAND THE ROLE OF THE DBA

a) What are some of the tasks that a procedural DBA might perform?

_____

_____

b) List three other tasks that can be part of the DBA's role.

_____

_____

_____

LAB 1.1 EXERCISE ANSWERS

1.1.1 ANSWERS

a) What is your current job title (or, if you're a student, what is your major)?

Answer: Your answers, of course, will vary.

The point of this question isn't just to remind yourself of your professional capacity, but to lead you to the next question. Hopefully, if you're reading this book, you have aspirations of becoming an Oracle DBA. Your current talents are important in contributing to this career path.

b) What are some of the paths that might lead you from your current work or study focus to the role of DBA?

Answer: You can become a DBA through several paths. Many DBAs start from some other position within an organization. They may have been programmers, front-end developers, system administrators, or data architects.

1.1.2 ANSWERS

a) What are some of the tasks that a procedural DBA might perform?

Answer: As a procedural DBA, your primary responsibilities will be the design, development, and implementation of code that supports complex constraint definitions. This code is maintained through database triggers, procedures, functions, and packages. A procedural DBA may also be asked to support front-end functionality and logic.

b) List three other tasks that can be part of the DBA's role.

Answer: The DBA can be responsible for many different components of the database environment. The key responsibilities are database security, backup and recovery, and tuning. This includes physically laying out the database files (that actually hold the data) for performance and high-availability. Other tasks include installing the database binaries (program files), preparing and testing a backup scenario, and performing imports and exports of data. Still other DBA tasks can include the installation of Oracle's networking and Web components, and even installing Oracle front-end tools—such as Oracle Developer Forms—on client machines.

LAB 1.1 SELF-REVIEW QUESTIONS

In order to test your progress, you should be able to answer the following questions.

1) There is one clear path to follow for becoming a DBA.

   a) _____ True
   b) _____ False

   Quiz answers appear in Appendix A, Section 1.1.

L A B   1 . 2

SOURCES FOR ORACLE DBA HELP

LAB OBJECTIVES

After this Lab, you will be able to:

✔ Prepare for Tasks
✔ Find Oracle Help

Before starting any task, you should be prepared with the techniques, tools, and a task plan (a list of task steps in their proper order of successful completion and the people responsible for those steps) that you will use to perform the task, and the knowledge of where to get help in case you run into trouble. There are many places for an Oracle DBA to get help. Of course, the first place to look for answers is in the Oracle documentation. Often the information you need is contained there. There are also third-party books that contain additional, summarized, or expert-oriented information on Oracle database topics.

Oracle also provides online and telephone support services. Some of these require you to have a Customer Support Identification (CSI) number. You get a CSI number by purchasing one of Oracle's support options. Oracle-provided support includes online and telephone assistance services. Online services include the MetaLink (metalink.oracle.com) and Oracle Technet (technet.oracle.com) Web sites. Both of these online services require you to register online, while MetaLink also requires you to have a CSI number. MetaLink's primary focus is to provide support. It can be used to enter support requests online, and to track your support requests. It also has information resources (such as a searchable knowledge base, technical forum, and searchable bug database) and a patch distribution facility. When you contact Oracle Support via MetaLink or telephone, you will receive a Technical Assistance Request (TAR) number to track the support request. Technet does not handle TARs, but it can be used as an additional support

---

The Fallback Plan

In spy movies, you often hear of the heroes relying on "Plan B." In your task plan, you will also need a fallback plan (or Plan B). This specifies what you will do if, during the execution of the task steps, you find that the task cannot be completed by the time it's due. Even if you are the best DBA in the world, something can still go wrong.

For example, you are given the task of performing an upgrade. You are told that you can start the upgrade at 22:00 Friday night and that the database has to be running again at 22:00 Sunday night.

In the process of developing your plan, you determine and confirm with the user that, more important than having an upgraded environment, they must have an environment (even the previous one) available to them at 22:00 Sunday night. If you are able to meet your deadline, use of your fallback plan will not be necessary. However, if your upgrade is not complete by the required deadline, you must restore the previous version. In that case, you will need to allow yourself enough time to complete the restoration.

If you don't have at least this level of a fallback plan, then your fallback plan defaults to: "If I don't have the upgraded environment running by 22:00 Sunday night, then I will submit my resume to a new company on Monday morning."

---

resource. Its primary focus is to provide information about Oracle technology. Visit Technet to get sample code downloads, view white papers on the latest Oracle components, and to join discussion groups.

In some operating systems, there is an Oracle-provided program, **oerr**, into which you can pass Oracle error numbers and receive information on the error. If your Oracle binaries are installed in UNIX or VMS (and some other operating systems, but not NT), you can try it yourself. The syntax for the command is:

```
$ oerr MessageType MessageNumber
```

In the error message "ORA-00904: invalid column name", **ORA** is the *MessageType* and **00904** is the *MessageNumber*.

■ *FOR EXAMPLE*

If a user calls you and says that they received the error ORA-01555, you can issue the following command at the command line in one of the supported environments:

```
$ oerr ora 01555
```

You would then get back the following information:

```
01555, 00000, "snapshot too old: rollback segment number %s with
name \"%s\" too small"

// *Cause: rollback records needed by a reader for consistent read
are

//          overwritten by other writers

// *Action: Use larger rollback segments
```

Another great place to get Oracle help is from the Oracle user community. There are many online listserv lists, magazines, user groups, and news groups that can offer you an environment to read about new techniques and discuss problems. Some Web sites to check are:

- www.ioug.org
- www.lazydba.com/listserv.pl

Note: Also, make sure to join at least one Oracle User's Group.

LAB 1.2 EXERCISES

1.2.1 PREPARE FOR TASKS

a) What should you do before beginning a task?

_____

_____

1.2.2 FIND ORACLE HELP

a) List three online resources for getting help or exchanging tips and techniques.

_____

_____

_____

b) What is a CSI number?

_____

_____

c) Visit the MetaLink site. If you have a CSI number, you may join MetaLink now. Once logged on to the site, choose *TARs* from the index panel on the left side of the browser window. In the frame on the right side of the browser window, you will see three choices: *TAR Search, Create a TAR,* and *Management Reports*. Click each of these and describe what each of the three areas is used for.

_____

_____

d) Visit Oracle's Technet site. In the index list on the left side of the browser window, choose *Technologies*. List three new technologies that are listed on that page. You may join Technet now.

_____

_____

e) What does the `oerr` command do?

_____

_____

f) If you are in an environment that supports the oerr command, try it now. Issue the following at the command line and describe the results:

```
$ oerr ora 00910
```

LAB 1.2 ANSWERS

1.2.1 ANSWERS

a) What should you do before beginning a task?

Answer: Before you begin a task, you should have your entire task plan organized. You should know what commands you are going to use, in what order they should be executed, what your fallback position is, and where you will find help in case there is a problem.

1.2.2 ANSWERS

a) List three online resources for getting help and exchanging tips and techniques.

Answer: There are many online resources where you can get help. Three of them are: MetaLink, Technet, and listserv lists.

b) What is a CSI number?

Answer: CSI stands for Customer Support Identification number. It is assigned to you when you purchase Oracle support. You will be asked for the CSI number each time you contact Oracle Support. When obtaining assistance from Oracle, you will often be given a Technical Assistance Request (TAR) number to use for following up on a technical issue.

c) Visit the MetaLink site. If you have a CSI number, you may join MetaLink now. Once logged on to the site, choose *TARs* from the index panel on the left side of the browser window. In the frame on the right side of the browser window you will see three choices: *TAR Search, Create a TAR,* and *Management Reports.* Click each of these and describe what each of the three areas is used for.

Answer:The three areas are for:

- *Tar Search—Reviewing open support requests.*

- *Create a TAR—Opening new support requests.*

- *Management Reports—Providing counts and statistics within a specific time period regarding your support requests.*

d) Visit Oracle's Technet site. In the index list on the left side of the browser window, choose *Technologies*. List three new technologies that are listed on that page. You may join Technet now.

Answer:At the time of this writing, three of the listed technologies were: XML, JAVA, and Migration Technologies.

e) What does the `oerr` command do?

Answer: `oerr` *is an Oracle command available in some operating systems, including UNIX and VMS. Given an Oracle error number, you can use this command to get additional information about an Oracle error.This can be very useful, especially if you do not have the Oracle error message books handy.*

f) If you are in an environment that supports the oerr command, try it now. Issue the following at the command line and describe the results:

```
$ oerr ora 00910
```

Answer: Issuing this command yields the following result:

00910, 00000, "specified length too long for its datatype"

// *Cause: for datatypes CHAR and RAW, the length specified was > 255;

//   otherwise, the length specified was > 2000.

// *Action: use a shorter length or switch to a datatype permitting a

//   longer length such as a VARCHAR2, LONG CHAR, or LONG RAW

The result is a description of the error corresponding to the error number 00910.This result contains Cause and Action information. Not all of the error numbers have such detailed information. Usually, less detailed information is supplied for simpler errors (try error 00904, for example).You should also know that it is not necessary to supply the leading zeros of the error number. For example, oerr ora 910 would work just as well as oerr ora 00910.

LAB 1.2 SELF-REVIEW QUESTIONS

In order to test your progress, you should be able to answer the following questions.

1) Which command will give you information for Oracle error ORA-01401 in some operating systems?

   a) _____ `$ help ORA-01401`
   b) _____ `$ oerr ora 1401`
   c) _____ `$ man 01401`
   d) _____ `$ CSI 01401`

2) A TAR number is used for:

   a) _____ Tracking Oracle support requests
   b) _____ Registering you with MetaLink
   c) _____ Unpacking an Oracle installation
   d) _____ Attaching a license to an Oracle installation

Quiz answers appear in Appendix A, Section 1.2.

CHAPTER 1

TEST YOUR THINKING

Chapter 1 is centered on the role of the DBA and gives some general ideas of how you as a DBA can organize and perform your tasks, including setting up your task plan and getting help.

1) Imagine that you have just been elected to be the DBA or Jr. DBA for an organization where you were previously a front-end developer. Your first task is to install a default Oracle database that does not have critical business impact. Knowing only what you know now, put together a plan and checklist for your task. The answer for this will vary based on your current level of experience. Put in a fallback position. You may also wish to include in your task plan the person or group responsible for each action with the listing of the action. Also, you may use a standard GANTT or PERT chart (diagramming systems used for tracking projects) if you know how.

C H A P T E R 2

CREATING YOUR DATABASE

CHAPTER OBJECTIVES

In this chapter, you will learn about:

- ✔ OFA Basics   Page 16
- ✔ Creating and Configuring an Oracle Database   Page 25

During the process of installing the Oracle software, you may have created a default database. In this chapter, you will be taken through the steps of manually creating a new database. This is the database that you will be using throughout the remaining chapters of this book. You will also locate the places in your operating system where the Oracle Database and configuration files are located. If you did not install the Oracle software yourself, or if you are working on a large multi-user machine, you may need to obtain some of the required information from your system administrator.

 The exercises in this book are intended for beginner DBAs. Perform them ONLY in an environment that is non-critical. Do not use a production environment (database or computer), or an environment where loss of service cannot be tolerated!

L A B   2 . 1

OFA BASICS

LAB OBJECTIVES

After this Lab, you will be able to:

✔ Identify your ORACLE_BASE Location
✔ Identify your ORACLE_HOME Directory
✔ Identify and Configure your Admin Directory
✔ Identify the Location for your Database Files

The Optimal Flexible Architecture (OFA) model was designed by Oracle to assist users in laying out their databases in a way that would support high performance and ease of maintenance. The Oracle white paper by Cary Millsap entitled "The OFA Standard" contains the specification in detail. For the purposes of this book, you will be making use of the characteristics of OFA that identify the logical location of the Oracle installation and associated files. Note that the Oracle Installer does not require that Oracle be installed according to OFA specifications and you will find different Oracle installations at varying levels of OFA compliance at different sites.

 Before commencing with these exercises, make sure to read the book's Introduction. Especially important is the section, "Important Notes about Completing the Exercises."

LAB 2.1 EXERCISES

2.1.1 IDENTIFY YOUR *ORACLE_BASE* LOCATION

The starting point for OFA is the Oracle Base (ORACLE_BASE) location. This is often a mount point, but can be a lower-level directory.

 For the work in this book, you should be logged on as the Oracle software owner or as an account with similar privileges. Otherwise, you may not have the correct permissions to see and use the various directories and tools.

Find your ORACLE_BASE location now. Start by seeing if you have an ORACLE_BASE environment variable.

In UNIX, you can use the `env` or `echo` commands to see your ORACLE_BASE. In NT, you will probably not have an ORACLE_BASE environment variable defined, but if you are using Oracle8i, you should be able to find a directory named Oracle directly below one of your drive letters. The directory named Oracle is your ORACLE_BASE location. In Oracle Server releases prior to 8i, the ORACLE_BASE directory is by default named ORANT, and appears directly below one of the drive letters.

If you cannot find the ORACLE_BASE location on your own, get the information from the person who installed the Oracle software.

■ *FOR EXAMPLE*

At the UNIX command line, issue the following command to find the location of ORACLE_BASE:

```
$ echo $ORACLE_BASE
```

a) What is the absolute path of your ORACLE_BASE?

_____

_____

b) What method did you use to get this information?

_____

_____

2.1.2 IDENTIFY YOUR ORACLE_HOME DIRECTORY

In an OFA-compliant directory structure, your Oracle Home (ORACLE_HOME) will be located below ORACLE_BASE. Using the echo command appropriate for your command-line environment, locate your ORACLE_HOME now.

In UNIX, you can issue the command:

```
$ echo $ORACLE_HOME
```

In NT using a default Oracle8i installation, look below ORACLE_BASE for a directory named Ora81. This will be your ORACLE_HOME location. In Oracle Server releases prior to 8i running on NT, the ORACLE_BASE and ORACLE_HOME defaults are both called ORANT and are located below one of the drive letters. Table 2.1 shows the default ORACLE_BASE and ORACLE_HOME locations in NT.

Table 2.1 ■ Sample NT Default ORACLE_BASE and ORACLE_HOME

Location	Oracle Pre-8i	Oracle8i
ORACLE_BASE	C:\ORANT	C:\ORACLE
ORACLE_HOME	C:\ORANT	C:\ORACLE\ORA81

Because most platforms can have multiple ORACLE_HOMEs, the ORACLE_HOME environment variable may not be set by default when you log on. Again, if you have trouble locating your ORACLE_HOME, you will have to check with the person who installed the Oracle software.

a) What is the absolute path of your ORACLE_HOME?

_____

_____

b) What method did you use to get this information?

_____

_____

2.1.3 IDENTIFY AND CONFIGURE YOUR ADMIN DIRECTORY

Not all Oracle installations use an admin directory. If it does exist, it should be found just below ORACLE_BASE. If you do not have an admin directory, create one now. It does not have to exist below ORACLE_BASE, but that is the OFA-compliant position for it.

Below each admin directory, there will be a directory for each database created on your system. Because your database is new to the system, you will have to add a directory for your database now as follows:

1) Create the admin directory if it does not already exist.

2) Create a directory below admin giving it the name of your database. **For organizational purposes of this book, your database will be referred to as db00.**

Allowing db00 to represent the name of your database, create a directory called db00 below the admin directory. If you wish to name the database something other than db00, that is fine.

3) Create the following directories below db00:
- adhoc
- adump
- arch
- bdump
- cdump
- create
- exp
- pfile
- udump

Unless otherwise noted, from this point on in this book, these directories will be referred to by their names. For example, the $ORACLE_BASE/admin/db00/arch directory will be referred to as "the arch directory."

a) What is the absolute path to your admin and associated database directories?

_____

_____

b) What is the absolute path to your pfile directory?

_____

_____

2.1.4 IDENTIFY THE LOCATION FOR YOUR DATABASE FILES

You need to find a location for the physical files that will make up your Oracle Database. For OFA compliance, Database files are put in directories as **MountPoint**/oradata/**DatabaseName**.

For instance, in UNIX, you might see the following directory structures:

```
/u01/oradata/db00
/u02/oradata/db00
/u03/oradata/db00
```

In NT using Oracle8i, you will find an Oradata directory below ORACLE_BASE. So in this environment, you might see the following directory structure:

```
e:\oracle\oradata\db00
```

Once you locate the ORADATA directory in your environment, add a directory below it for your database name. So, you should have a directory similar to …/oradata/db00.

a) What is the absolute path to the location of your database files?

_____

_____

LAB 2.1 EXERCISE ANSWERS

2.1.1 ANSWERS

a) What is the absolute path of your ORACLE_BASE?

Answer: The location of ORACLE_BASE will be specific for each installation. In UNIX, it will appear similar to /u01/app/oracle. In NT, in may appear as e:\oracle.

b) What method did you use to find this information?

Answer: Again, this will depend on your environment. In UNIX, there may be an environment variable set to ORACLE_BASE. In that case, you might use the command: echo $ORACLE_BASE. If there is no ORACLE_BASE environment variable, you may have to check with the person who installed your software.

2.1.2 ANSWERS

a) What is the absolute path of your ORACLE_HOME?

Answer: This location is another one that is specific to your environment.

*It should be the location of **ORACLE_BASE**/product/**VersionNumberOfOracle Server**. So, if you have several versions of Oracle installed, you might have several ORACLE_HOMEs.*

For example, in UNIX, if you have versions 7.3.4 and 8.1.6 installed, you might
see the ORACLE_HOME directories:

```
/u01/app/oracle/product/7.3.4
```

and

```
/u01/app/oracle/product/8.1.6
```

In an NT Oracle8i installation, you might see the ORACLE_HOME directory:

```
e:\Oracle\Ora81
```

b) What method did you use to get this information?

Answer: This answer will depend on your situation.

*In UNIX, there may be an environment variable set to ORACLE_HOME. In that case,
you might use the command: echo $ORACLE_HOME. If there is no ORACLE_HOME
environment variable, you will have to check with the person who installed your software.*

2.1.3 ANSWERS

a) What is the absolute path to your admin and associated database directories?

*Answer: For OFA compliance, the admin directory falls underneath the ORACLE_BASE
location.*

The admin directory contains one directory for each database on your system. For
example, in UNIX, you might see the following directories:

```
/u01/app/oracle/admin/db00
/u01/app/oracle/admin/prod
/u01/app/oracle/admin/devel
```

b) What is the absolute path to your pfile directory?

Answer: Using the above examples, your pfile directory would be in:

```
/u01/app/oracle/admin/db00/pfile
```

2.1.4 ANSWERS

a) What is the absolute path to the location of your Database files?

Answer: There will probably be several directories that store your Database files.

In this book, you will be using only one directory location for your Database files. They are usually located under the ORADATA directory. In UNIX, they will be in a directory similar to one of the following:

```
/u02/oradata/db00
/u02/oradata/prod
/u02/oradata/devel
```

In NT, they will probably be found in directories similar to:

```
e:\oracle\oradata\db00 (For Oracle8i)
```

or

```
e:\orant\database (For Oracle7.3.4-Oracle8.0)
```

LAB 2.1 SELF-REVIEW QUESTIONS

1) OFA is which of the following?

a) _____ A tool for monitoring the database
b) _____ A model for the layout of Oracle software and Database files
c) _____ A data dictionary view that when queried shows the location of Oracle-related database files
d) _____ An operating system command that deletes Oracle-related Database files

2) The Oracle Installer requires you to install the Oracle software according to the OFA.

a) _____ True
b) _____ False

3) Match the definition to the logical location:

a) _____ Top-level location of OFA model

b) _____ Location of Oracle product-specific software

c) _____ Location of database-related directories that in turn hold Database files

d) _____ OFA location for trace, configuration, and other database files related to a specific database

1) admin
2) ORACLE_BASE
3) ORADATA
4) ORACLE_HOME

4) Which of the locations shown in Question 3 may be set as environment variables? (Choose all that apply.)

a) _____ admin

b) _____ ORACLE_BASE

c) _____ ORADATA

d) _____ ORACLE_HOME

Quiz answers appear in Appendix A, Section 2.1.

LAB 2.2

CREATING AND CONFIGURING AN ORACLE DATABASE

LAB OBJECTIVES

After this Lab, you will be able to:

✔ Edit the Instance Configuration File
✔ Write Scripts to Create the Database
✔ Create the Database Using the Create Scripts
✔ Test Database Viability
✔ Set the ROLLBACK_SEGMENTS Parameter
✔ Review the Scripts that Create the Data Dictionary

At the end of this lab, you will have created and tested the database that you will use throughout the remainder of this book. Before launching into the lab exercises, you'll need a brief overview of the Oracle database architecture.

There are two main parts to the Oracle Server architecture: the Instance and the Database. The Instance is made up of two components: a memory area called the System Global Area (SGA) that gets allocated when you tell the Instance to start and a set of programs called the background processes that also begin running at Instance startup. The SGA holds areas called the Database Buffer Cache, the Shared Pool, and the Redo Log Buffer. The Shared Pool contains the Dictionary Cache and the Library Cache. In Oracle8, there is an additional optional area in the SGA called the Large Pool. These areas will be discussed in later exercises.

The second piece in the Oracle database architecture is the Oracle Database. The Database consists of a set of files stored on disk. There are three types of files that make up the Database: datafiles, which hold the actual database data; control files, which contain state and layout information about the database; and redo log files, which contain redo log entries used for recovery if there is a database crash.

> *In this book, when the word "Database" appears with an upper-case "D", it will refer to the set of files discussed above (control files, datafiles, and redo log files). When the word "database" appears with a lower-case "d", it will refer to the database management system (such as in the phrase, "Can I please get an account to connect to the database?").*

As shown in Table 2.2, there are three different modes for startup. The first two start only the Instance and are normally used for maintenance purposes. The third mode opens the database files for access to the users via the Oracle Server.

Table 2.2 ■ Startup Modes

Mode	Description
startup nomount	Starts the Instance—Creates the SGA and runs the background processes after reading the parameters in the init.ora (Instance configuration) file.
startup mount	Starts the Instance and mounts the database—Reads the control file and identifies the Database files.
startup open	Starts the Instance and allows access to the Database for users via the Oracle Server.
startup force	Performs a shutdown abort, followed by a startup open. Note that startup force is an option, not a mode.

There are several types of shutdown for the database, as shown in Table 2.3.

The last piece of information you will need before getting to the exercises concerns the logon accounts and tools you'll be using to perform DBA activities. For all of the exercises in this chapter, you'll be issuing commands to the database from the Oracle tool called Server Manager. In most environments, the command to start Server Manager is svrmgrl, which stands for "Server Manager line mode." Once in Server Manager, you can exit by typing the command, "exit". In pre-Oracle8i databases in NT, the command is svrmgr30 for Oracle8.0.5 and Oracle8.0.4, or svrmgr23 for Oracle7.3.4. You'll need to check in the ORACLE_HOME/bin directory to see which one to use for your work. In NT, you will be doing this work from within an MS-DOS window. The exercises in this

Table 2.3 ■ Shutdown Types

Type	Description
shutdown normal	Prohibits sessions from being created and waits for any current session to log out, then shuts down cleanly.
shutdown immediate	Prohibits sessions from being created, rolls back all uncommitted transactions, disconnects any remaining connected sessions, and shuts down cleanly.
shutdown transactional	Similar to shutdown immediate, except that instead of rolling back uncommitted transactions, they are allowed to complete. Shutdown transactional is not available in pre-Oracle8 versions.
shutdown abort	Shuts down the database in a very ungraceful manner similar to a crash. Note that the Database will need to undergo Instance recovery the next time it starts up, which it will do automatically.

book are written for command-line, character-based tools rather than the GUI utilities that are provided with more recent versions of Oracle. This is done for two main reasons. The first is that you will not always have access to the GUI tools. Practicing the commands in a character-based environment helps ensure that you will be prepared for more situations as a DBA. The second reason is that working this way helps provide a more in-depth understanding of what's going on behind the scenes in the Oracle database.

The DBA accounts that are automatically created in the database are shown in Table 2.4. Note that when a default database is created with the Oracle Installer, you may be prompted for some of these values.

For compatibility and ease of reading, the Server Manager line mode tool will be used in many of the exercises throughout this book. Be aware though that in Oracle8i, you can use SQL*Plus for most of the tasks that Server Manager would normally do. Using SQL*Plus is a great improvement over Server Manager because you can make use of the SQL*Plus buffer and editing capabilities in your DBA tasks. If you use Oracle8i's SQL*Plus, use the character based version (In NT that will be In an MS-DOS window) for this chapter.

Table 2.4 ■ Default DBA Accounts

Username	Default Password	Description
SYS	CHANGE_ON_INSTALL	SYS owns the data dictionary tables, the place where all the information about database objects is stored. You should only connect to the database as SYS if you are explicitly instructed to do so in this book or in the Oracle documentation.
SYSTEM	MANAGER	SYSTEM was originally created to maintain database objects that support the Oracle Developer suite of tools. SYSTEM can perform most of the actions that SYS can and will be used most of the time for the exercises in this book.
INTERNAL	ORACLE (in some environments, INTERNAL)	INTERNAL is not truly a database account, but is used when performing certain maintenance work against—and starting and stopping—the database. Note that for this book's exercises, if you are prompted for a password when connecting INTERNAL use the password ORACLE (as shown in the createdb00_01.sql script below). Oracle states that connecting INTERNAL will no longer be supported as of Oracle version 8.2. From then on, you will connect as SYS AS SYSDBA.

LAB 2.2 EXERCISES

2.2.1 EDIT THE INSTANCE CONFIGURATION FILE

The Instance configuration file, often called the init.ora file, holds parameters that Oracle uses when starting the Instance. In this exercise, you will prepare the init.ora file for use in creating your database.

1) Create a text file called init.ora in your pfile directory. Put the parameter lines as shown in the steps below into your init.ora. The parameters in this init.ora file are the most basic that can work across Oracle database versions 7.3.4–8.1.6. For each database version, there are many more parameters that can be added to aid in performance and recovery. You will be adding some of them to the init.ora file throughout this book. Note that anything after a # in the configuration file is a comment.

```
##############################################################
## file: init.ora
## purpose: minimal init.ora file template
## created: by: dscherer date: April 25, 1999
##############################################################
db_name = db00
db_block_buffers = 60
shared_pool_size = 3500000
log_checkpoint_interval = 10000
log_checkpoint_timeout = 1800
processes = 100
log_buffer = 32768
db_block_size = 2048
```

2) Save the file and make a copy of it called init.ora.00 in the pfile directory. You will keep this as a backup.

3) Open the init.ora file for editing and make the following changes. You may name your database something other than db00, but it's recommended that you keep it short (five characters). If you call your database something other than db00, then replace:

```
db_name = db00
```

with

```
db_name = TheNameOfYourDatabase
```

   a) What is the name of your database?

   _____

   _____

4) Add the parameter for your control files. You should always specify at least two control files—preferably on two physically different mirrored drives. For the database used in this book, you may put the control files in the same directory as your datafiles—that is, your ORADATA directory.

An example of a control_files entry for a UNIX environment is:

```
control_files =
 (/u01/oradata/db00/control01.ctl,
  /u02/oradata/db00/control02.ctl
 )
```

An example of a control_files entry for an NT environment is:

```
control_files =
  (e:\oracle\oradata\db00\control01.ctl,
   e:\oracle\oradata\db00\control02.ctl
  )
```

   b) What are the locations of your control files?

_____

_____

5) Add a compatible parameter that specifies which version of the Oracle database software you are using. This specifies which version of Oracle Server features you will allow to be used in your database. Some sample entries are:

```
compatible = 7.3.4
compatible = 8.0.5
compatible = 8.1.6
```

Of course, you will only add one compatible line to your init.ora file.

   c) What version is your database installation?

_____

_____

Now you will add parameters for the location of trace and log files.

6) Add a background_dump_dest parameter that resolves to your bdump direc-tory. Among other things, the background_dump_dest location holds a file called alert*DatabaseName*.log. The alert log holds information about critical database errors, startups and shutdowns, and other database server-related issues. An example of this parameter is:

```
background_dump_dest=/u01/app/oracle/admin/db00/bdump
```

   d) What is the location of your background_dump_dest?

   _____

   _____

7) Add a core_dump_dest parameter that resolves to your cdump directory. For example:

```
core_dump_dest=/u01/app/oracle/admin/db00/cdump
```

Do not add a core_dump_dest parameter to an NT init.ora file.

   e) What is the location of your core_dump_dest?

   _____

   _____

8) Add a user_dump_dest parameter that resolves to your udump directory. For example:

```
user_dump_dest=/u01/app/oracle/admin/db00/udump
```

   f) What is the location of your user_dump_dest?

   _____

   _____

■ *FOR EXAMPLE*

After having completed the steps in this exercise, you should have an init.ora file similar to the one that follows, but with customization for your environment. The file should be located in your admin/db00/pfile directory.

In UNIX, the init.ora file might look like:

```
########################################################
##          file:  init.ora
##       purpose:  minimal init.ora file template
##       created:  by: dscherer date: April 25, 1999
##      modified:  by: dscherer date: April 27, 1999
## description:  Added additional startup parameters.
########################################################
db_name=db00
control_files=
        (/u01/oradata/db00/control01.ctl,
         /u01/oradata/db00/control02.ctl
        )
background_dump_dest=/u01/app/oracle/admin/db00/bdump
core_dump_dest=/u01/app/oracle/admin/db00/cdump
user_dump_dest=/u01/app/oracle/admin/db00/udump
compatible = 8.1.6
db_block_buffers = 60
shared_pool_size = 3500000
log_checkpoint_interval = 10000
log_checkpoint_timeout = 1800
processes = 100
log_buffer = 32768
db_block_size = 2048
```

In NT, the init.ora file might look like:

```
########################################################
##          file:  init.ora
##       purpose:  minimal init.ora file template
##       created:  by: dscherer date: April 25, 1999
##      modified:  by: dscherer date: April 27, 1999
## description:  Added additional startup parameters.
########################################################
db_name = db00
control_files =
        (e:\oracle\oradata\db00\control01.ctl,
         e:\oracle\oradata\db00\control02.ctl
        )
```

```
background_dump_dest = e:\oracle\admin\db00\bdump
user_dump_dest = e:\oracle\admin\db00\udump
compatible = 8.1.6
db_block_buffers = 60
shared_pool_size = 3500000
log_checkpoint_interval = 10000
log_checkpoint_timeout = 1800
processes = 100
log_buffer = 32768
db_block_size = 2048
```

Wherefore Art Thou, Oh init.ora?

There is one common parameter—ifile—that you will not use in these exercises. The ifile parameter is used to point to another file that contains additional configuration information. This is used in a parallel server configuration where two Instances share some of the same configuration settings, but also have settings that are specific to each Instance. Parallel server configuration is not covered in this book.

Prior to Oracle8i, the default location of the init.ora file was non-OFA-compliant. The init.ora file was stored in the ORACLE_HOME/dbs directory and was named init<SID>.ora. For example, the db00 init.ora file could be named /u01/app/oracle/product/dbs/initdb00.ora. With Oracle8i, the init.ora file is placed in its OFA-compliant location and is named init.ora, but the Instance still looks for it at startup in its non-OFA-compliant location. This is dealt with differently on each platform. In UNIX, an init<SID>.ora symbolic link, pointing to the OFA-compliant file, is created in ORACLE_HOME/dbs. In NT, the ifile parameter is employed. With a default database (created with the Oracle Installer), an init<SID>.ora file is created in the non-OFA-compliant location. That file contains one parameter ifile. The ifile parameter points to the OFA-compliant init.ora file.

In the exercises in this book, you will be using only the OFA-compliant location. This is why you will always have to explicitly tell the Instance where the init.ora (or pfile) is located using the PFILE= directive with the STARTUP command.

g) How big is the Shared Pool going to be?

_____

_____

h) Where is the alert log going to be created?

_____

_____

2.2.2 WRITE SCRIPTS TO CREATE THE DATABASE

Now that you have the init.ora file and all of the needed directories created, it's time for you to write the scripts that will create the database. There are two scripts. The first will contain the CREATE DATABASE statement. The second script will issue calls that run Oracle-provided scripts.

It's important that you create both scripts that are defined in this lab (2.2.2) before attempting to create your database. If you do not prepare these scripts prior to database creation, it will lead to confusion in Lab 2.2.3.

1) In the admin/db00/create directory, create a SQL*Plus script called createdb00_01.sql that contains a CREATE DATABASE statement. Remember to put a header at the top of your script, identifying what the script contains. Use the following template script to get you going. Just replace the location values in the template scripts with the correct locations for your environment.

The location of the /admin/db00/pfile directory can be laborious to type and you will be using it quite a bit in this book's exercises. You may wish to create a PFILE operating system environment variable to use when starting your database. You can use it from within Server Manager as in:

In UNIX:

```
STARTUP NOMOUNT PFILE = $PFILE
```

In NT:

```
STARTUP NOMOUNT PFILE = %PFILE%
```

The templates for the two scripts below (createdb00_01.sql and createdb00_02.sql) are provided on the Web at www.phptr.com/ phptrinteractive

```
REM ********************************************************
REM *      filename: createdb00_01.sql      version: 1
REM *       purpose: Creates a database named db00
REM *          args: none
REM *       created: by: dscherer date: April 26, 1999
REM *         notes: In this script, the following
REM *                should be set to match your
REM *                environment:
REM *                /u01/oradata/db00 represents your
REM *                ORADATA directory.
REM ********************************************************
SET ECHO ON
SET TERMOUT ON
SPOOL createdb00_01.log
CONNECT internal/oracle
STARTUP NOMOUNT PFILE=$PFILE
CREATE DATABASE db00
LOGFILE
  GROUP 1 ('/u01/oradata/db00/redo_01a.log',
           '/u01/oradata/db00/redo_01b.log'
           ) size 100K,
  GROUP 2 ('/u01/oradata/db00/redo_02a.log',
           '/u01/oradata/db00/redo_02b.log'
           ) size 100K
MAXLOGFILES 32
MAXLOGMEMBERS 2
MAXLOGHISTORY 1
DATAFILE '/u01/oradata/db00/system01.dbf'
  SIZE 75M
MAXDATAFILES 254
MAXINSTANCES 1;
SPOOL OFF
```

a) In a few sentences, briefly describe what you think this script will do.

_____

_____

2) In the admin/db00/create directory, create a second SQL*Plus script called createdb00_02.sql, which contains calls to the Oracle-provided scripts that create the additional database objects—including the data dictionary needed to make the database work. Just replace the location values in the template scripts with the correct locations for your environment.

```
REM  ******************************************************
REM  *      filename: createdb00_02.sql      version: 1
REM  *      purpose: Creates the data dictionary
REM  *               and other additional database
REM  *               objects.
REM  *         args: none
REM  *      created: by: dscherer date: April 2, 2000
REM  *        notes: In this script, the following
REM  *               should be set to match your
REM  *               environment:
REM  *               /u01/oradata/db00 represents your
REM  *               ORADATA directory.
REM  *               /u01/app/oracle/product/8.1.6/
REM  *               represents your ORACLE_HOME
REM  *               directory.
REM  ******************************************************
SET ECHO ON
SET TERMOUT ON
SPOOL createdb00_02.log
CONNECT internal/oracle
STARTUP PFILE = $PFILE
CREATE ROLLBACK SEGMENT SYSROL
   TABLESPACE system
   STORAGE (INITIAL 100K NEXT 100K);
ALTER ROLLBACK SEGMENT sysrol ONLINE;
REM ********* TABLESPACE FOR ROLLBACK *********
CREATE TABLESPACE RBS
   DATAFILE '/u01/oradata/db00/rbs01.dbf' SIZE 40M
   DEFAULT STORAGE (INITIAL 128k
                    PCTINCREASE 0
                    );
REM ********* TABLESPACE FOR USER *********
CREATE TABLESPACE USERS
   DATAFILE '/u01/oradata/db00/users01.dbf'
   SIZE 25M
   DEFAULT STORAGE (INITIAL 128K
                    MAXEXTENTS UNLIMITED
                    PCTINCREASE 0
                    );
```

```
REM ********** TABLESPACE FOR TEMPORARY **********
CREATE TABLESPACE TEMP
   DATAFILE '/u01/oradata/db00/temp01.dbf'
   SIZE 25M
   DEFAULT STORAGE (INITIAL 128K
                    MAXEXTENTS UNLIMITED
                    PCTINCREASE 0
                    )
   TEMPORARY;
REM ********** TABLESPACE FOR INDEX **********
CREATE TABLESPACE INDX
   DATAFILE '/u01/oradata/db00/indx01.dbf'
   SIZE 25M
   DEFAULT STORAGE (INITIAL 128K
                    MAXEXTENTS UNLIMITED
                    PCTINCREASE 0
                    );
REM ********** TABLESPACE FOR TOOLS **********
CREATE TABLESPACE tools
   DATAFILE '/u01/oradata/db00/tools01.dbf' size 25M
   DEFAULT STORAGE (INITIAL 128K
                    MAXEXTENTS UNLIMITED
                    PCTINCREASE 0
                    );
REM ******* CREATE ADDITIONAL ROLLBACK SEGMENTS *******
CREATE ROLLBACK SEGMENT RB01 TABLESPACE RBS
   STORAGE (INITIAL 100K NEXT 100K OPTIMAL 300K);
CREATE ROLLBACK SEGMENT RB02 TABLESPACE RBS
   STORAGE (INITIAL 100K NEXT 100K OPTIMAL 300K);
CREATE ROLLBACK SEGMENT RB03 TABLESPACE RBS
   STORAGE (INITIAL 100K NEXT 100K OPTIMAL 300K);
CREATE ROLLBACK SEGMENT RB04 TABLESPACE RBS
   STORAGE (INITIAL 100K NEXT 100K OPTIMAL 300K);
ALTER ROLLBACK SEGMENT rb01 ONLINE;
ALTER ROLLBACK SEGMENT rb02 ONLINE;
ALTER ROLLBACK SEGMENT rb03 ONLINE;
ALTER ROLLBACK SEGMENT rb04 ONLINE;
REM ***** CONFIGURE SYS *****
ALTER USER SYS
   TEMPORARY TABLESPACE temp;
REM ****************************************
REM ****** CREATE THE DATA DICTIONARY *****
REM ******    AND PROCEDURAL OPTION    *****
REM ****************************************
REM For the catalog.sql and catproc.sql
REM   scripts that follow, you may need to
```

**LAB
2.2**

```
REM    make the following changes:
REM In Oracle8.0 for NT use:
REM    @ORACLE_HOME\rdbms80\admin\ScriptName.sql
REM In Oracle7.3.4 for NT use
REM    @ORACLE_HOME\rdbms73\admin\ScriptName.sql
REM In UNIX (and Oracle8i for NT) use
REM @ORACLE_HOME\rdbms\admin\ScriptName.sql
REM ****************************************
@/u01/app/oracle/product/8.1.6/rdbms/admin/catalog.sql
@/u01/app/oracle/product/8.1.6/rdbms/admin/catproc.sql
CONNECT system/manager
@/u01/app/oracle/product/8.1.6/sqlplus/admin/pupbld.sql
CONNECT internal/oracle
REM ******** LAST BIT OF CLEANUP **********
ALTER ROLLBACK SEGMENT sysrol OFFLINE;
ALTER USER SYSTEM
   DEFAULT TABLESPACE tools
   TEMPORARY TABLESPACE temp;
REM ***************************************************
REM *** The commands below this point are used
REM ***    only to create the environment for this
REM ***    book. They do not normally need to be
REM ***    included in a database creation script.
REM ***************************************************
REM *** CREATE ACCOUNT TO BE USED WITH THIS BOOK ***
CREATE USER pth01 IDENTIFIED BY books
   DEFAULT TABLESPACE users
   TEMPORARY TABLESPACE temp;
GRANT CONNECT, RESOURCE TO pth01;
REM ***************************************************
SPOOL OFF
```

Remember, the init.ora file, scripts, and final database are designed to be used with the exercises in this book. When you are ready to implement databases for your development and production environments, you will need to base sizing, configuration, and layout on the specific needs of those databases.

Replace the names in bold face with the true directory names on your system and save the file.

b) In a few sentences, briefly describe what you think this script will do.

_____

_____

c) Looking at all of the statements in this script, where do you see that OFA compliance is not adhered to, but would be very useful.

_____

_____

2.2.3 CREATE THE DATABASE USING THE CREATE SCRIPTS

If you run into problems with these steps, you may need to clean your environment of all the files that the scripts created and start again.

Now you get to make use of all the hard work you did in Lab 2.2.2. You get to run the scripts and create the Database.

1) Make sure you are in the admin/db00/create directory.

2) The ORACLE_SID environment variable is used to identify the name of an Instance on the host machine. In this case, you are going to use it prior to opening Server Manager so that Server Manager knows against which Instance you want to perform your tasks. In the environment you are configuring for the exercises in this book, the ORACLE_SID (also called the SID, or Instance name) and the Database name (represented by the db_name parameter in the init.ora file) are the same.

You should always check that your ORACLE_SID environment variable is set properly before performing work In Server Manager. You can check the ORACLE_SID variable with the echo commands described earlier.

Make sure your ORACLE_SID and ORACLE_HOME environment variables point to the correct Instance and location.

    a) Write the statement to set up your ORACLE_SID environment variable.

    _____

    _____

    b) Now write the statement you used to test that the ORACLE_SID environment variable is set properly.

    _____

    _____

    c) Write the statement to set up your ORACLE_HOME environment variable.

    _____

    _____

    d) Write the statement that you used to test that the ORACLE_HOME environment variable is set properly.

    _____

    _____

3) From the command line, start Server Manager in line mode.

    `e:\Oracle\Ora81`

If You're Using NT...

In the next step, you will start running the create scripts. On the NT platform, there are a few additional steps to perform. Before you run the create scripts, you must create an NT service. You will do this from the command line.

Issue the command:

```
del e:\Oracle\Ora81\database\pwddb00.ora
```

where `e:\Oracle\Ora81\` is your ORACLE_HOME. This command will remove an existing password file.

The next command (oradim—also called Instance Manager) should be issued on one line and will create an NT service. It is a long command and is shown here wrapping over several lines because of the book's page size. The command is shown for versions 7.3, 8.0, and 8i.

In Oracle8i, issue:

```
oradim -new -sid DB00 -intpwd oracle -startmode manual
-pfile e:\Oracle\admin\db00\pfile\init.ora
```

where e:\Oracle is your **ORACLE_BASE.**

A file is created to report on the execution of the oradim command. For Oracle8i, it is created in ***ORACLE_HOME***\database\oradim.log (or, in this sample, e:\Oracle\Ora81\database\oradim.log).

In Oracle8.0, issue:

```
oradim80 -new -sid DB00 -intpwd oracle -startmode
manual -pfile e:\ORANT\admin\db00\pfile\init.ora
```

where e:\ORANT is your **ORACLE_BASE.**

In Oracle8.0, the execution log file is created as ***ORACLE_HOME***\rdbms80\oradim80.log (or, in this sample, e:\ORANT\rdbms80\oradim80.log).

In Oracle7.3, issue:

```
oradim73 -new -sid DB00 -intpwd oracle -startmode
manual -pfile e:\ORANT\admin\db00\pfile\init.ora
```

Where e:\ORANT is your **ORACLE_BASE.**

In Oracle7.3, the execution log file is created as ***ORACLE_HOME***\rdbms73\oradim73.log (or, in this sample, e:\ORANT\rdbms73\oradim73.log).

Next, make sure that your service is running. Go to the **Start->Settings->Control Panel** (In Windows 2000—levels Professional and higher—use **Start->Settings->Control Panel->Administrative Tools**) and double-click the Services icon. Scroll through the list of services until you reach **OracleServiceDB00.** It should say Started, and in the Startup column, it should say Manual. If the service is not running, click the Start button (in Windows NT) or the Start Service button (in the toolbar at the top of the Services window in Windows 2000).

4) Now that you have set up your environment variables and have started Server Manager in line mode, you are ready to run the scripts.

You should allocate enough time to work from this point to the end of the chapter without shutting down your machine or your sessions. One of the scripts can take 20 minutes to two hours to run. Of course, you do not have to wait at the computer while it runs, but when it is done, there are some additional tasks for you to do. Allocate two to three hours of time for the rest of this chapter. All of these steps will be done in Server Manager line mode.

Now run the script called createdb00_01.sql. This script may take 10 to 20 minutes.

    e) What message do you get back in Server Manager when the CREATE DATABASE statement is done running?

Check the spooled log file. If you see any error messages, correct the CREATE DATABASE statement, save the file, and try again.

Frequently Encountered Errors

1) The error message is similar to "ORA-01031: insufficient privileges" and may be seen in some installations because of the way that some privileges are set in your environment. If you get this error, you should issue a SHUTDOWN ABORT in Server Manager and then exit Server Manager. Next add the following line to your init.ora file:

`REMOTE_LOGIN_PASSWORDFILE=exclusive`

Begin the creation process again by opening Server Manager and re-running `createdb00_01.sql`.

2) You may receive the error message "LRM-00109: could not open parameter file 'E:\orant\DATABASE\INITdb00.ORA" along with the error message "ORA-01078: failure in processing system parameters". If so, the Instance could not find your init.ora file. In this case, issue a SHUTDOWN ABORT and make sure that a PFILE environment variable is defined. Use the `echo` command to check as described above. If you get the message again, you can change the line in the `createdb00_01.sql` and `createdb00_02.sql` scripts to use the full path to your init.ora file. So, `PFILE=$PFILE` (or `PFILE=%PFILE%`) would be replaced by something similar to `PFILE=/u01/app/oracle/admin/pfile/init.ora` (or `e:\oracle\admin\db00\pfile\init.ora`).

Begin the creation process again by re-running `createdb00_01.sql`.

5) Issue the following command:

```
SELECT name
   FROM v$database;
```

If you get back one row stating the name of your database, then proceed to the next step. If not, revisit the previous steps and check your work to make sure all the scripts are correct.

6) Once you have received a successful test in Step 2.2.3.5, run the script called createdb00_02.sql in Server Manager. This may run for 20 minutes to an hour or more.

If You're Using NT... (Revisited)

Now that your database is successfully created, you can alter your NT service so that it starts automatically when the machine starts. This will eliminate the need for you to open the NT Services Window and start the service each time you boot your machine. Since the service already exists, you use the Oradim command to edit it.

To configure the service to start automatically issue one of the following commands in an MS-DOS Window.

In Oracle8i issue:

```
oradim -edit -sid DB00 -startmode auto
```

In Oracle8.0 issue:

```
oradim80 -edit -sid DB00 -startmode auto
```

In Oracle7.3 issue:

```
oradim73 -edit -sid DB00 -startmode auto
```

Check the associated log file (as described in the earlier sidebar, "If You're Using NT...") for any errors. The next time you start your machine, the Service will start automatically.

2.2.4 TEST DATABASE VIABILITY

Now you will issue a few SQL statements to check that your database is running okay.

At this point, the Instance and the Database have been started and are open. Each operating system has a command that allows you to see which processes are currently running. In some UNIX environments, you can issue the command ps -ef | grep ora_ (the ps command options vary with different types of UNIX. For example, in Linux, the command would be ps ax | grep ora_), but how about in NT? There is no way to look at the actual background processes since they all run under one program.

In any operating system, you can get a list of the running background processes by issuing the following statement while connected as an account with DBA privileges.

```
SELECT name, description
  FROM v$bgprocess
 WHERE paddr != '00'
 ORDER BY name;
```

Issue the statement now, from within Server Manager while connected INTERNAL.

    a) List which background processes you found running. List both the name and description.

NAME	DESCRIPTION

Using the following query, get a list of the tablespaces in your database:

```
SELECT tablespace_name
  FROM dba_tablespaces
 ORDER BY tablespace_name;
```

Issue the statement now.

b) Write down the result set from the tablespace query.

NAME	DESCRIPTION

2.2.5 SET THE ROLLBACK_SEGMENTS PARAMETER

Now you are going to locate information about some objects in the database called *rollback segments*. You are going to see which ones are online and which ones are offline. Then you are going to add a parameter to the init.ora file to assure that the correct ones are brought online automatically when the database starts up.

Instance Acquisition of Rollback Segments across Oracle Versions

The algorithm that the database uses to acquire rollback segments at startup is different in Oracle8i than it is in earlier versions. There is more information on this in the Lab 2.2 Exercise Answers section.

---

1) In Server Manager, issue the following SQL statement against the data dictionary:

```
SELECT  segment_name
   FROM  dba_rollback_segs
  WHERE  status = 'ONLINE'
    AND  segment_name != 'SYSTEM';
```

a) There should be four rollback segments online. List them.

---

2) Now shutdown your database by issuing the following command in Server Manager, but do not close your Server Manager session:

```
SHUTDOWN IMMEDIATE
```

3) Now restart the database by issuing the following statement in Server Manager:

```
STARTUP PFILE=$PFILE
```

4) Now re-issue the SQL statement listed in Step 2.2.5.1.

b) Which rollback segments do you find online now?

_____

_____

_____

_____

Shutdown the database again, leaving the Server Manager session open as you did in Step 2.2.5.2.

5) Copy your init.ora file to init.ora.01 in your pfile directory. If you made other incremental saves, then you might call it init.ora.02 or whatever the next highest version number is. Now open init.ora for editing and add a new parameter that will tell Oracle which rollback segments to automatically place online. Substitute each **NAMEn** for the rollback segments you listed in Step 2.2.5.1.

```
rollback_segments=(NAME1, NAME2, NAME3, NAME4)
```

Save and close the init.ora file.

Startup the database again as you did in Step 2.2.5.3.

c) Again issue the query that shows which rollback segments are online and list them.

_____

_____

2.2.6 REVIEW THE SCRIPTS THAT CREATE THE DATA DICTIONARY

Two of the scripts that are called from within the createdb00_02.sql script are catalog.sql and catproc.sql. These scripts in turn call other scripts. One of those scripts is standard.sql.

a) Briefly describe what catalog.sql does.

_____

_____

_____

_____

b) Following the path to catalog.sql from within createdb00_02.sql, find the location of standard.sql and write it here.

_____

_____

c) Briefly describe what you think standard.sql does.

_____

_____

There are some reminders about environment settings located in Appendix D. You should review them now.

LAB 2.2 EXERCISE ANSWERS

2.2.1 ANSWERS

a) What is the name of your database?

Answer: To keep in line with the book, you may have called it db00. Otherwise, you will have put the name you chose for your database here.

b) What are the locations of your control files?

Answer: This will depend on your environment. Your answers should be similar to the examples shown in the exercise. Make sure to write the location of your control files. You will need this information later.

c) What version is your database installation?

Answer: Look at the documentation, or determine the version by viewing your ORACLE_HOME environment variable (the version number generally appears as the name of this directory). Make sure that you have the COMPATIBLE parameter set accordingly, since it will severely affect the functionality of your database.

d) What is the location of your background_dump_dest?

Answer: background_dump_dest should be located in the bdump directory.

In UNIX, continuing with the example, the parameter might look like:

```
background_dump_dest=/u01/app/admin/db00/bdump
```

In NT Oracle8i, the parameter might look like:

```
background_dump_dest=e:\oracle\admin\db00\bdump
```

The background_dump_dest parameter specifies the location for the database alert log and the location for trace files that are created when one of the Instance's background processes produces an error. The files are created with a .trc extension.

e) What is the location of your core_dump_dest?

Answer: This parameter should point to your cdump directory.

In UNIX, that might look like:

```
core_dump_dest=/u01/app/admin/db00/cdump
```

In NT, core_dump_dest is an invalid parameter since it is mainly used in environments like UNIX, which create a core file containing debugging information when a fatal error occurs within a running program.

f) What is the location of your user_dump_dest?

Answer: This parameter should point to your udump directory.

In UNIX, that might look like:

```
user_dump_dest=/u01/app/admin/db00/udump
```

In NT, it might look like:

```
user_dump_dest=e:\oracle\admin\db00\udump
```

This directory holds trace files created from user sessions. These can include trace files that you specify to be created—such as for the purpose of getting information to assist you in tuning your application's SQL statements.

g) How big is the Shared Pool going to be?

Answer: The Shared Pool is going to be 3.5M, as specified in the shared_pool_size parameter.

h) Where is the alert log going to be created?

Answer: The alert log will be created in the directory specified in the background_dump_dest directory. The alert log in the case of the example database will be alert_db00.log.

2.2.2 ANSWERS

a) In a few sentences, briefly describe what you think this script will do.

Answer: This script contains a CREATE DATABASE statement. It runs when you are connected as INTERNAL or SYS AS SYSDBA. It simply creates an Oracle Database. The physical files created with this database include a datafile, control files as specified by the control_files parameter in the init.ora file, and two groups of redo log files.

b) In a few sentences, briefly describe what you think this script will do?

*Answer: This script will create additional pieces for the database to support clients logging on and doing work. It does that by directly issuing DDL statements that create additional tablespaces and rollback segments, setting defaults for the SYS and SYSTEM accounts, and by calling other SQL*Plus scripts.*

c) Looking at all of the statements in this script, where do you see that OFA compliance is not adhered to, but would be very useful?

Answer: One place where it is fairly obvious that the OFA model was not considered is with the statements commented out that relate to pre-Oracle8i databases in NT. In those environments, ORACLE_BASE and ORACLE_HOME were, by default, the same. So, executables for different versions of the database existed in the same directory. When they wanted to separate different versions, they would have to add the version number to the name of the directory. So, you see an rdbms73 directory and an rdbms80 directory instead of just an rdbms directory under the product-specific ORACLE_HOME directory.

2.2.3 ANSWERS

a) Write the statement to set up the ORACLE_SID environment variable.

Answer: In UNIX korn shell, for example, this would be:

```
$ export ORACLE_SID=db00
```

In NT, it would be:

```
set ORACLE_SID=db00
```

b) Now write the statement you used to test that the ORACLE_SID environment variable was set correctly.

Answer: In UNIX, you can use:

```
$ echo   $ORACLE_SID
```

In NT, you can use:

```
echo %ORACLE_SID%
```

c) Write the statement to set up your ORACLE_HOME environment variable.

Answer: In certain UNIX shells, it might look similar to:

```
$ export ORACLE_HOME=/u01/app/oracle/product/8.1.6
```

In NT using Oracle8i, it might look something like:

```
set ORACLE_HOME=e:\oracle\ora81
```

d) Write the statement that you used to test that the ORACLE_HOME environment variable was set properly.

Answer: In UNIX, you can use:

```
$ echo   $ORACLE_HOME
```

In NT, you can use:

```
echo %ORACLE_HOME%
```

e) What message do you get back in Server Manager when the CREATE DATABASE statement is done running?

Answer: If your statement ran without errors, you should receive the single message:

```
Statement processed.
```

a) List which background processes you found running. List both the name and description.

Answer: Your query should produce a list that includes at least the PMON, SMON, DBWR, and LGWR processes. In pre-Oracle8 databases, you may not get the CKPT process started automatically. If that is the case, you can get it to start by adding the parameter:

```
checkpoint_process=true
```

to your init.ora file and restarting your database. In pre-Oracle8i installations, your database writer process may be called DBWR instead of DBW0.

NAME	DESCRIPTION
CKPT	Checkpoint
DBW0	Database writer
LGWR	Log writer
PMON	Process monitor
SMON	System monitor

b) Write down the result set from the tablespace query.

Answer: Your query should have returned the following tablespaces:

```
TABLESPACE_NAME

---------------

INDX

RBS

SYSTEM

TEMP

TOOLS

USERS
```

2.2.5 ANSWERS

a) There should be four rollback segments on the list. List them.

Answer: These should be as follows:

```
SEGMENT_NAME
-----------
RB01
RB02
RB03
RB04
```

b) Which rollback segments do you find online now?

Answer: Oddly enough, this list can be different, depending on which version of Oracle you're using.

In versions of Oracle prior to Oracle8i, you will probably not see any rollback segments listed online (the SYSTEM rollback segment was online, but it was filtered out in the WHERE clause). A change in Oracle8i eliminates the need for the rollback_segments parameter in most installations. So, in Oracle8i, you may see all of the rollback segments online.

c) Again issue the query that shows which rollback segments are online and list them.

Answer: The rollback_segments parameter specifies which rollback segments will be brought online at Instance startup. So, all four rollback segments that you listed in Question a) should be in this list of online rollback segments.

2.2.6 ANSWERS

a) Briefly describe what catalog.sql does.

Answer: The catalog.sql script performs several tasks. Among them is creating the data dictionary views.

b) Following the path to catalog.sql from within createdb00_02.sql, find the location of standard.sql and write it here.

*Answer: **ORACLE_HOME**/rdbms/admin. For example: e:\Oracle\Ora81\rdbms\admin.*

c) Briefly describe what you think standard.sql does.

Answer: standard.sql is responsible for creating identifiers, data types, and other core components of PL/SQL.

LAB 2.2 SELF-REVIEW QUESTIONS

1) Which of the following make up an Oracle Instance? (Choose all that apply)

   a) _____ RBS01
   b) _____ SGA
   c) _____ Datafiles
   d) _____ Background processes
   e) _____ Redo logs
   f) _____ Control files

2) Which of the following three make up an Oracle Database? (Choose all that apply)

   a) _____ RBS01
   b) _____ Datafiles
   c) _____ Instance
   d) _____ Background processes
   e) _____ Redo logs
   f) _____ Control files

3) What does the compatible parameter specify?

   a) _____ Which client applications are compatible with Oracle
   b) _____ The Oracle license feature's compatibility
   c) _____ Which version of features are allowed in your Oracle database
   d) _____ The number of redo logs that are compatible with the control files
   e) _____ The SGA size

4) Which of the following are the three main parts of the SGA?

   a) _____ Database Buffer Cache, DBW0, Shared Pool
   b) _____ Database Buffer Cache, Redo Log Buffer, Shared Pool
   c) _____ DBW0, Redo Buffer, Shared Pool
   e) _____ DBW0, LGWR, Shared Pool

5) Which of the following are the four background processes that must be running in all Oracle versions (7.3-8i)?

   a) _____ CKPT, DBW0/DBWR, LGWR, CKPT
   b) _____ DBW0/DBWR, LGWR, SNP0, SVR0

c) _____ D000, LGWR, SMON, SVR0
d) _____ D000, LGWR, PMON, SVR0
e) _____ DBW0/DBWR, LGWR, PMON, SMON

6) What's the main difference between the DBA account's SYS and SYSTEM?

a) _____ SYSTEM is the only one that can create new users
b) _____ SYS is the only one that can create new users
c) _____ SYS owns the data dictionary
d) _____ SYSTEM owns the data dictionary
e) _____ SYS controls Database Writer
f) _____ SYSTEM controls the Database Writer

7) Which of the following are the four shutdown types?

a) _____ ABORT, EXTERNAL, FORCE, INTERNAL
b) _____ ABORT, IMMEDIATE, INTERNAL, TEMPORARY
c) _____ ABORT, IMMEDIATE, NORMAL, TRANSACTIONAL
d) _____ IMMEDIATE, INTERNAL, NORMAL, TRANSACTIONAL
e) _____ IMMEDIATE, INTERNAL, NORMAL, OPEN
f) _____ IMMEDIATE, INTERNAL, MOUNT, TRANSACTIONAL

8) Which of the following are the three startup modes?

a) _____ EXTERNAL, MOUNT, OPEN
b) _____ MOUNT, NOMOUNT, TEMPORARY
c) _____ IMMEDATE, MOUNT, NOMOUNT
d) _____ MOUNT, NOMOUNT, OPEN
e) _____ INTERNAL, MOUNT, OPEN

9) What does the ifile parameter in the init.ora file signify?

a) _____ It points to a file with additional configuration parameters
b) _____ It lists the Instance's datafiles
c) _____ It is used to determine how many files the Database may consist of
d) _____ It contains the values TRUE or FALSE, stating whether or not this Instance is allowed to start

10) What are the two parts of the Shared Pool?

a) _____ Database Buffer Cache and Redo Log Buffer
b) _____ Database Buffer Cache and Library Cache
c) _____ Dictionary Cache and Library Cache
d) _____ Dictionary Cache and Redo Log Buffer
e) _____ Database Buffer Cache and Dictionary Cache

Quiz answers appear in Appendix A, Section 2.2.

CHAPTER 2

TEST YOUR THINKING

In this chapter, you set up your directory structure and created a new database. Of course, the goals with this database and its configuration were fairly simple. Each CREATE DATABASE script you write will be customized for the specific application and use it is destined to support.

1) Choose a scenario that is likely to occur in your business environment and write a paragraph or two describing it in a way that would assist you in the initial configuration of the database. What kinds of things do you think would be important in the planning of your Database? If you don't have a real-life environment to pull information from, make up an environment where you would like to work and imagine what needs that database would have.

C H A P T E R   3

ORACLE NETWORKING: CONFIGURING BASIC NET8/SQL*NET COMPONENTS

CHAPTER OBJECTIVES

In this chapter, you will learn about:

✔ Setting Up Networking Configuration Files	Page 58
✔ Managing the Oracle Listener	Page 67
✔ Configuring the Multi-Threaded Server	Page 76

Now that your database is running, the next step involves setting up the basic Oracle networking components. This additional step makes the database available to users—such as those you will create in Chapter 10, "Privileges and Resource Groups" over a network. The topic of Oracle networking involves many different components and many different implementations. This chapter focuses on basic networking components, including the dedicated server configuration and multi-threaded server configuration using the TCP/IP protocol.

LAB 3.1

SETTING UP NETWORK CONFIGURATION FILES

LAB OBJECTIVES

In this lab, you will:

✔ Manually Configure the tnsnames.ora File
✔ Manually Configure the listener.ora File

LAB 3.1 EXERCISES

3.1.1 MANUALLY CONFIGURE THE TNSNAMES.ORA FILE

Chapter 3 is concerned with setting up basic Oracle networking configuration. It is included at the beginning of the Oracle DBA Interactive Workbook to emulate the flow of tasks involved in the preparation of a new database. This chapter is different from the others in the book in that it is not required to be completed before starting work in subsequent chapters. There are many general networking issues that fall outside the scope of this book, but can affect the way that SQL*Net/Net8 work. Because of this, you may wish to complete Chapter 3 after you have completed the other chapters in this book.

The steps involved in making an Oracle database available through a network are relatively simple. Database communication is made possible by *Net8* (a set of networking components). These components can support connections from the same machine that the database is on, or from remote machines.

You Say Potato, I Say Net8

Prior to Oracle8.x, there was a set of networking components called SQL*Net. SQL*Net is not available with Oracle8.x and Net8 is not available with Oracle7.x. So, although these two sets should be considered separate entities, they perform the same base level functionality for the different Oracle Server versions and will both be referred to as Net8 in this book.

One of the important components of Oracle networking is the Oracle listener. The listener is the process responsible for receiving database connection requests and redirecting them to another process, which in turn becomes the main point of contact between the client and the database. The process that ultimately services user requests is called a *server process*. It is the responsibility of the server process to perform such tasks as reading data from disk into the Database Buffer Cache and sorting query results.

There are two possible configurations for the server process. In the *dedicated server configuration*, one server process is started for each client connection to the database. This server process is then dedicated to serving only that connection's request. In the *multi-threaded server configuration*, shared servers perform most of the same tasks as the dedicated server. The main difference is that, where a dedicated server only supports one client, a shared server supports one or more clients. The ability to support multiple client connections can be useful if the number of requests made by each client connection is low. Therefore, a dedicated server configuration would be useful for operations such as a batch load of data into the database, whereas a multi-threaded server configuration would be more appropriate for supporting many clients, each of which periodically performs transactions on the database that affect small amounts of data.

The information needed to establish database connections is stored in several configuration files. The following two configuration files will be discussed in this chapter:

- tnsnames.ora
- listener.ora

Note that there are several other configuration files that are used, depending on your Oracle networking needs. For example, the sqlnet.ora file is used for configuring logging and tracing for database connection problems, and setting Oracle Advanced Security parameters, among others. For the simple network configuration in theses exercises, you will work with only the tnsnames.ora and listener.ora configuration files.

These files can be found in a location known as the TNS_ADMIN directory. The location of this directory depends on the version of the Oracle Server that is installed. For versions 7.x and 8.1.x, the TNS_ADMIN directory is usually at ORACLE_HOME\network\admin; for version 8.0.x, it is usually at ORACLE_ HOME\net80\admin. Occasionally, you will find an installation that uses an environment variable named TNS_ADMIN to point to the location of the network configuration files. If a TNS_ADMIN environment variable is used, the DBA must make sure that the configuration files are moved to the new TNS_ADMIN location.

a) What is the location of your TNS_ADMIN directory?

_____

The *listener.ora* file simply contains configuration information for the Oracle listener. The *tnsnames.ora* file is used in defining *TNS service names*. "TNS," which stands for Transparent Network Substrate, serves as a single, common interface to most industry-standard networking protocols. TNS service names are resolved in the tnsnames.ora file, which contains information on where to locate particular databases. For example, you might define a TNS service name called DEV. In tnsnames.ora, the configuration information for DEV may indicate that the listener for this database is located at Port 1521 on IP address 111.222.333.444 (or the name of the machine at that address) and listens for connection requests to a database called "dev". Note that in these exercises, the tnsnames.ora file is configured on the database server. For many client or front-end environments, there is usually a tnsnames.ora file to support connections to the database. Oracle is slowly moving away from using these files that support TNS service names, and moving towards the use of the Oracle Names Server. For more information on the Oracle Names Server, see the Oracle document "Net8 Administrator's Guide."

In these exercises, you will set up two TNS service names. The first will allow you to connect to your own database through Net8. The second is optional, and will allow you to connect to a second, remote database.

A template for two TNS service name definitions is shown below:

```
###################################
#        FILENAME: tnsnames.ora      #
# LAST MODIFIED: March 24, 2000      #
###################################
example00 =
  (DESCRIPTION =
    (ADDRESS_LIST =
        (ADDRESS =
           (PROTOCOL = TCP)
           (HOST = development)
           (PORT = 1521)
        )
    )
    (CONNECT_DATA =
      (SID = db00)
    )
  )
example01 =
  (DESCRIPTION =
    (ADDRESS_LIST =
        (ADDRESS =
           (PROTOCOL = TCP)
           (HOST = production)
           (PORT = 1521)
        )
    )
    (CONNECT_DATA =
      (SID = db01)
    )
  )
```

If you have access to a database other than your own, you can configure connectivity to it by performing the following steps on the "example01" TNS service name in the above template:

- If there is an existing tnsnames.ora file in your TNS_ADMIN directory, back it up. (If you have problems with the tnsnames.ora file after making the edits in this chapter, you can restore the original from the backup.) In keeping with the backup file naming standard used in this book, you should name it tnsnames.ora.01.

- If you do not already have a file called tnsnames.ora in your TNS_ADMIN directory, then create a new one with a text editor. Create it as shown in the above template. If you already have a tnsnames.ora file, then append it with the text from the template above.

- Change "example01" to "*<SID>*", where <SID> is the SID of the Instance on the remote machine. Note that, since this is a logical name, you can call it anything that you want; it does not have to be the same as the name of the database (however, for purposes of simplification, it is often the same as the database name). You could, for example, leave the name as "example01" and still use it to locate a database called "db01".
- Change "Host = Production" to "Host = *name of the machine or network name for the machine where the database is located*". You can either use the name or the IP address. It is recommended that you use the name if you know what it is.
- Change "Port = 1521" to "Port = *the port number of the listener*". Note that 1521 is the default port for an Oracle listener and should not be changed unless another service is already using that port or you are instructed to do so in the Oracle documentation.
- Change "db01" to "*<SID>*". This is the name of the Instance that you will be connecting to.
- Save the file and close your text editor.

Once you have entered configuration information for this optional TNS service name into tnsnames.ora, you can open SQL*Plus and attempt to connect to the database it represents using the following syntax:

```
CONNECT <username>/<password>@<TNSservicename>
```

In the next exercise, you will configure and start the Oracle listener for your own database. You will configure a TNS service name for the database that you created in Chapter 2.

b) Using the steps outlined above for configuring the "example01" TNS service name, configure the "example00" TNS service name to locate the database you created in Chapter 2. Show the final version of the tnsnames.ora file.

_____

_____

3.1.2 MANUALLY CONFIGURE THE LISTENER.ORA FILE

In these exercises, you will configure the listener for your own database. The listener.ora file, which is the configuration file for the listener, is kept in the TNS_ADMIN directory. It contains information such as the name of the listener, the name of the databases for which it accepts connection requests, and the location of log files produced by the listener.

- Locate your listener.ora file and make a backup copy of it.
- Delete the original copy of the listener.ora file, then create a new one and open it for editing.
- Add the following template information to the new file:

```
####################################
#       FILENAME: listener.ora      #
# LAST MODIFIED: March 24, 2000     #
####################################
LISTENER =
        (ADDRESS =
          (PROTOCOL = TCP)
          (HOST = production)
          (PORT = 1521)
        )
    )
STARTUP_WAIT_TIME_LISTENER = 0
CONNECT_TIMEOUT_LISTENER = 10
LOG_DIRECTORY_LISTENER = e:\Oracle\Ora81\network\log
LOG_FILE_LISTENER = listener
SID_LIST_LISTENER =
  (SID_LIST =
    (SID_DESC =
      (SID_NAME = db00)
      (ORACLE_HOME = e:\Oracle\Ora81)
    )
  )
```

- Now review and edit this template where applicable:
  - The "LISTENER =" states the name of your listener. This is also known as the listener alias.

- • Replace all occurrences of "db00" with the name of your Instance (SID)
- • Change "HOST = production" to "HOST = <network name or machine name where the listener is running>"
- • Change "ORACLE_HOME = e:\Oracle\Ora81" to "ORACLE_HOME = <your ORACLE_HOME directory>"
- • Change "LOG_DIRECTORY_LISTENER = e:\Oracle\Ora81\network\log" to "LOG_DIRECTORY_LISTENER = <your ORACLE_HOME location>\network\log" (or "LOG_DIRECTORY_LISTENER = <your ORACLE_HOME location>\net80\log" if you are running Oracle8.0.x).
- • Save the listener.ora file and close the text editor.

LAB 3.1 EXERCISE ANSWERS

3.1.1 ANSWERS

a) What is the location of your TNS_ADMIN directory?

Answer: Your TNS_ADMIN directory will usually be located in either ORACLE_HOME\network\admin or ORACLE_HOME\net80\admin. It's a good idea to check your environment for a TNS_ADMIN variable. In UNIX with the korn shell, you can use following command: `echo $TNS_ADMIN`*. It is rare to find the variable set for an NT environment, but if it is set, you will find it in the Windows NT Registry within the HKEY_LOCAL_MACHINE-> SOFTWARE->ORACLE node.*

b) Using the steps outlined above for configuring the "example01" TNS service name, configure the "example00" TNS service name to locate the database you created in Chapter 2. Show the final version of the tnsnames.ora file.

Answer: The final version of your tnsnames.ora file will look similar to the following:

```
####################################
#        FILENAME: tnsnames.ora        #
# LAST MODIFIED: March 24, 2000       #
####################################
db00 =
   (DESCRIPTION =
     (ADDRESS_LIST =
         (ADDRESS =
            (PROTOCOL = TCP)
            (HOST = production)
            (PORT = 1521)
         )
     )
     (CONNECT_DATA =
        (SID = db00)
     )
   )
dev =
   (DESCRIPTION =
     (ADDRESS_LIST =
         (ADDRESS =
            (PROTOCOL = TCP)
            (HOST = development)
            (PORT = 1521)
         )
     )
     (CONNECT_DATA =
        (SID = dev)
     )
   )
```

LAB 3.1 SELF-REVIEW QUESTIONS

To test your progress, you should be able to answer the following questions.

1) Net8 is an application development environment similar to Oracle Forms or Oracle JDeveloper.

   a) _____ True
   b) _____ False

2) Which of the following is the responsibility of the listener?

   a) _____ It manages the datafiles
   b) _____ It provides TNS service name resolution information
   c) _____ It waits for and manages database connection requests
   d) _____ It reads data from the Database files and puts the information in memory

3) What is the tnsnames.ora file used for?

   a) _____ It manages the datafiles
   b) _____ It provides TNS service name resolution information
   c) _____ It waits for and manages database connection requests
   a) _____ It reads data from the Database files and puts the information in memory

4) The tnsnames.ora file is the Instance configuration file read by the Oracle Instance upon startup to help it decide, for example, how much memory to allocate to the Shared Pool.

   a) _____ True
   b) _____ False

5) Which of the following are some of the responsibilities of dedicated server processes? (check all that apply)

   a) _____ Reading data stored on disk into the Database Buffer Cache
   b) _____ Routing connection requests to the database
   c) _____ Sorting query results
   d) _____ Resolving TNS service names

6) The TNS_ADMIN location is where configuration files for Net8 components are typically held.

   a) _____ True
   b) _____ False

Quiz answers appear in Appendix A, Lab 3.1.

LAB 3.2

MANAGING THE ORACLE LISTENER

LAB OBJECTIVES

After this lab, you will be able to:

✔ Start and Stop the Listener
✔ Issue Other Listener Commands
✔ Perform a Loopback Test

LAB 3.2 EXERCISES

Now that you have created or edited the listener.ora file, you are ready to start the listener. Administrative communication to the listener is accomplished via a utility called "Listener Control." In UNIX, this utility is called from the command line by the name lsnrctl. For Oracle8.0.x on Windows NT, the command is lsnrctl80; if you are running this type of environment, substitute lsnrctl80 wherever lsnrctl appears in the exercises below.

To indicate to Listener Control what you want to do, provide an argument to the lsnrctl command. At the command line in your operating system (in NT this will be in an MS-DOS window), issue the following command:

lsnrctl help

You will receive a response similar to the following:

```
C:\>lsnrctl help

LSNRCTL for 32-bit Windows: Version 8.1.6.0.0 - Production on
24-MAR-00 17:42:28
```

The following operations are available
An asterisk (*) denotes a modifier or extended command:

start	stop	status
services	version	reload
save_config	trace	dbsnmp_start
dbsnmp_stop	dbsnmp_status	change_password
debug	test	quit
exit	set*	show*

"lsnrctl help" produces a list of all arguments that can be used with the Listener Control utility. The exercises throughout the remainder of this chapter will refer back to this list of arguments.

**LAB
3.2**

3.2.1 START AND STOP THE LISTENER

For remote users to be able to connect to your database, the listener for your database needs to be running. The listener listens on a specific port—by default, Port 1521—for database connection requests. When it receives a request, it either redirects it to a dispatcher process or to a new dedicated server process. Note that it is possible to have a free dedicated server process waiting for a new request. You may wish to read more about these "pre-spawned dedicated server processes" in the Oracle documentation.

Start the listener by issuing the following command at the operating system command line:

```
lsnrctl start
```

Status information similar to the following should appear on the screen:

```
C:\>lsnrctl start

LSNRCTL for 32-bit Windows: Version 8.1.6.0.0 - Production on
24-JUN-2000 12:04:39

(c) Copyright 1998, 1999, Oracle Corporation.  All rights
reserved.

Starting tnslsnr: please wait...

TNSLSNR for 32-bit Windows: Version 8.1.6.0.0 - Production

System parameter file is C:\ORACLE\ORA81\network\admin\
listener.ora
```

```
Log messages written to
C:\ORACLE\ORA81\network\log\listener.log

Listening on:
(DESCRIPTION=(ADDRESS=(PROTOCOL=tcp)(HOST=rocky)(PORT=1521)))

Connecting to (ADDRESS=(PROTOCOL=TCP)(HOST=rocky)(PORT=1521))
STATUS of the LISTENER
--------------------------
Alias                     LISTENER
Version                   TNSLSNR for 32-bit Windows:
Version 8.1.6.0.0 - Production
Start Date                24-JUN-2000 12:04:44
Uptime                    0 days 0 hr. 0 min. 2 sec
Trace Level               off
Security                  OFF
SNMP                      OFF
Listener Parameter File
E:\ORACLE\ORA81\network\admin\listener.ora
Listener Log File
E:\ORACLE\ORA81\network\log\listener.log
Services Summary...
   db00             has 1 service handler(s)
The command completed successfully
```

You should see the phrase "The command completed successfully" as one of the last lines. If you do not, make sure you've edited the listener.ora file correctly and have entered the lsnrctl command correctly. Don't go on to the other exercises in this chapter until this is working properly.

a) Based on the information in your listener.ora file, find the location of your listener log file.

To stop the listener, issue the following command:

```
lsnrctl stop
```

b) What is the response you get after issuing this command? Did your listener stop properly? How can you tell?

3.2.2 ISSUE OTHER LISTENER COMMANDS

As you saw when you issued the command "lsnrctl help," there are many other arguments that can be used with lsnrctl. You will try some of these in the following exercises.

First, verify that the listener is running. To check this, issue the following command:

```
lsnrctl status
```

If you received a response similar to "The command completed successfully", then the listener is running properly. Otherwise, you should start the listener now.

Next, consider the "show" argument. This argument displays additional information about the configuration of the listener; it requires a parameter to specify which element of the configuration you want to see. For example, to see information about the log status (which shows whether the listener will log information about its activities to the listener log file), you issue the command: `lsnrctl show log_status`. To view the list of all the `lsnrctl show` parameters, issue the following command:

```
lsnrctl show
```

You should receive a response similar to the following:

```
C:\>lsnrctl show

LSNRCTL for 32-bit Windows: Version 8.1.6.0.0 - Production on 25-
MAR-00 10:18:53


(c) Copyright 1998 Oracle Corporation.  All rights reserved.

The following operations are available after show
An asterisk (*) denotes a modifier or extended command:

rawmode            displaymode          trc_file
trc_directory      trc_level            log_file
log_directory      log_status           current_listener
connect_timeout    startup_waittime     snmp_visible
use_plugandplay    direct_handoff       save_config_on_stop
```

a) What is the full command for finding the name of the listener's log file?

_____

_____

b) Retrieve information about the listener with the lsnrctl status command. What does the "Alias" line signify?

_____

_____

3.2.3 PERFORM A LOOPBACK TEST

Now that your listener is running, you can perform a *loopback test* to make sure that it can indeed service connection requests to your database. A loopback test is performed by starting SQL*Plus and connecting to the database, via the listener, using the TNS service name you configured for the "example00" entry in the tnsnames.ora file template (Exercise 3.1). In that exercise, the service name was configured as "db00".

Before performing the loopback test, verify that the listener is running. Next, start SQL*Plus and connect to your database as the user SYSTEM using the TNS service name you configured for example00 in the tnsnames.ora template. If your test was unsuccessful, review the previous exercises to make sure that your tnsnames.ora and listener.ora file are configured correctly and that your listener started without error.

a) Why is it useful to perform a loopback test?

_____

_____

b) How will you test to see if the listener is started?

_____

_____

TNSPING

For some Oracle installations, there is a command called "tnsping". This command can be used to perform a test that is somewhat different than the loopback test performed in this exercise. Tnsping does not attempt to connect to the database, but rather simply ensures that the listener is present (i.e., started) on the machine. If you have this utility, it will be located in the ORACLE_HOME\bin directory. Its syntax is: **tnsping <address> [<count>]**. The <address> is the TNS service name, and [<count>] is an optional parameter representing the number of times you want tnsping to test connectivity. The following example shows the results of using tnsping to connect to the "db00" database five successive times:

```
C:\>tnsping db00 5

TNS Ping Utility for 32-bit Windows: Version
2.3.4.0.0 - Production on 25-MAR-00
 10:51:05

Copyright (c) Oracle Corporation 1995.  All rights
reserved.

Attempting to contact
(ADDRESS=(PROTOCOL=TCP)(Host=127.0.0.1)(Port=1521))

OK (20 msec)
OK (20 msec)
OK (40 msec)
OK (20 msec)
OK (30 msec)
```

LAB 3.2 EXERCISE ANSWERS

3.2.1 ANSWERS

a) Based on the information in your listener.ora file, find the location of your listener log file.

Answer: The listener log file is in the location specified by the "LOG_DIRECTORY_LIS-TENER" line in the listener.ora file. In the template listener.ora file provided above, the directory is: e:\Oracle\Ora81\network\log. The name of the listener log file is specified in the "LOG_FILE_LISTENER" line. In the above template, the name of the file is specified as: listener. The log file for this listener then is: e:\Oracle\Ora81\network\log\listener.log.

b) What is the response you get from the system after issuing this command? Did your listener stop properly? How can you tell?

Answer: After issuing the `lsnrctl stop` *command, you should receive a response similar to the following:*

```
C:\>lsnrctl stop

LSNRCTL for 32-bit Windows: Version 8.1.6.0.0 - Production
on 24-JUN-2000 12:07:56

(c) Copyright 1998, 1999, Oracle Corporation.  All rights
reserved.

Connecting to
(ADDRESS=(PROTOCOL=TCP)(HOST=rocky)(PORT=1521))

The command completed successfully
```

You can tell that there were no problems in shutting down the listener because the message "**The command completed successfully**" *appeared in the final message line.*

3.2.2 ANSWERS

a) What is the full command for finding the name of the listener's log file?

Answer: The command for finding the name of the listener's log file is:

```
lsnrctl show log_file
```

b) Retrieve information about the listener with the lsnrctl status command. What does the "Alias" line signify?

Answer: The "Alias" line represents the name of the listener. Remember that you can set up more than one listener on a machine. If there are multiple listeners, they must be named differently. Note that if a listener has a name other than the default

(LISTENER), then you must include the name of the listener when you issue lsnrctl com-mands. For example, if you configure your listener to have the name LSNR_DB00, then you would issue the following command to start the listener: `lsnrctl start lsnr_db00`. *It is rare to find more than one listener running on a machine, but a senior level DBA may use this configuration for load balancing or to ensure connectivity.*

3.2.3 ANSWERS

a) Why is it useful to perform a loopback test?

Answer: It is useful to perform a loopback test to get an initial indication as to whether or not the listener is configured properly.

b) How will you test to see if the listener is started?

Answer: You can test to see if the listener is started by issuing the lsnrctl status command.

LAB 3.2 SELF-REVIEW QUESTIONS

To test your progress, you should be able to answer the following questions.

1) What is the command for starting the listener?

    a) _____ start listener
    b) _____ svrmgrl start
    c) _____ listener control startup
    d) _____ lsnrctl start

2) To get help for the Listener Control utility, you simply issue the command: `lsnrctl`

    a) _____ True
    b) _____ False

3) Issuing the `lsnrctl show` command will display the values of all the listener configuration parameters.

    a) _____ True
    b) _____ False

4) There is no difference between performing a loopback test with the SQL*Plus method versus using the tnsping command.

    a) _____ True
    b) _____ False

5) Which of the following are lsnrctl options? (check all that apply)

    a) _____ services

    b) _____ reload

    c) _____ log_file

    d) _____ trc_level

    e) _____ dbsnmp_status

6) Which of the following are lsnrctl show parameters? (check all that apply)

    a) _____ services

    b) _____ reload

    c) _____ log_file

    d) _____ trc_level

    e) _____ dbsnmp_status

Quiz answers appear in Appendix A, Lab 3.2.

<u>L A B   3 . 3</u>

CONFIGURING THE MULTI-THREADED SERVER

> ## LAB OBJECTIVES
>
> After this lab, you will be able to:
>
> ✔ Configure and View Information about the MTS Environment

LAB 3.3 EXERCISES

A multi-threaded server can be configured to support an environment where user interactions with the database are small. For example, a telemarketer may call up a customer record (usually containing a relatively small amount of information) and not perform another transaction until the customer agrees to purchase an item. It is helpful in this case to use the multi-threaded server configuration, since fewer system resources are required when connections share servers than when they each use their own dedicated server. Note that Instances in MTS configuration connections can still be made via dedicated servers if needed.

3.3.1 CONFIGURE AND VIEW INFORMATION ABOUT THE MTS ENVIRONMENT

To configure the database to allow multi-threaded server connections, you simply need to add or edit some parameters of your init.ora file. As always, make a backup copy of your init.ora file before making any changes.

When the database is configured to allow connections via shared servers, there are at least two additional background processes that start with the Instance. The first is the shared server itself, which is named Snnn. Since more than one shared server can be started, the name of the background process reflects the number of shared servers started. So, an Instance with two shared servers will have two background processes: S000 and S001.

Shared servers work in conjunction with another background process, called the *dispatcher*, which gets started with the Instance in this configuration. The dispatcher process issues requests and receives responses on behalf of the shared server processes, and is named Dnnn. An Instance running with two dispatchers will have two additional background processes called D000 and D001.

These two components—shared servers and dispatchers—pass information via *response and request queues*, which are located in the SGA. When an application attempts to connect to the database, the listener receives the request and redirects it to one of the dispatchers. From that time on, the client application communicates with the database via the dispatcher. When the client makes a request of the database, the dispatcher places the request in the request queue. The shared server process performs the requested action (such as selecting a row in a table) and places the result in the response queue. The dispatcher routes the response back to the client application, after retrieving it from the response queue.

To allow multi-threaded server connections, the init.ora file must contain the following parameters:

- mts_dispatchers—This specifies the number of dispatcher processes that will be started at Instance startup, as well as the protocol that they will be receiving requests on.

- mts_max_dispatchers—This specifies the maximum number of dispatchers that the Instance can run simultaneously. The number of dispatchers can be increased beyond the value of the mts_dispatchers parameter by issuing an ALTER SYSTEM statement, but cannot be increased beyond the number specified in this (mts_max_dispatchers) parameter.

- mts_servers—This specifies the number of shared servers that will be started at Instance startup.

- mts_max_servers—This specifies the maximum number of shared servers that the Instance can run simultaneously. If needed, the Oracle Server will add servers dynamically up to the number specified in this parameter.

Perform a shutdown immediate on your database. If your init.ora file already contains these parameters, then you will edit them as described next. If it does not contain these parameters, then you will need to add them. Set the values of these parameters to the following:

mts_dispatchers="tcp,2"

mts_max_dispatchers=10

mts_servers=2

mts_max_servers=10

Restart your database.

You will now be able to see information about the shared servers and dispatchers. Remember that these two components are background processes to the Instance. In most environments, you can issue a command to see the processes running in the operating system. For example, in some types of UNIX, the dispatcher processes can be seen with the following command:

```
ps -ef | grep ora_d0
```

The result will be similar to the following:

```
root   5261   1   0   19:21:57 ?        0:00 ora_d000_db00
root   2049   1   0     Mar 21 ?        0:00 ora_d001_db00
```

In any environment, additional information about the dispatchers and shared servers is available in two views:

- V$DISPATCHER—This view contains general information about the dispatchers. There is one row in the table for each dispatcher process.
- V$SHARED_SERVER—This view contains general information about shared server processes.

a) Connect to the database as the user SYSTEM and describe the V$DISPATCHER view. Write a query to find the name of the dispatchers.

_____

_____

You can stop dispatcher processes using the following command:

```
ALTER SYSTEM SHUTDOWN IMMEDIATE '<dispatcher_name>';
```

b) Choose one of the running dispatchers from the result of the query in Question a). Write the SQL statement to shut it down, then execute the statement.

_____

_____

Issue the query from Question a) and confirm that the dispatcher has been shut down.

c) As the user SYSTEM, write a query against the V$SHARED_SERVER view to determine the names of the shared servers.

_____

_____

3.3.1 ANSWERS

a) Connect to the database as the user SYSTEM and describe the V$DISPATCHER view. Write a query to find the name of the dispatchers.

Answer: To "find the name of the running dispatchers" issue the query shown below. You'll see here that there are two dispatcher processes: D000 and D001. These correlate to the two dispatchers that were specified to start with the Instance per the line in the init.ora file: mts_dispatchers="tcp,2".

```
SQL> SELECT name
  2     FROM v$dispatcher;
```

NAME

D000

D001

b) Choose one of the running dispatchers from the result of the query in Question a). Write the SQL statement to shut it down, then execute the statement.

Answer: Your statement should look similar to this.

```
ALTER SYSTEM SHUTDOWN IMMEDIATE 'D001';
```

c) As the user SYSTEM, write a query against the V$SHARED_SERVER view to determine the names of the shared servers.

Answer: Your query and results should look similar to those shown below. These results indicate that there are two shared server processes: S000 and S001. These correlate to the two shared servers that were specified to start with the Instance per the line in the init.ora file: mts_servers=2.

```
SQL> SELECT name
  2     FROM v$shared_server;


NAME
----

S000

S001
```

LAB 3.3 SELF-REVIEW QUESTIONS

To test your progress, you should be able to answer the following questions.

I) What are the two additional background processes that get started in a multi-threaded server configuration?

    a) _____ Listener and dispatcher
    b) _____ Dispatcher and tnsnames.ora
    c) _____ Shared server and dispatcher
    d) _____ Shared sever and listener

2) When the Oracle server is running with a multi-threaded server configuration, connections cannot be serviced by dedicated servers.

    a) _____ True
    b) _____ False

3) Issuing the command `lsnrctl show` will display the values of all the listener configuration parameters.

    a) _____ True
    b) _____ False

Quiz answers appear in Appendix A, Lab 3.3.

LAB 3.3

CHAPTER 3

TEST YOUR THINKING

1) Suppose you perform a loopback test using SQL*Plus and you receive the message "ERROR:ORA-01017: invalid username/password; logon denied." Based solely on this error message, would you say that the loopback test was successful? Explain your answer.

2) Suppose you perform a loopback test using SQL*Plus and you receive the message "ERROR: ORA-12154: TNS:could not resolve service name." Based solely on this error message, would you say that the loopback test was successful? Explain your answer.

3) Considering the kind of work that is done in your workplace, describe one scenario that would benefit from the use of dedicated servers, and one that would benefit from using shared servers.

CHAPTER 4
TABLESPACES

CHAPTER OBJECTIVES

In this chapter, you will learn about:

- ✔ Tablespaces: Logical Areas of Storage   Page 85
- ✔ How Tablespaces Relate to the Oracle Database
  and How to Manipulate Them   Page 91

Now that you have successfully installed your Oracle database, you can begin to look at its structures. This chapter is the first of several that will discuss data storage issues. The configuration of a database's data storage is crucial to both its performance and its administration. The more planning that goes into the configuration of the database's structures, the easier it is for a DBA to maintain and tune the database.

You will soon discover that there are logical and physical constructs of an Oracle database which work hand in hand with each other. In this book, logical constructs are defined as those constructs that are created to help maintain data storage, yet do not themselves contain physical data, per se. Examples of logical constructs are tablespaces, segments, extents, and data blocks. Physical constructs are referred to here as those constructs that actually contain database object data. Two examples of physical constructs are datafiles and redo logs.

To perform most of the exercises in this chapter, you will need DBA privileges. This is true about doing similar tasks in a real-world environment. Oracle comes with three pre-created DBA accounts: SYSTEM, SYS, and INTERNAL. If you do not have DBA privileges, you will receive the message:

```
ORA-01031: insufficient privileges
```

In general, it is a good idea to create an additional account with DBA privileges and use this new account to perform DBA-related tasks. You learn how to create this account in Chapter 9, "User Creation," and how to grant DBA privileges to it in Chapter 10, "Privilege and Resource Groups." For the next few chapters, however, you perform DBA-related tasks using one of the pre-created Oracle DBA accounts mentioned above.

LAB 4.1

TABLESPACES:
LOGICAL AREAS OF STORAGE

LAB OBJECTIVES

After this lab, you will know:

- ✔ What a Tablespace Is
- ✔ What a Tablespace Is Used For

WHAT A TABLESPACE IS

Most databases contain multiple tables and one or more *tablespaces*. Figure 4.1 depicts these relationships.

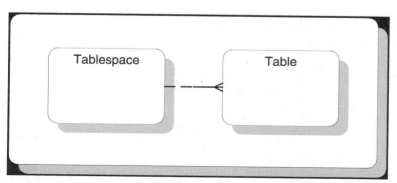

Figure 4.1 ■ An Entity Relationship Diagram showing the relationship between tables and tablespaces.

> **How Data Relates to a Tablespace**
>
> A *tablespace* is a database construct that is realized by one or more files called "datafiles." Data is not physically stored in a tablespace. It is stored in one or more datafiles. The general concept of a *file* is a named grouping of data on a storage medium, like a disk. In some configurations, a datafile can span multiple disks. The size of a datafile is initially determined by the DBA upon creation. It can be as large as the largest file permitted by the operating system. The configuration of the machine on which the database is running determines exactly how the information in the datafile is distributed across the disk.

A tablespace can contain many tables, indexes, and so forth. It has a size that is initially assigned by the DBA. As data is inserted and updated, the amount of free space in the tablespace diminishes. As the space used reaches 100%, the DBA may choose to archive rows or expand the tablespace by extending one or more existing datafiles or by adding a new datafile to the tablespace. Datafiles are discussed in greater detail in Chapter 8, "Datafiles."

Although a tablespace cannot span more than one database, Oracle8i allows tablespaces to be shared by more than one database. If they are shared, the data in them cannot be updated. They are read-only.

WHAT A TABLESPACE IS USED FOR

One of the goals a DBA keeps in mind when designing the layout of a database is to configure the database such that database objects are separated, to reduce the amount of administration and physical disk I/O (input/output) necessary. This type of planning can result in an improvement of throughput. This separation also helps the DBA ensure that problem areas will remain isolated and will not affect the entire database.

Every database has at least one tablespace (known as the SYSTEM tablespace). The SYSTEM tablespace holds the *data dictionary,* which holds tables that contain information about the database, otherwise known as metadata. Only special kinds of objects should be stored in the SYSTEM tablespace. Some of these are discussed in this book.

Other tablespaces should be created that contain grouped, or like, data. For instance, a tablespace may contain data owned by similar users/accounts, generally referred to as "schemas," or used by similar applications. Alternatively, they can be grouped by the size of the objects. Remember, one of the goals when making decisions about tablespaces is to separate database objects (in this case, you should separate those schemas or application data that belong together from those that do not) to increase performance and administration ease.

LAB 4.1 EXERCISES

4.1.1 WHAT A TABLESPACE IS

    a) List two differences between a datafile and a tablespace.

    _____

    _____

    b) In relation to datafiles, is a tablespace logical or physical?

    _____

    c) What is the relationship of datafiles to tablespaces?

    _____

    _____

4.1.2 WHAT A TABLESPACE IS USED FOR

Type the following SELECT statement:

```
SELECT tablespace_name, status
  FROM dba_tablespaces;
```

    a) List the tablespaces you see, along with their current status.

    _____

    _____

Examples of tablespace names can be USERS, RBS, TEMP, and INDX. In the examples in this book, the USERS tablespace is used as the default tablespace for all users who have been granted permission to create objects such as tables and indexes. Once the default tablespace is specified and a user creates objects, those objects are stored in the default tablespace. The RBS tablespace is used for rollback segments (which are described in Chapter 12, "Rollback Segments"). The TEMP tablespace is used as temporary storage for performing large sort operations. The INDX tablespace is used to store index data. These naming conventions can be overridden by a DBA using the techniques shown in this book.

LAB 4.1 EXERCISE ANSWERS

4.1.1 ANSWERS

a) List two differences between a datafile and a tablespace.

Answer:

1) *Database objects that store data are held in tablespaces. Their data, though, is physically stored in the operating system files—known as datafiles—that are associated with the tablespaces via a CREATE TABLESPACE or ALTER TABLESPACE command.*

2) *Datafiles are physical, while tablespaces are logical.*

b) In relation to datafiles, is a tablespace logical or physical?

Answer: A tablespace is logical.

c) What is the relationship of datafiles to tablespaces?

Answer: One or more datafiles can belong to one tablespace.

4.1.2 ANSWERS

a) List the tablespaces you see, along with their current status.

Answer: After executing this query, you should receive a result similar to the following:

```
SQL> SELECT tablespace_name, status
  2    FROM dba_tablespaces;
```

TABLESPACE_NAME	STATUS
SYSTEM	ONLINE
USERS	ONLINE
RBS	ONLINE
TEMP	ONLINE
TOOLS	ONLINE
INDX	ONLINE

6 rows selected.

All of the tablespaces you see listed are online, or "active." A tablespace can have one of two statuses: "ONLINE" or "OFFLINE." When a tablespace is online, it is available to the database Instance. For example, data may be read from the datafiles associated with an online tablespace. When a tablespace is offline, it is *not* available for such activity. For example, a DBA might choose to perform a backup (an action which saves some or all of the data in the Database, usually to disk or tape), where he or she has set one or more of the tablespaces offline in order to do so. You learn how to deactivate, or take tablespaces offline, in subsequent exercises.

Reasons for creating new tablespaces include, but are not limited to, the following:

- A "client database application" is an interface which a user uses to make requests to and receive information from a database server. If you add a new client database application to your database system, you may also need to create that application's objects (tables, indexes, and so forth). It is usually to your benefit to separate this new application's data logically and physically into one or more of its own tablespaces.

- Remember the examples of tablespaces shown earlier in this chapter: one tablespace is called *USERS* and another is called *INDX*? If an application's data is stored in one tablespace and its indexes are stored in another tablespace, and each tablespace's physical files are on separate disks, throughput is increased because separating data from its indexes allows for simultaneous read/write action from multiple devices. Data access is thus made more efficient.

LAB 4.1 SELF-REVIEW QUESTIONS

To test your progress, you should be able to answer the following questions.

1) Using the SYSTEM tablespace to support all users, applications, and operations performed on the database is more than sufficient to meet the requirements of good database storage layout.

   a) _____ True
   b) _____ False

2) Oracle8i tablespaces can be shared by other Oracle8i databases.

   a) _____ True
   b) _____ False

3) Which tablespace does every database have?

   a) _____ INDX
   b) _____ USERS
   c) _____ SYSTEM
   d) _____ TEMP

4) What kind of information does the tablespace you selected in Question 3) contain that no other tablespace contains?

   a) _____ Indexes
   b) _____ The data dictionary
   c) _____ Temporary objects
   d) _____ Schema object data

5) What are some goals a DBA should keep in mind during database storage layout? Check all that apply.

   a) _____ Reduce the amount of administration necessary
   b) _____ Reduce the amount of disk I/O necessary
   c) _____ Improve throughput
   d) _____ Separate database objects into grouped, or like, data

6) What type of data might the tablespaces, other than *SYSTEM,* be comprised of? Check all that apply.

   a) _____ Indexes for database objects
   b) _____ The data dictionary
   c) _____ Schema database objects
   d) _____ The system rollback segment

Quiz answers appear in Appendix A, Lab 4.1.

LAB 4.2

HOW TABLESPACES RELATE TO THE ORACLE DATABASE AND HOW TO MANIPULATE THEM

LAB OBJECTIVES

After this lab, you will be able to:

✔ Understand the Relationship of Tablespaces to Physical Files
✔ Create a Tablespace
✔ Delete a Tablespace

UNDERSTAND THE RELATIONSHIP OF TABLESPACES TO PHYSICAL FILES

At this point, you should understand the relationship of tablespaces to datafiles in that tablespaces are logical space management structures that are composed of one or more disk or *physical* files. Oracle refers to these physical files as *datafiles*, the files that hold the physical data contained in the objects in the tablespaces. Again, one single tablespace can be composed of one or more datafiles. See Figure 4.2 for a depiction of these relationships.

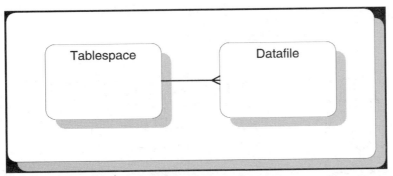

Figure 4.2 ■ The relationship between tablespaces and datafiles.

In the chapters that follow, you discover how tablespaces are further logically divided to support increased data access speed.

A datafile cannot span more than one tablespace.

CREATE A TABLESPACE

You create a new tablespace with the CREATE TABLESPACE command, which has the following syntax:

```
CREATE TABLESPACE <tablespace_name>
  DATAFILE <datafile_name> SIZE <size_of_datafile>
  DEFAULT STORAGE
    (INITIAL <size_of_initial_extent>
    NEXT <size_of_next_extent>
    MINEXTENTS <minimum_number_of_extents>
    MAXEXTENTS <maximum_number_of_extents>
    PCTINCREASE <extent_growth_rate>
    )
  PERMANENT;
```

Bracketed (<>) words used in the syntax diagrams should be substituted with your actual values. The CREATE TABLESPACE command options are explained later in this chapter.

The PERMANENT keyword in this command tells Oracle that you would like objects to be stored in this tablespace (e.g., tables or indexes). If the tablespace is to be used for temporary sort operations, then you may use the TEMPORARY keyword. Using this keyword means that you do not intend to store application objects in the tablespace. If this keyword is not specified in the CREATE TABLESPACE command, the default is PERMANENT.

DELETE A TABLESPACE

If *all* the data in a particular tablespace is no longer needed, you can reclaim the disk space associated with that tablespace by *dropping* the tablespace and its associated datafile(s). You can then remove the datafile(s) from the disk using an operating system command (like del (Windows) or rm (UNIX)).

Dropping a tablespace should not be done indiscriminately. A great deal of planning should go into making the decision to drop a tablespace because you do not want to delete any data that will be needed later.

■ *FOR EXAMPLE:*

You can drop a tablespace by typing the following command:

```
DROP TABLESPACE <tablespace_name>;
```

LAB 4.2 EXERCISES

4.2.1 UNDERSTAND THE RELATIONSHIP OF TABLESPACES TO PHYSICAL FILES

a) What is the relationship of tablespaces to datafiles?

_____

_____

b) How many tablespaces can a datafile relate to? Why?

_____

_____

4.2.2 CREATE A TABLESPACE

Log on to the database as the user SYSTEM (password is MANAGER). Enter the following command, substituting your locations for the placeholders:

```
CREATE TABLESPACE new_data
   DATAFILE 'e:\oracle\oradata\db00\new_data01.dbf'
      SIZE 1M DEFAULT STORAGE (INITIAL 25K NEXT 10K
                                MINEXTENTS 1 MAXEXTENTS 100
                                PCTINCREASE 0
                              );
```

Note that in UNIX, forward slashes are used in the datafile definition instead of back slashes.

a) What message did the Oracle Server return to you once you typed this statement?

_____

_____

Now, type the following SELECT statement:

```
SELECT tablespace_name, status
   FROM dba_tablespaces;
```

b) What difference do you see between the result you receive after typing this query now and the result you received when you typed this query in Lab 4.1.2?

_____

_____

Type the following query:

```
SELECT file_name, tablespace_name, status
   FROM dba_data_files
  WHERE tablespace_name = 'NEW_DATA';
```

c) What is the result of this query?

_____

_____

d) Based on the CREATE TABLESPACE statement shown earlier in this lab, will the objects be permanent or temporary?

_____

_____

Type the following query:

```
SELECT contents
  FROM dba_tablespaces
 WHERE tablespace_name = 'NEW_DATA';
```

e) How will the objects in the NEW_DATA tablespace be stored?

_____

_____

4.2.3 DELETE A TABLESPACE

Before you delete a tablespace, you should make it unavailable by taking it offline.

Enter the following DDL command in Server Manager:

```
ALTER TABLESPACE new_data OFFLINE;
```

Now check the status of the NEW_DATA tablespace by executing the following query:

```
SELECT tablespace_name, status
  FROM dba_tablespaces
 WHERE tablespace_name = 'NEW_DATA';
```

a) What is the current status of the NEW_DATA tablespace?

_____

_____

Now, drop the NEW_DATA tablespace by issuing the following DDL command:

```
DROP TABLESPACE new_data;
```

Check the result of this action by issuing the following query:

```
SELECT tablespace_name
  FROM dba_tablespaces;
```

    b) What is the result of these two actions?

_____

_____

LAB 4.2 EXERCISE ANSWERS

4.2.1 ANSWERS

a) What is the relationship of tablespaces to datafiles?

Answer: Tablespaces are composed of one or more datafiles.

b) How many tablespaces can a datafile relate to? Why?

Answer: Oracle architecture dictates that a datafile can support only one tablespace.

4.2.2 ANSWERS

a) What message did the Oracle Server return to you once you typed this statement?

Answer: Server Manager should have returned the message "Statement processed.", which, for purposes of this particular statement, is equivalent to a message like "Tablespace created."

Each tablespace is named in the CREATE TABLESPACE command. You must use a separate CREATE TABLESPACE command for each tablespace you create. The name for the tablespace being created above is NEW_DATA. The DATAFILE keyword is used to specify the datafile(s) that will comprise the new tablespace. In the example, the new tablespace will be comprised of only one datafile (so far), which is e:\oracle\oradata\db00\data01.dbf. The size of the datafile in bytes immediately follows. A "K" (for kilobytes) or an "M" (for megabytes) can follow the number representing the size of the datafile. A tablespace's default storage definition provides the storage that an object (such as a table) will automatically use if two conditions exist:

1. Storage is not specified via the object's CREATE command.
2. The object being created is placed in that tablespace.

The next parameters listed require a bit of understanding about the further logical divisions of a tablespace. These further divisions will be explained in greater detail in subsequent chapters. But for your understanding of this CREATE TABLESPACE statement, some of the logical divisions are listed here:

1. A tablespace can contain zero or more *segments*.
2. A segment is composed of one or more *extents*.
3. An extent is composed of one or more *data blocks*.

Figure 4.3 shows a broad overview of segments, extents, and data blocks, which will be discussed much more thoroughly in subsequent chapters. Here they provide you with an introductory pictorial representation of the relationships between these constructs.

 Starting with Oracle8.x, if you are using partitioning, then your tables may each have more than one segment. However, partitioning is beyond the scope of this book's discussion.

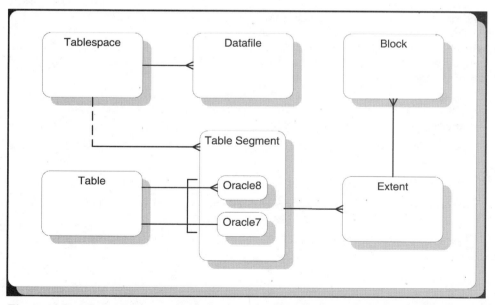

Figure 4.3 ■ Broad overview of Oracle segments, extents, and data blocks

The INITIAL keyword in this example of the CREATE TABLESPACE statement refers to the initial default size of the *first* extent. In this example, our initial extent has been set to a size of 25K and our next (or incremental) extent has been set to a size of 10K.

The MINEXTENTS option allows you to set aside additional extents beyond the initial extent at the time an object is created in the tablespace. The minimum number of extents to reserve, including your initial extent in the NEW_DATA tablespace, is one. And, of course, MAXEXTENTS is the maximum number of total extents allowed. Here, that limit has been set to 100. You can also specify MAXEXTENTS UNLIMITED.

You should be careful about using the MAXEXTENTS UNLIMITED option. For example, a rollback segment created without a specific storage option will, by default, use the storage option of the tablespace that contains it. Therefore, if the containing tablespace uses the MAXEXTENTS UNLIMITED storage option, then the rollback segment will inherit this same storage option. It is not a good idea for rollback segments to be created this way because certain transactions that continue to run for a long time may create new extents until the tablespace is full.

The PCTINCREASE parameter specifies the growth factor for additional or incremental extents. The example shown earlier displays a value of zero. This means that an additional extent created after the NEXT extent, if a NEXT extent value is specified, for any object will be created using the same size as the extents created before it. If this value is greater than zero, then each incremental extent will be the specified percentage larger than the one before it. For instance, if the PCTINCREASE value is set to 10, then each extent created after the next extent will be 10 percent larger than the one created before it. When used, this option can help the DBA reduce the need for a large number of extents, resulting in a more manageable database layout.

b) What difference do you see between the result you receive after typing this query now and the result you received when you typed this query in Lab 4.1.2?

Answer: You should now be able to see your NEW_DATA tablespace listed.

c) What is the result of this query?

Answer: The result you receive upon executing this query should resemble the following:

```
SQL> SELECT file_name, tablespace_name, status
  2    FROM dba_data_files
  3    WHERE tablespace_name = 'NEW_DATA';
```

```
FILE_NAME                                          TABLESPACE_NAME
STATUS
-------------------------------------------------------------
e:\oracle\oradata\db00\new_data01.dbf
NEW_DATA
AVAILABLE
```

The result of this query tells you the path and filename of your new datafile that corresponds to your new tablespace, and lets you know that the new database file is "Available" to be read from or written to.

d) Based on the CREATE TABLESPACE statement shown earlier in this lab, will the objects be permanent or temporary?

Answer: Because there is no explicit PERMANENT or TEMPORARY storage parameter in the statement, the default value is used and objects will be stored permanently in the new tablespace. If you try to create a table in a tablespace explicitly marked "TEMPORARY", you will receive the following error message:

ORA-02195: Attempt to create PERMANENT object in a TEMPORARY tablespace

e) How will the objects in the NEW_DATA tablespace be stored?

Answer: Upon executing this query, you should receive a result similar to the following:

```
SQL> SELECT contents
  2    FROM dba_tablespaces
  3    WHERE tablespace_name = 'NEW_DATA';
```

```
CONTENTS
---------
PERMANENT
```

The objects in the NEW_DATA tablespace will be stored permanently.

4.2.3 ANSWERS

a) What is the current status of the NEW_DATA tablespace?

Answer: After executing the two statements above, you should receive results similar to the following:

```
SQL> ALTER TABLESPACE new_data OFFLINE;
Tablespace altered.
```

```
SQL> SELECT tablespace_name, status
  2    FROM dba_tablespaces
  3    WHERE tablespace_name = 'NEW_DATA';
```

TABLESPACE_NAME	STATUS
NEW_DATA	OFFLINE

Your tablespace is now offline (inactive).

b) What is the result of these two actions?

Answer: The result of these two actions should produce the following:

```
SQL> DROP TABLESPACE new_data;
```

Tablespace dropped.

```
SQL> SELECT tablespace_name
  2    FROM dba_tablespaces;
```

TABLESPACE_NAME
SYSTEM
USERS
RBS
TEMP
TOOLS
INDX

6 rows selected.

You are no longer able to see your NEW_DATA tablespace. It has been dropped.

Consider the following alternative statement:

```
DROP TABLESPACE new_data INCLUDING CONTENTS;
```

NEW_DATA is the name of the tablespace being dropped. The option INCLUDING CONTENTS allows you to drop the tablespace even if it contains data. Most DBAs avoid this clause as it removes an important safety net. Without this option, the tablespace could only be dropped if it were empty. Notice you did not use the INCLUDING CONTENTS option when dropping your tablespace. So, why did your statement work? The INCLUDING CONTENTS option is only necessary if data exists in the tablespace. You never created any objects in your tablespace, therefore it was empty and could be dropped(deleted) directly.

LAB 4.2 SELF-REVIEW QUESTIONS

To test your progress, you should be able to answer the following questions.

1) A datafile belongs to as many tablespaces as are necessary to satisfy its disk space requirements.

    a) _____ True
    b) _____ False

2) Anyone who can create a session in the database can also manipulate tablespaces to support his or her objects.

    a) _____ True
    b) _____ False

3) The correct syntax for creating a tablespace is:

    a) _____ CREATE TABLESPACE <tablespace_name>;
    b) _____ CREATE TABLESPACE <tablespace_name> DATAFILE '<datafile_name>';
    c) _____ CREATE TABLESPACE <tablespace_name> DATAFILE '<datafile_name>'
                     SIZE <size_of_datafile>;
    d) _____ CREATE TABLESPACE <tablespace_name> AS SELECT * FROM
                      <second_tablespace_name>;

4) A tablespace can be dropped even if it contains data by including the following option:

    a) _____ DROP ALL DATA
    b) _____ ON CASCADE
    c) _____ WITH OBJECTS
    d) _____ INCLUDING CONTENTS

5) Even if you have created a tablespace, it is not automatically active until you submit an explicit command to activate it, or bring it online.

    a) _____ True
    b) _____ False

6) If no keyword is specified (e.g., PERMANENT or TEMPORARY) in a CREATE TABLESPACE command then, by default, objects created in that tablespace will be stored temporarily.

    a) _____ True
    b) _____ False

Quiz answers appear in Appendix A, Lab 4.2.

C H A P T E R   4

TEST YOUR THINKING

Throughout this chapter's exercises, you have obtained information about your tablespaces by querying certain data dictionary views like DBA_TABLESPACES, and DBA_DATA_FILES. A data dictionary view allows you to view metadata (data about data) concerning database objects. Create a tablespace using all of the options you've learned thusfar and select from the corresponding data dictionary views mentioned above to verify that your tablespace and corresponding datafile(s) are active. Then drop the tablespace (remembering to take it offline before you do so). Once you've dropped the tablespace, try to re-create it using the syntax from Lab 4.2.2 and using the same datafile name(s).

1) What happens?
2) Once a tablespace has been dropped, does that mean all corresponding datafiles have been deleted from the system?
3) Why do you think it might be useful to take a tablespace offline before you attempt to alter it?

C H A P T E R 5

SEGMENTS
AND EXTENTS

CHAPTER OBJECTIVES	
In this chapter, you will learn about:	
✔ Segments	Page 104
✔ Extents	Page 111

In the previous chapter, we discussed logical constructs called tablespaces. Each tablespace contains even smaller logical constructs. In this chapter, we touch upon two of them: segments and extents. In Chapter 6, "Data Blocks," in the last part of the discussion on logical constructs, we introduce data blocks. For now, it is important to understand the logical storage layout of an Oracle database and how each unit affects not only the rate of growth of the database, but also how operations and transactions are effectively managed and executed.

You will soon discover that the monitoring and maintenance of the logical storage layout of a database is an ongoing process. As a DBA, you will be constantly fine-tuning particular parameters and settings, and must always be aware of factors such as changes in the volume of transactions, as well as characteristic changes in the data entered. In support of this, the more knowledge you have about the business requirements the database supports, the more equipped you will be to design and maintain that database's logical storage.

 All of the commands that you issue in this chapter's exercises should be done in SQL*Plus as user SYSTEM.

L A B 5 . 1

SEGMENTS

LAB OBJECTIVES

After this lab, you will be able to:

✔ Define a Segment
✔ Identify Common Segment Types

LAB 5.1 EXERCISES

5.1.1 DEFINE A SEGMENT

Segments work as the most direct logical storage construct for database objects that store data. That is, for every database object that stores data (such as tables and indexes), there exists at least one segment. Prior to Oracle 8.0, there was only one segment per data-storing object. With Oracle 8.0 (and subsequent versions), tasks such as data warehousing require partitioning of such data-storing objects as tables and indexes with large amounts of data to relate to multiple segments in order to assist in the maintenance and performance of those objects. In these cases, those segments are referred to as "partitioned." For the exercises in this book, we will assume only one segment per data-storing object. The segment is created automatically when you create the database object and has the same name as the object it supports.

For example, *data segments* (which in this book you will see sometimes referred to as *table segments*) store the data associated with the tables owned by a particular account, while *index segments* store the data associated with indexes on those tables, and so forth.

a) What kind of information does a segment store?

_____

_____

b) Can a tablespace simply exist without any segments? Why or why not?

_____

_____

c) How many database objects can one segment support?

_____

To efficiently manage segments, a DBA must know the objects each client application will use, the type and volume of data that will be associated with those objects, and in what manner the data will be retrieved. A segment resides in one and only one tablespace. As a consequence, it will correspond with one or more of the datafiles relating to that tablespace.

d) Where is a segment logically assigned?

_____

_____

e) Where is the data in a segment physically placed?

_____

_____

5.1.2 IDENTIFY COMMON SEGMENT TYPES

The two common types of segments that we will focus on are _table (or data) segments_ and _rollback segments_. Other common types of segments are _index segments_ and _temporary segments_.

**LAB
5.1**

Type the following query while logged into SQL*Plus as user SYSTEM:

```
SELECT DISTINCT segment_type
  FROM dba_segments;
```

a) List the most common types of segments.

_____

_____

b) Do you see the most common types of segments listed in your
result set?

_____

_____

Refer back to Figure 4.3 for a depiction of the relationships between segments,
tablespaces, and datafiles.

Each segment type and the type of information each is associated with might be
explained as follows:

- Data segments—Store data for the users' tables.
- Rollback segments—Store information about database
  transactions. If for some reason a set of transactions needs to be
  canceled, or *rolled back*, the Oracle Server uses the undo data that
  is stored in the rollback segments to complete that action.
  Rollback segments are also used to provide read consistency. (We
  will discuss rollback segments in greater detail in Chapter 12,
  "Rollback Segments.")
- Index segments—Store data for indexes created for a table.
- Temporary segments—Dynamically created work areas used for
  executing certain SQL operations, such as sorting operations (like
  ORDER BY), that cannot be performed in memory.

c) Briefly describe the kind of information each type of segment
stores or is used for.

_____

_____

Type the following at the SQL*Plus command line:

```
SET PAUSE ON

SELECT SUBSTR(segment_name, 1, 30) segment_name,
       segment_type, tablespace_name
   FROM dba_segments;
```

Here simply note the different names and types of segments as they relate to their corresponding tablespaces. You do not have to list them.

Type the following queries at the SQL*Plus command line (once again, you do not have to note the names of all segments and extents you see. The sample statements below should be executed so that you gain an idea of what kind of information is stored in the data dictionary for these types of storage units):

```
SELECT *
  FROM dba_free_space
  ORDER BY file_id, block_id;

SELECT free.tablespace_name, free.block_id, free.bytes
  FROM dba_free_space free, dba_data_files file
  WHERE free.file_id = file.file_id
  ORDER BY 1, 2;

SELECT owner, segment_name, extents, max_extents
  FROM dba_segments
  ORDER BY 1, 2;

SELECT tablespace_name, COUNT(*), segments,
       SUM(bytes) BYTES
  FROM dba_segments
  GROUP BY tablespace_name;

SELECT *
  FROM dba_extents;

SELECT SUM(bytes)/SUM(blocks)
  FROM dba_free_space;
```

LAB 5.1 EXERCISE ANSWERS

5.1.1 ANSWERS

a) What kind of information does a segment store?

Answer: A segment stores the data for a database object.

b) Can a tablespace simply exist without any segments? Why or why not?

Answer: A tablespace contains no segments when it is first created. The moment an object is created within that tablespace, a segment is allocated to that tablespace to store the data for that object.

c) How many database objects can one segment support?

Answer: A segment can support only one database object.

d) Where is a segment logically assigned?

Answer: A segment is logically assigned to a tablespace.

e) Where is the data in a segment physically placed?

Answer: A segment logically resides in a tablespace, but its data is physically placed in one or more datafiles.

5.1.2 ANSWERS

a) List the most common types of segments.

Answer: The most common types of segments are: data/table, rollback, index, and temporary.

b) Do you see the most common types of segments listed in your result set?

Answer: Upon issuing this query, you should have received a result similar to the following:

```
SQL> SELECT DISTINCT segment_type
  2    FROM dba_segments;
```

```
SEGMENT_TYPE
------------------
CACHE
CLUSTER
INDEX
LOBINDEX
LOBSEGMENT
ROLLBACK
TABLE

7 rows selected.
```

Here you should see the common segment types, table, rollback, and index, listed in your result set. Note that in Oracle versions previous to 8.x, LOBINDEX and LOBSEGMENT do not exist. At this point, it is only necessary for you to concentrate on the segments that have been discussed in this chapter. Do not concern yourself right now with the purpose of the other segment types listed here. The other segment types you see may vary depending on the version of Oracle and type of installation used.

c) Briefly describe the kind of information each type of segment stores or is used for.

Answer:

1. A data segment stores data for a particular table.

2. A rollback segment stores undo information for transactions. Information in the rollback segments is used when a set of transactions needs to be canceled, or rolled back.

3. An index segment stores information for indexes.

4. A temporary segment is used for sort operations that cannot be completed in memory.

LAB 5.1 SELF-REVIEW QUESTIONS

To test your progress, you should be able to answer the following questions.

1) Tablespaces do not truly need segments to store data information for the objects they correspond to.

a) _____ True
b) _____ False

2) A segment can contain information for more than one database object.

a) _____ True
b) _____ False

3) A segment can span many tablespaces.

a) _____ True
b) _____ False

4) Temporary segments store information for table objects that you only plan to keep for a short, specified period of time (i.e., temporarily).

a) _____ True
b) _____ False

5) Match the type of segment on the left with the number of the corresponding description on the right:

a) _____ Rollback
b) _____ Temporary
c) _____ Table

1) Contains information about an index for a table
2) Contains data for a table object
3) Contains undo information for database transactions

d) _____ Index

4) Used for assisting in certain SQL sort operations

Quiz answers appear in Appendix A, Lab 5.1.

L A B   5 . 2

EXTENTS

LAB OBJECTIVES

After this Lab, you will be able to:

✔ Define an Extent
✔ Understand Segment and Extent Parameters
✔ Understand Free Space

LAB 5.2 EXERCISES

5.2.1 DEFINE AN EXTENT

Each segment contains one or more *extents*. An *extent* is a contiguous set of Oracle data blocks, the smallest unit of storage in Oracle (data blocks are discussed in Chapter 6, "Data Blocks"). Extents are contained in segments. The type of segment an extent supports determines the way the extent is used and managed by the Oracle Server. See Figure 5.1 for a depiction of the relationship between a table's extents and segments.

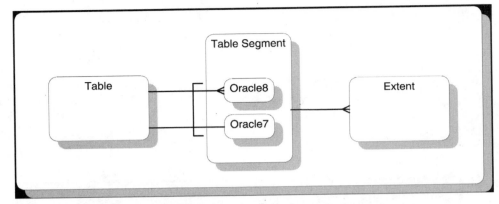

Figure 5.1 ■ The relationship between a table's extents and segments.

a) What type of information does an extent typically contain?

_____

_____

Because a segment consists of extents, once the existing extents in a segment run out of space to hold new data, the Oracle Server allocates an additional extent. This extension process continues as necessary until either the tablespace is full or the maximum number of extents per segment has been reached.

 If a segment has more than one extent, there is no guarantee that those extents will be contiguous. When a tablespace contains many non-contiguous extents for multiple segments, the result is tablespace fragmentation.

To obtain an additional extent, the Oracle Server searches through the tablespace that contains the segment. During its search, it tries to find a set of contiguous data blocks that is at least the size of the extent to be allocated.

b) What happens if a segment is running out of space?

_____

_____

c) What conditions could prevent a segment from *extending*?

5.2.2 UNDERSTAND SEGMENT AND EXTENT PARAMETERS

In the previous chapter, you created a tablespace and were required to specify certain default storage parameters like INITIAL, NEXT, MINEXTENTS, MAXEXTENTS, and PCTINCREASE. These types of storage parameters are available for all kinds of CREATE <object> statements. If you create a database object (such as with the CREATE TABLE statement) without specifying storage parameters for it, the object will inherit the storage parameters of the tablespace it is stored in. Alternatively, these storage parameters can be specified explicitly for the object upon its creation.

Once a segment has been created, you cannot change its INITIAL and MINEXTENTS values.

When a segment is created, it must contain at least one extent. Rollback segments require at least two initial extents.

a) Can a segment be created without an extent? Why or why not?

Type the following DDL statement while logged on as user PTH01:

```
CREATE TABLE employee
  (ssn NUMBER(9)
    constraint EMPLOYEE_PK PRIMARY KEY,
  last_name VARCHAR2(35),
  first_name VARCHAR2(20),
  salary NUMBER(6,2)
  );
```

Now log into SQL*Plus as user SYSTEM and type the following query to find out the names of all segments that are in your schema:

```
SELECT segment_name, segment_type
  FROM dba_segments
 WHERE owner = 'PTH01';
```

b) Write down the result of this query, noting the name and type of your segments.

_____

_____

Now type the following query to find out how many extents were created for this table:

```
SELECT segment_name, extent_id
  FROM dba_extents
 WHERE segment_name LIKE 'EMPLOYEE%'
   AND owner = 'PTH01';
```

c) How many extents do you see listed in your result set?

_____

_____

Reconnect as user PTH01 and type the following DDL statement:

```
CREATE INDEX EMPLOYEE_NAME ON employee
   (last_name, first_name);
```

Log on once again as user SYSTEM and type the following query:

```
SELECT segment_name, extent_id
  FROM dba_extents
 WHERE segment_name = 'EMPLOYEE_NAME'
   AND owner = 'PTH01';
```

d) How many extents were created for your new index?

_____

_____

e) Which storage parameters can you alter after you've created a segment?

_____

_____

f) What determines the size of a segment?

_____

_____

The default storage parameter settings for each tablespace can be found in the DBA_TABLESPACES data dictionary view. Remember from Chapter 4, "Tablespaces," that a data dictionary view allows you to view metadata (data about data) concerning database objects.

g) Which data dictionary view contains information about the default storage parameters for each tablespace?

_____

_____

5.2.3 UNDERSTAND FREE SPACE

Log into SQL*Plus as user SYSTEM and type the following at the command line:

```
SELECT tablespace_name
  FROM dba_tablespaces;
```

a) List all of the tablespaces that you have.

_____

_____

To find out the total amount of free space currently available in the USERS tablespace, execute the following query:

```
SELECT SUM(bytes)
  FROM dba_free_space
 WHERE tablespace_name = 'USERS';
```

b) What is the result of this query? How much free space is available for this tablespace?

_____

_____

Repeat this query for each of the other tablespaces you listed in your answer to Question a).

A *free extent* is a contiguous set of blocks in the tablespace that is not currently allocated to a segment. A tablespace may contain multiple extents allocated to segments and one or more *free extents*. When a segment is dropped, (indirectly, when a tablespace is dropped), its associated extents are made *free*.

c) What is a free extent?

_____

_____

d) How does an extent become free?

_____

_____

Though extents may be free and contiguous, they are not automatically coalesced (combined) with one another unless one of two events occurs:

- The default PCTINCREASE for the tablespace has been set to a nonzero value and the SMON background process has performed its periodic action of coalescing neighboring free extents.

- The COALESCE clause of the ALTER TABLESPACE command has been issued.

■ *FOR EXAMPLE*

A sample ALTER TABLESPACE command is shown here:

```
ALTER TABLESPACE new_data COALESCE;
```

While connected as user SYSTEM, type the following at the SQL*Plus command line:

```
ALTER TABLESPACE users COALESCE;
```

Now retype the query you executed in Question b):

```
SELECT  SUM(bytes)
  FROM dba_free_space
 WHERE tablespace_name = 'USERS';
```

e) What is the result of this query? How much free space is available for this tablespace?

_____

_____

f) Write the command you would issue to insert a row into the EMPLOYEE table.

_____

_____

g) Connect to the database as user PTH01 and issue the command. Re-issue the query from Question e). Did you remember to reconnect as user SYSTEM? How much free space is available for this tablespace? Is there any difference between the value you receive here and the value you received in Question e)?

_____

_____

h) Write the command you would use to get rid of all the rows in the EMPLOYEE table without getting rid of the table itself.

_____

_____

i) Connect to the database as user PTH01 and issue the command. Re-issue the query from Question g). Did you remember to reconnect as user SYSTEM? How much free space is available for this tablespace? Is there any difference between the value you receive here and the value you received in Question g)?

_____

_____

j) Write the command you would use to get rid of the EMPLOYEE table.

_____

_____

k) Connect to the database as user PTH01 and issue the command. Re-issue the query from Question i). Did you remember to reconnect as user SYSTEM? How much free space is available for this tablespace? Is there any difference between the value you receive here and the value you received in Question i)?

_____

_____

l) Describe the events that enable free and contiguous extents to be coalesced.

_____

_____

LAB 5.2 EXERCISE ANSWERS

5.2.1 ANSWERS

a) What type of information does an extent typically contain?

Answer: An extent typically contains data that corresponds to the type of segment the extent belongs to. For example, if an extent belongs to a table segment, it contains data for that table, while an extent that belongs to a rollback segment contains information about database transactions, and so forth.

b) What happens if a segment is running out of space?

Answer: If a segment is running out of space, the Oracle Server allocates an additional extent.

It is important to note that although extents do not have to be, and often are not, contiguous, data blocks used to form an extent MUST be contiguous.

c) What conditions could prevent a segment from extending?

Answer: A segment may be prevented from extending if the tablespace is full or a segment's maximum number of extents has been reached. At that moment, the DBA may consider extending the tablespace or increasing the value of the MAXEXTENTS storage parameter.

5.2.2 ANSWERS

a) Can a segment be created without an extent? Why or why not?

Answer: A segment cannot be created without an extent. It never exists without at least one extent, and a rollback segment must have at least two initial extents.

b) Write down the result of this query, noting the name and type of your segments.

Answer: Upon executing this query, you may have received a result similar to the following:

```
SQL> SELECT segment_name, segment_type
  2    FROM dba_segments
  3   WHERE owner = 'PTH01';
```

```
SEGMENT_NAME        SEGMENT_TYPE
------------        ------------
EMPLOYEE            TABLE
EMPLOYEE_PK         INDEX
```

c) How many extents do you see listed in your result set?

Answer: Upon executing this query, you may have received a result similar to the following:

```
SQL> SELECT segment_name, extent_id
  2    FROM dba_extents
  3    WHERE segment_name like 'EMPLOYEE%'
  4      AND owner = 'PTH01';

SEGMENT_NAME        EXTENT_ID
------------        ---------
EMPLOYEE                0
EMPLOYEE_PK             0
```

You should see two extents listed in your result set: one for the new table, and one for its new primary key index. Each initial extent is assigned an EXTENT_ID value of 0.

d) How many extents were created for your new index?

Answer: Upon executing this query, you may have received a result similar to the following:

```
SQL> SELECT segment_name, extent_id
  2    FROM dba_extents
  3    WHERE segment_name = 'EMPLOYEE_NAME'
  4      AND owner = 'PTH01';

SEGMENT_NAME        EXTENT_ID
--------------      ----------
EMPLOYEE_NAME           0
```

You should see that one extent has been created for your new index.

e) Which storage parameters can you alter after you've created a segment?

Answer: You can alter the NEXT, MAXEXTENTS, and PCTINCREASE storage parameters after you've created a segment.

f) What determines the size of a segment?

Answer:

1) When creating a database object, the size of a segment is determined by the DBA explicitly specifying segment storage parameters.

2) If those parameters are not specified, then the database object will automatically inherit the segment storage parameters specified for the tablespace it is contained in. These types of segment storage parameters are sometimes referred to as the "default" storage parameters.

This brief discussion on segment parameters regarding extents is included mainly to inform you that just because a tablespace has been created with a particular set of parameters does not mean that every database object you create within that tablespace must use the same parameters. However, many DBAs now practice placing like-sized objects into the same tablespace to assist in the reuse of fragmented free extents.

■ FOR EXAMPLE

An example of a CREATE TABLE statement with segment storage parameters specified follows:

```
CREATE TABLE orders
   (orderid NUMBER(3)
      constraint orders_orderid_nn
      CHECK (orderid IS NOT NULL),
   orderdate DATE,
   shipdate DATE,
   client VARCHAR2(3)
      constraint orders_client_nn
      CHECK (client IS NOT NULL),
   amount_due NUMBER(10,2),
   amount_paid NUMBER(10, 2)
   )
STORAGE (INITIAL 5M NEXT 5M
         PCTINCREASE 0 MINEXTENTS 1
         MAXEXTENTS 121
         )
TABLESPACE users;
```

Do not alter the PCTINCREASE value without also reviewing the value for the NEXT parameter. The size of each successive extent is calculated by looking at the size of the most recently allocated extent in the segment.

g) Which data dictionary view contains information about the default storage parameters for each tablespace?

Answer: The DBA_TABLESPACES data dictionary view contains information about the default storage parameters for each tablespace.

5.2.3 ANSWERS

a) List all of the tablespaces that you have.

Answer: Upon executing this query, your result set should look similar to the following:

```
SQL> SELECT tablespace_name
  2    FROM dba_tablespaces;

TABLESPACE_NAME
-------------------------------
SYSTEM
USERS
RBS
TEMP
TOOLS
INDX

6 rows selected.
```

b) What is the result of this query? How much free space is available for this tablespace?

Answer: After executing this query, you should have received a result similar to the following:

```
SQL> SELECT SUM(bytes)
  2    FROM dba_free_space
  3    WHERE tablespace_name = 'USERS';

SUM(BYTES)
----------
   5152768
```

Do not worry if your received sum total does not exactly match the value you see here.

c) What is a free extent?

Answer: A free extent is a contiguous set of blocks in the tablespace that is not currently allocated to a segment.

d) How does an extent become free?

Answer: An extent becomes free when its associated segment is dropped.

Deleting data from a table does not release its segment's extents. It simply removes the data from the extents. Extents become free when the segment is dropped.

e) What is the result of this query? How much free space is available for this tablespace?

Answer: After coalescing the free space in the USERS tablespace and re-executing this query, you should have received a result similar to the following:

```
SQL> SELECT SUM(bytes)
  2    FROM dba_free_space
  3    WHERE tablespace_name = 'USERS';

SUM(BYTES)
----------
   5152768
```

The total number of bytes did not change because between the last time you executed this query and this time (after coalescing your tablespace), you did not execute any DML statements to alter data. If you had, fragmentation may have occurred, creating the necessity to coalesce.

f) Write the command you would issue to insert a row into the EMPLOYEE table.

Answer: One possible command you could write to insert a row into the EMPLOYEE table is:

```
INSERT INTO employee (ssn, last_name, first_name, salary)
            VALUES (123456789, 'Newton', 'Frances', 5500);
```

g) Connect to the database as user PTH01 and issue the command. Re-issue the query from Question e). Did you remember to reconnect as user SYSTEM? How much free space is available for this tablespace? Is there any difference between the value you receive here and the value you received in Question e)?

Answer: Upon issuing this query, you should have received a result similar to the following:

```
SQL> SELECT SUM(bytes)
  2     FROM dba_free_space
  3     WHERE tablespace_name = 'USERS';
```

SUM(BYTES)

    5152768

There should be no difference between the value you receive here and the value you received in Question e). The reason for this will be explained shortly.

h) Write the command you would use to get rid of all rows in the EMPLOYEE table without getting rid of the table itself.

Answer: One possible command you could write to get rid of all rows in the EMPLOYEE table without getting rid of the table itself is:

```
TRUNCATE TABLE employee;
```

i) Connect to the database as user PTH01 and issue the command. Re-issue the query from Question g). Did you remember to reconnect as user SYSTEM? How much free space is available for this tablespace? Is there any difference between the value you receive here and the value you received in Question g)?

Answer: Upon issuing this query, you should have received a result similar to the following:

```
SQL> SELECT SUM(bytes)
  2     FROM dba_free_space
  3     WHERE tablespace_name = 'USERS';
```

SUM(BYTES)

    5152768

Again, there should be no difference between the value you receive here and the value you received in Question g).

j) Write the command you would use to get rid of the EMPLOYEE table.

Answer: One possible solution for a command you could write to get rid of the EMPLOYEE table is:

```
DROP TABLE employee;
```

k) Connect to the database as user PTH01 and issue the command. Re-issue the query from Question i). Did you remember to reconnect as user SYSTEM? How much free space is available for this tablespace? Is there any difference between the value you receive here and the value you received in Question i)?

Answer: Upon issuing this query, you should have received a result similar to the following:

```
SQL> SELECT SUM(bytes)
  2     FROM dba_free_space
  3     WHERE tablespace_name = 'USERS';

SUM(BYTES)
----------
   5183488
```

You should notice that the value you receive here is 30720 bytes larger than the value you received in Question i). When you dropped the EMPLOYEE table owned by user PTH01, you not only freed the space claimed by the EMPLOYEE table extent, you also freed the space claimed by the table's two associated indexes: EMPLOYEE_PK and EMPLOYEE_NAME. Since each of these objects contained only one extent with a size value of 10240 bytes, the sum total byte value of these three objects was 30720. This value is exactly the same as the number of bytes reclaimed as free space in the USERS tablespace. If an object and its associated indexes each have only one extent, and data has been entered for this object, note that deleting data with the TRUNCATE command does not diminish the sum total byte value of space claimed by these extents. The byte value for the space claimed for these extents is going to be the same as it was upon the object's and indexes' creation, regardless of whether they contain data or not. Only when you delete the object entirely is space reclaimed from that object and its indexes.

l) Describe the events that enable free and contiguous extents to be coalesced.

Answer: The events that enable free and contiguous extents to be coalesced are:

1) The default PCTINCREASE for the tablespace has been set to a nonzero value, enabling the SMON background process to periodically coalesce neighboring free extents.

2) The ALTER TABLESPACE command has been issued with the COALESCE clause.

When searching for free space, the database will only go through the process of coalescing free extents if it cannot find a large enough existing free extent. To obtain a list of free extents, query the DBA_FREE_SPACE data dictionary view.

Lab 5.2 Self-Review Questions

To test your progress, you should be able to answer the following questions.

1) Segments consist of contiguous and non-contiguous extents.

a) _____ True
b) _____ False

2) Extents consist of contiguous and non-contiguous data blocks.

a) _____ True
b) _____ False

3) An extent can span multiple segments.

a) _____ True
b) _____ False

4) All segments require at least one initial extent, but rollback segments require two.

a) _____ True
b) _____ False

5) Which storage parameters can be altered after a segment is created?

a) _____ INITIAL, NEXT, and PCTINCREASE
b) _____ INITIAL, MAXEXTENTS, and TEMPORARY
c) _____ NEXT, MAXEXTENTS, and PCTINCREASE
d) _____ NEXT, MINEXTENTS, and PERMANENT

6) The following data dictionary view can be queried to discover the number of available free extents in a particular tablespace.

a) _____ DBA_TABLESPACES
b) _____ DBA_FREE_SPACE
c) _____ DBA_SEGMENTS
d) _____ DBA_EXTENTS

Quiz answers appear in Appendix A, Lab 5.2.

CHAPTER 5

TEST YOUR THINKING

1) What is the difference between the kind of information contained in the different data dictionary views: DBA_TABLESPACES, DBA_SEGMENTS, and DBA_EXTENTS?

2) What would happen if you were to set the PCTINCREASE value for a database object to a nonzero value?

3) Discuss the issue of space management, given your knowledge gained in Chapters 4, "Tablespaces," and 5, "Segments and Extents," and what you believe the differences between performing this action on a high-transactional versus a low-transactional database might be.

CHAPTER 6

DATA BLOCKS

CHAPTER OBJECTIVES

In this chapter, you will learn about:

✔ Units of Storage Called Data Blocks   Page 130
✔ Block-Level Storage Parameters   Page 145

The data block, the smallest subdivision in our discussion of data storage, is one of the most central and integral parts of a database. In this chapter, we will help you understand how interrelated the logical and physical constructs of a database are.

L A B   6 . 1

UNITS OF STORAGE CALLED DATA BLOCKS

LAB OBJECTIVES

After this lab, you will be able to:

✔ Define a Block
✔ Understand the Makeup of a Block
✔ Recognize the Physical Record Format

LAB 6.1 EXERCISES

6.1.1 DEFINE A BLOCK

A *block* is the smallest unit of storage for Oracle data. The size of a block in a starter database installed by the Oracle Installer is typically defaulted to 2048 bytes (2K) or 4096 bytes (4K), depending on the installation environment.

Find out the size of a block in your current installation environment.

Type the following at the SQL*Plus command line while connected as user SYSTEM:

```
SELECT segment_name, bytes, blocks, bytes/blocks
  FROM dba_extents
 WHERE ROWNUM = 1;
```

a) Write down the results of this query. What is the current size, in bytes, of a block in your environment?

_____

_____

Now type the following at the SQL*Plus command line:

```
SELECT value
  FROM v$parameter
 WHERE name = 'db_block_size';
```

b) Write down the results of this query. Compare the results from this query with the results from the query in Question a). What do you observe?

_____

_____

c) What are the most common default block sizes for a starter database?

_____

_____

Remember from Chapter 5, "Segments and Extents," that the number of blocks initially assigned to an Oracle object depends on either the storage parameters for the tablespace in which that object was created or the storage parameters that were specified when the object was created. In other words, the number of blocks is assigned based upon the size allocated to the extents in the CREATE <object > statement.

d) What determines the number of blocks initially assigned to an Oracle object?

_____

_____

Using the CREATE TABLE statement example from Chapter 5, "Segments and Extents," create a table and explicitly specify storage parameters for it .

Type the following at the SQL*Plus command line as user PTH0I:

```
CREATE TABLE orders
   (orderid NUMBER(3)
      CONSTRAINT orders_orderid_nn
        CHECK (orderid IS NOT NULL),
    orderdate DATE,
    shipdate DATE,
    client VARCHAR2(3)
      CONSTRAINT orders_client_nn
        CHECK (client IS NOT NULL),
    amount_due NUMBER(10,2),
    amount_paid NUMBER(10,2)
    )
   STORAGE (INITIAL 5M NEXT 5M
            PCTINCREASE 0 MINEXTENTS 1
            MAXEXTENTS 121
             )
   TABLESPACE users;
```

You should receive a confirmation message like "Table created." If you do not receive this message, check that the statement was typed correctly and try it again.

Next, type the following query to see what the storage parameters are for this object:

```
SELECT table_name, initial_extent, next_extent,
       pct_increase, min_extents, max_extents
  FROM dba_tables
 WHERE table_name = 'ORDERS';
```

e) Write down the results of this query.

_____

_____

Notice in your CREATE TABLE statement that you explicitly assign this table to the USERS tablespace.

Now, type the following query to see what the default storage parameters for the USERS tablespace are:

```
SELECT tablespace_name, initial_extent, next_extent,
       pct_increase, min_extents, max_extents
  FROM dba_tablespaces
 WHERE tablespace_name = 'USERS';
```

f) Write down the results of this query. What differences do you see between the query from DBA_TABLES (Question e) and this query from DBA_TABLESPACES?

_____

_____

Now type the following query to find out the number of blocks currently assigned to the ORDERS table:

```
SELECT segment_name, blocks
  FROM dba_segments
 WHERE segment_name = 'ORDERS';
```

g) Write down the results of this query. What is the number of blocks currently in use by the ORDERS table?

_____

_____

The block size is specified at the time the database is created and cannot be altered for the life of that database. To specify the data block size during database creation, specify the size using the DB_BLOCK_SIZE parameter in the init.ora file as outlined in Chapter 2, "Creating Your Database."

Several contiguous data blocks comprise an extent (as shown in Figure 6.1).

h) How would you specify the block size at database creation time?

_____

_____

i) Write the statement that should be placed in the init.ora file at database creation time for a database with a 32K block size.

_____

_____

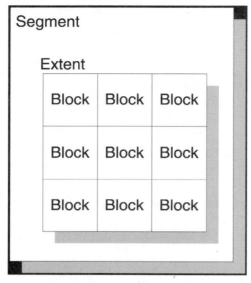

Figure 6.1 ■ **The relations between all units of storage discussed in this chapter thus far.**

j) What is the relationship of blocks to extents?

_____

_____

k) Look at the results from Questions a) and b). At what times can these queries result in different values?

_____

_____

6.1.2 UNDERSTAND THE MAKEUP OF A BLOCK

A data block consists of the following:

- Header
- Table Directory
- Row Directory

- Free Space
- Row Data

LAB 6.1

A DBA begins estimating the amount of space a database will need by understanding the various parts of a data block. Table 6.1 provides an overview of these parts.

a) What are the parts of a data block?

_____

_____

b) What kind of information does each part contain?

_____

_____

6.1.3 RECOGNIZE THE PHYSICAL RECORD FORMAT

The rows that are inserted into a block each have a format. Planning for the number of rows that can be stored in each data block is a key issue for a DBA in

Table 6.1 ▪ Parts of a data block

Block Portion	Block Portion Description
Header	Contains general block information like the block address, segment type, and number of transaction entries.
Table Directory	Used with cluster segments. Contains information about the tables in the cluster. A "cluster" is a group of tables that are related and often stored together in the same area of a disk.
Row Directory	Contains row information about the actual rows in the block.
Free Space	Space that can be used for adding new rows and extending rows that need more space due to growth.
Row Data	The actual data contained in rows or parts of rows of a table or index.

terms of space management. The *row directory* (refer back to Table 6.1) may also be referred to as the *row header,* while the *row data* (refer back to Table 6.1) contains the actual column data as defined by the CREATE TABLE command. To calculate the number of rows that can be stored in each data block, you need to ascertain an accurate estimate of the average row size.

The row header occupies three to five bytes. Table 6.2 provides a breakdown of the information contained within the row header, with each part's corresponding required number of bytes.

Chaining, the splitting of rows across data blocks, will be discussed shortly. For now, it is important to note that two bytes are required for each row's record header in the row header. One byte is required in the row header to list the total number of columns contained within the particular row being inserted. The physical sequence of columns does not necessarily correspond with the logical sequence specified in the CREATE TABLE statement. The physical location for a column with a data type of Long or Raw is always at the end of the row.

a) What parts does the row header consist of?

_____

_____

b) What kind of information does each part contain?

_____

_____

Table 6.2 ■ Parts of the row header

Row Header Part	Number of Bytes Required
Record Header—general overhead	2
Number of Columns	1
Cluster Index (for those blocks that contain information about clusters; optional)	1
Chaining Address (for records larger than block) or	1
Column Value with Long or Raw Data Type (again, optional)	

c) How many bytes does the row header occupy? Why?

_____

_____

The layout of the column data in the row body of the row data looks like the following:

Column Header	*Physical Column*	*Column Header*	*Physical Column*
Length of Column	Data	Length of Column	Data

The actual length of a column is contained in a *column header* that precedes each physical column. This header occupies a certain number of bytes, depending on the data type of its corresponding column.

- 1 byte—Number, Char, and Date.
- 3 bytes—Varchar, Varchar2, Long, Raw, and Long Raw.

d) Describe the layout of the column data.

_____

_____

e) What information is contained in the column header?

_____

_____

f) What determines the length of the column header?

_____

_____

LAB 6.1 EXERCISE ANSWERS

6.1.1 ANSWERS

a) Write down the results of this query. What is the current size, in bytes, of a block in your environment?

Answer: After executing this query, you should receive a result similar to the following:

```
SQL> SELECT segment_name, bytes, blocks, bytes/blocks
  2     FROM dba_extents
  3   WHERE ROWNUM = 1;
```

SEGMENT_NAME	BYTES	BLOCKS	BYTES/BLOC
FILE$	10240	5	2048

```
1 row selected.
```

The SEGMENT_NAME is less important here than discovering the size in bytes of one data block. So, do not worry if your SEGMENT_NAME does not exactly match what you see here. In this example, the current data block size, in bytes, is 2048 (2K). Alternatively, you could have simply checked the value for the DB_BLOCK_SIZE initialization parameter in your init.ora file.

b) Write down the results of this query. Compare the results from this query with the results from the query in Question a). What do you observe?

Answer: After executing this query, you should receive a result similar to the following:

```
SQL> SELECT value
  2     FROM v$parameter
  3   WHERE name = 'db_block_size';
```

VALUE
2048

Remember that the block size for this database was defined as 2048 bytes (or 2K) when the database was created. The values returned in both queries are the same. There can be only one block size for an Oracle database, so the value shown in

Question a)—*representing the size of blocks in a specific segment*—*and the value shown in Question b)*—*representing the block size defined for the database*—*must be the same.*

c) What are the most common default block sizes for a starter database?

Answer: The most common default block sizes for a starter database are 2K and 4K, depending on the installation environment.

d) What determines the number of blocks initially assigned to an Oracle object?

Answer: The number of blocks assigned to an Oracle object depends on either the storage parameters for the tablespace in which that object was created or the storage parameters for the object itself (if any were specified when the object was created or defaulted).

e) Write down the results of this query.

Answer: After executing this query, you should receive a result similar to the following:

```
SQL> SELECT table_name, initial_extent, next_extent,
  2         pct_increase, min_extents, max_extents
  3    FROM dba_tables
  4   WHERE table_name = 'ORDERS';
```

TABLE_NAME	INITIAL_EX	NEXT_EXTEN	PCT_INCREA	MIN_EXTENT	MAX_EXTENT
ORDERS	5242880	5242880	0	1	121

```
1 row selected.
```

f) Write down the results of this query. What differences do you see between the query from DBA_TABLES (Question e) and this query from DBA_TABLESPACES?

Answer: After executing this query, you should receive a result similar to the following:

```
SQL> SELECT tablespace_name, initial_extent, next_extent,
  2         pct_increase, min_extents, max_extents
  3    FROM dba_tablespaces
  4   WHERE tablespace_name = 'USERS';
```

TABLESPACE_NAME	INITIAL_EX	NEXT_EXTEN	PCT_INCREA	MIN_EXTENT	MAX_EXTENT
USERS	131072	10240	0	1	2147483645

1 row selected.

> *The two queries return different kinds of information regarding storage. While the query from DBA_TABLES returns the storage settings for a specific table, the query from DBA_TABLESPACES returns the default storage parameters for objects created in the USERS tablespace. The values for the initial extent, next extent, and maximum extents parameters are different between the result sets of the queries from DBA_TABLES and DBA_TABLESPACES. Notice that the ORDERS table uses the storage parameters that were specified during its creation.*

g) Write down the results of this query. What is the number of blocks currently in use by the ORDERS table?

Answer: After executing this query, you should receive a result similar to the following:

```
SQL> SELECT segment_name, blocks
  2     FROM dba_segments
  3   WHERE segment_name = 'ORDERS';
```

SEGMENT_NAME	BLOCKS
ORDERS	2560

1 row selected.

There are 2560 blocks currently in use by the ORDERS table.

h) How would you specify the block size at database creation time?

Answer: You would specify the block size by setting a value for the initialization parameter, DB_BLOCK_SIZE, in your initialization parameter file (init.ora).

■ FOR EXAMPLE

Go to the directory where your parameter file, init.ora, is stored. An example of the path in an NT environment might be:

```
E:\Oracle\admin\db00\pfile\init.ora
```

Open your init.ora file and look at the value for the DB_BLOCK_SIZE parameter. If you've created your database using instructions from this book, this value should be 2048.

i) Write the statement that should be placed in the init.ora file at database creation time for a database with a 32K block size.

Answer: Your statement should resemble the following:

```
db_block_size = 32768
```

 Do not change the DB_BLOCK_SIZE parameter unless you are doing so in the init.ora file of a database currently being created. In an existing database, this parameter should not be altered.

j) What is the relationship of blocks to extents?

Answer: An extent consists of several contiguous data blocks.

k) Look at the results from Questions a) and b). At what times can these queries result in different values?

Answer: These queries should never result in different values. The data block size can only be one value for the entire life of a database.

6.1.2 ANSWERS

a) What are the parts of a data block?

Answer: The parts of a block are the header, table directory, row directory, free space, and row data.

b) What kind of information does each part contain?

Answer: The information contained in each part includes the following:

Header—Block information like the block address, segment type, and number of transaction entries.

Table Directory—Information about the tables that use the block.

Row Directory—Row information about the actual rows in the block.

Free Space—Space that can be used for adding new rows.

Row Data—The actual data contained in rows or parts of rows of a table or index.

See Figure 6.2 below for a logical depiction of what a data block divided by its various parts looks like.

6.1.3 ANSWERS

a) What parts does the row header consist of?

Answer: The row header consists of:

<u>*Mandatory*</u>

1. *The record header.*

2. *The area used for storing the number of columns.*

<u>*Optional*</u>

1. *Cluster index (if necessary).*

2. *Chaining address or column value with Long or Raw data type.*

b) What kind of information does each part contain?

1. *The record header—General overhead information (always two bytes).*

2. *Number of columns—Stores the number of columns contained in the row.*

3. *Cluster index—Used for those blocks that contain information about clusters.*

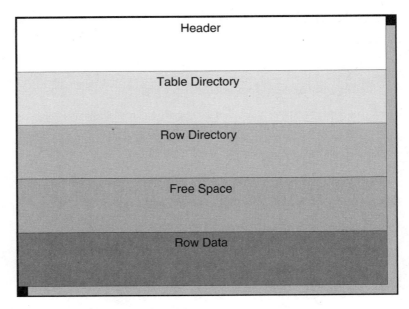

Figure 6.2 ■ The parts of a data block.

4. Chaining address—For rows larger than the block OR Column value with Long or Raw data type—Physically stored at the end of the row.

c) How many bytes does the row header occupy? Why?

Answer: The row header occupies three to five bytes. It occupies a minimum of three bytes due to the record header (two bytes) and space for storing number of columns (one byte). It can take up to one to two more bytes if it contains a space for storing the cluster index (one byte) and/or information about a chaining address or a column value with a Long or Raw data type (one byte).

d) Describe the layout of the column data.

Answer: A column header is followed by a physical column, which is then followed by another column header and another physical column, until the layout of the row is complete.

e) What information is contained in the column header?

Answer: The length of a column is contained in the column header.

f) What determines the length of the column header?

Answer: The data type of the column header's corresponding column determines the length of the column header.

LAB 6.1 SELF-REVIEW QUESTIONS

To test your progress, you should be able to answer the following questions.

1) The block size can easily be changed after database creation.

    a) _____ True
    b) _____ False

2) An extent is comprised of several contiguous and non-contiguous data blocks.

    a) _____ True
    b) _____ False

3) The actual data contained in rows of a table is stored in the header of a data block.

    a) _____ True
    b) _____ False

4) Transaction entries are typically stored in the free space of a data block.

    a) _____ True
    b) _____ False

5) Match the data block part on the left with the corresponding number of the description on the right:

    a) _____ Table Directory

    b) _____ Row Data

    c) _____ Header
    d) _____ Free Space

    e) _____ Row Directory

1) Contains general block information like the block address and segment type
2) Contains information about the tables that use the block
3) Space that can be used for adding new rows
4) Contains row information about the actual rows used in the block
5) The actual data contained in rows or parts of rows of a table or index

Quiz answers appear in Appendix A, Lab 6.1.

LAB 6.2

BLOCK-LEVEL STORAGE PARAMETERS

LAB OBJECTIVES

After this lab, you will be able to:

✔ Understand Block-Level Storage Parameters
✔ Understand Row Migration and Row Chaining
✔ Understand Free Lists

LAB 6.2 EXERCISES

6.2.1 UNDERSTAND BLOCK-LEVEL STORAGE PARAMETERS

Just as there are segment/extent-level storage parameters, there are also data block-level storage parameters. These parameters assist the DBA, as all other types of storage-level parameters do, in the task of planning proper storage design and maintenance. Some of the goals a DBA should keep in mind in block storage management are:

1. Pack as many rows as possible into the block to reduce I/O – thereby increasing performance.
2. Reduce row chaining and row migration.
3. Avoid the number of times a block is placed onto and taken off of the free list.

The parameters for block-level storage are PCTUSED, PCTFREE, INITRANS, MAX-TRANS, and FREELISTS.

a) What are the parameters for block level storage?

■ *FOR EXAMPLE:*

PCTUSED—Used when creating or altering a table or cluster.

PCTFREE—Used when creating or altering a table, cluster, or index.

PCTFREE

The value of the PCTFREE ("percent free") parameter tells the Oracle Server what percent of the data block to reserve for probable changes or updates to the existing rows in that data block. For instance, if you create a table with a PCTFREE value of 20, then you are telling the Oracle Server that 20 percent of that data block must be kept free to accommodate changes to the rows already in that block. Reaching the PCTFREE threshold will therefore disallow the insertion of new rows into that block when there is only 20 percent of free space left in the block. When the Oracle Server disallows the insertion of new rows into a block, it is said that the block has been taken off of the free list.

We will discuss more about PCTFREE when we discuss *row migration* and *row chaining* later in this lab.

PCTUSED

Whereas PCTFREE specifies when blocks should be taken off the free list to reserve space for row updates, PCTUSED specifies when a block should be put back on the free list, allowing it to again receive new/inserted rows. In our previous example, PCTFREE holds a value of 20. Assume also that PCTUSED holds a value of 40. The block starts out on the free list. Once the insertion of new rows fills the block to 80 percent (in other words, the PCTFREE parameter threshold of 20 has been reached), the block is taken off the free list. No more inserts are allowed into that block. The rest of the block will be reserved for updates to the existing rows in the block, allowing the existing rows to grow within the block they were inserted into. The block will again be placed on the free list when deletions to the existing rows leave the block containing a percentage of data that is less than or equal to the value of PCTUSED—in this case, 40 percent.

INITRANS

INITRANS is the initial number of concurrent transaction entries supported in each block header when the block is allocated. In other words, it is the initial number of transactions than can concurrently perform DML on a data block. The default value is 1, the minimum is 1 (default and minimum values are 2 for indexes), and the maximum is 255.

MAXTRANS

The MAXTRANS parameter is the maximum number of concurrent transaction entries allowed in a block. The default value is 255, the minimum is 1, and the maximum is 255.

The FREELISTS parameter will be discussed later in this lab.

b) What action does each block-level parameter support?

_____

_____

c) Why is it important for a DBA to plan for PCTUSED and PCTFREE settings?

_____

_____

These parameters can be specified during some CREATE and ALTER statements, and apply to all of a segment's blocks.

Drop the ORDERS table by typing the following statement:

```
DROP TABLE orders;
```

Now re-create the ORDERS table using a statement that illustrates the inclusion of block-level storage parameters (highlighted with italics):

```
CREATE TABLE orders
  (orderid NUMBER(3)
     CONSTRAINT orders_orderid_nn
       CHECK (orderid IS NOT NULL),
   orderdate DATE,
   shipdate DATE,
```

```
      client VARCHAR2(3)
         CONSTRAINT orders_client_nn
            CHECK (client IS NOT NULL),
      amount_due NUMBER(10,2),
      amount_paid NUMBER(10,2)
   )
PCTFREE 5 PCTUSED 65
   STORAGE (INITIAL 5M NEXT 5M PCTINCREASE 0
               MINEXTENTS 1 MAXEXTENTS 121
               FREELISTS 10
            )
TABLESPACE users;
```

d) In which kinds of statements can these parameters be specified?

_____

_____

e) Notice in the example that values were not specified for either the INITRANS or MAXTRANS parameters. What, then, will the values be for this statement?

_____

_____

Type the following query to find out all of the storage parameters currently being used for the ORDERS table:

```
SELECT table_name, initial_extent, next_extent,
       pct_increase, min_extents, max_extents, pct_free,
       pct_used, freelists
  FROM dba_tables
 WHERE table_name = 'ORDERS';
```

f) Write down the result of this query.

_____

_____

6.2.2 UNDERSTAND ROW MIGRATION AND ROW CHAINING

Row migration or *row chaining* may occur if enough room is not available in the block for row expansion. A good rule of thumb is, if you expect an object to experience a high number of updates that extend row size, you should specify a high PCTFREE, otherwise a low PCTFREE will suffice.

ROW MIGRATION

When a block's row is updated with a value for a column that was previously either NULL or of a smaller variable length than the new value, the new value may no longer fit in the data block. In that case, the Oracle Server must move the whole row to a second block.

The old data block stores the address of the new data block so that an index generated on the table will still be able to locate the row. Even though the row no longer resides in the first data block, the Oracle Server reads both the original data block (to obtain the new address of the second data block) and the new data block (to read the actual row(s)). This process of moving an entire row from its original data block to another is called *row migration*.

a) What is row migration?

_____

_____

b) What causes it to occur?

_____

_____

c) Where is the address for a row that has been migrated stored?

_____

_____

d) How is data retrieved from the migrated row?

_____

_____

ROW CHAINING

Sometimes after an update, a whole row cannot fit into the original block nor a new block. In this case, only part of the row can be moved. This process of splitting the row across multiple blocks is known as *row chaining*.

When either row migration or row chaining has occurred, a query must perform at least two disk reads to locate the entire row. One read gets the original data block and subsequent reads get the new data blocks. Multiple reads can significantly decrease performance.

PCTFREE helps to reduce row migration and row chaining by reserving enough free space in the data block for probable updates to existing rows, and therefore reduces the number of reads necessary to retrieve each row. However, it is not completely foolproof. If a row is too large to fit into a block from the very beginning, then the row will be chained upon insert. This will often happen with rows that contain columns of data type Long or Raw.

   e) What is row chaining?

   _____

   _____

   f) What causes it to occur?

   _____

   _____

   g) How does PCTFREE relate to row migration and row chaining?

   _____

   _____

   h) What can be done at database creation time to help avoid row chaining later on?

   _____

   _____

6.2.3 UNDERSTAND FREE LISTS

The PCTFREE and PCTUSED parameters work together with *free lists*. Notice in the CREATE TABLE statement above that a FREELISTS parameter was included. When a table is created, lists of data blocks that have been allocated for that table are also created. Free lists contain lists of blocks with free space for inserting rows.

a) What is a free list?

_____

_____

b) What does it contain?

_____

_____

If a block has not yet reached its PCTFREE threshold, it remains on the free list, since it still contains free space for inserting rows. Once it reaches that threshold (for example, in the statement above, 5) it is taken off the free list and reserved for possible updates to its existing rows. Once it reaches its PCTUSED threshold (in the case of the above statement, 65) the block is put back on the free list and is allowed to accept newly inserted rows. As updates and deletes on the data block take place, space availability in the block fluctuates and the block moves on and off the free list. If blocks move on and off the free list too frequently, it can cause performance degradation since the action of moving blocks on and off the free list causes overhead. So, when setting PCTFREE and PCTUSED, you must balance how much space to reserve for row growth versus attempting to pack the block as fully as possible to reduce the necessary number of reads.

c) How does a block get onto the free list?

_____

_____

d) How does a block get taken off of the free list?

_____

_____

The FREELISTS parameter specifies the number of free lists to be allocated to a segment. If a large number of inserts have to be carried out in parallel, this parameter is particularly important. Ten free lists have been specified in the above CREATE TABLE statement. The maximum number of free lists allowed is 22.

e) What does the FREELISTS parameter specify?

_____

_____

LAB 6.2 EXERCISE ANSWERS

6.2.1 ANSWERS

a) What are the parameters for block-level storage?

Answer: The parameters for block-level storage are PCTFREE, PCTUSED, INITRANS, MAXTRANS, and FREELISTS.

b) What action does each parameter support?

Answer: As outlined below:

PCTFREE—Tells the Oracle Server what percent of the data block to reserve for possible changes or updates to the existing rows in that data block.

PCTUSED—Provides an upper limit or percentage of a block that can be filled with new rows before the Oracle Server begins to add new rows to a block.

INITRANS—The initial number of concurrent transaction entries supported in each block header when the block is allocated.

MAXTRANS—The maximum number of concurrent transaction entries allowed in a block.

c) Why is it important for a DBA to plan for PCTUSED and PCTFREE settings?

Answer: It is important for a DBA to plan for PCTUSED and PCTFREE settings primarily so that he or she may be able to:

1) Reduce occurrences of row chaining and row migration.

2) Fill each block with data, while balancing the two I/O-related issues associated with data retrieval and free list management.

d) In which kinds of statements can these parameters be specified?

Answer: These parameters can be specified in CREATE or ALTER statements, specifically for tables and clusters (and indexes as well, if you are setting the value for the PCTFREE parameter).

e) Notice in the example that values were not specified for either the INITRANS or MAXTRANS parameters. What, then, will the values be for this statement?

Answer: These values will take the default values of

INITRANS = 1

MAXTRANS = 255

f) Write down the result of this query.

Answer: The result you receive should look similar to the following:

```
SQL> SELECT table_name, initial_extent, next_extent,
  2         pct_increase,min_extents, max_extents,
  3         pct_free, pct_used, freelists
  4    FROM dba_tables
  5   WHERE table_name = 'ORDERS';
```

TABLE_NAME	INITIAL_EXTENT	NEXT_EXTENT	PCT_INCREASE
MIN_EXTENTS	MAX_EXTENTS	PCT_FREE PCT_USED	FREELISTS

TABLE_NAME	INITIAL_EXTENT	NEXT_EXTENT		PCT_INCREASE
ORDERS	5242880	5242880		0
1	121	5	65	10

6.2.2 ANSWERS

a) What is row migration?

Answer: Row migration is the moving of an entire row from one block to another.

b) What causes it to occur?

Answer: It occurs as a result of an update that leaves the row too large to fit in its original block.

c) Where is the address for a row that has been migrated stored?

Answer: The address for a row that has been migrated is actually stored in the original block.

d) How is data retrieved from the migrated row?

Answer: To retrieve data from a migrated row, the Oracle Server must perform two reads; one against the original data block (to obtain the new address of the second data block) and one against the new data block (to read the actual row(s)).

e) What is row chaining?

Answer: Row chaining is the splitting of a row across multiple blocks.

f) What causes it to occur?

Answer: Row chaining takes place when the update to or insert of a row leaves it so large that it cannot fit entirely into the original block or a new block, forcing the Oracle Server to split it across two or more blocks.

g) How does PCTFREE relate to row migration and row chaining?

Answer: PCTFREE helps to reduce row migration and row chaining by reserving enough free space in the data block for probable updates to existing rows.

h) What can be done at database creation time to help avoid row chaining later on?

Answer: To help avoid row chaining, you can set a larger value for the DB_BLOCK_SIZE parameter in your init.ora file at database creation time.

6.2.3 ANSWERS

a) What is a free list?

Answer: A free list is a list of data blocks that has been allocated to a recently created object.

b) What does it contain?

Answer: It contains a list of blocks with free space for inserting rows.

c) How does a block get onto the free list?

Answer: A block goes onto the free list when, as a result of deletions and/or updates, it falls to or below its PCTUSED threshold.

d) How does a block get taken off of the free list?

Answer: A block gets taken off of the free list when it reaches its PCTFREE threshold. At this point, it is no longer available for inserts.

e) What does the FREELISTS parameter specify?

Answer: The FREELISTS parameter specifies the number of free lists to be allocated to a segment.

LAB 6.2 SELF-REVIEW QUESTIONS

To test your progress, you should be able to answer the following questions.

1) Both PCTFREE and PCTUSED parameters can be specified during a CREATE INDEX statement.

    a) _____ True
    b) _____ False

2) A data block is removed from the free list when it has reached its PCTFREE threshold.

    a) _____ True
    b) _____ False

3) Both row migration and row chaining create the necessity for two reads in obtaining data for one row.

    a) _____ True
    b) _____ False

4) Which of the below scenarios describes row chaining? Check all that apply.

    a) _____ A row has been moved from one block to another.
    b) _____ A row has been moved off the free list.
    c) _____ A row has been split between two or more data blocks.
    d) _____ A row has been inserted into multiple data blocks.

5) The PCTFREE parameter is used to account for inserts in the data block.

    a) _____ True
    b) _____ False

6) If you have a database with a low number of updates, you definitely want to specify a high PCTFREE.

    a) _____ True
    b) _____ False

Quiz answers appear in Appendix A, Lab 6.2.

CHAPTER 6

TEST YOUR THINKING

This project will give you practice in planning data block storage for data-storing objects.

Using the CREATE TABLE statement example from Lab 6.2:

For each of the two phases below, create the following sample university tables: new_course, new_enrollment, new_section, new_instructor, new_zipcode, and new_student.

Pay special attention to the values you choose for each of your PCTUSED, PCTFREE, and FREELISTS parameters as prescribed in each phase. Explain your choices.

PHASE I (The first six months)

In the first six months, there will be 500 courses. For each course, there will be three sections. There will be 100 instructors, no enrollments, and no students. new_course, new_instructor, new_section, and new_zipcode tables stay fairly static (i.e., not many inserts and/or updates once the data is entered). The new_student and new_enrollment tables have a high level of inserts, updates, and deletes.

PHASE II (After the first six months)

1) After six months, the school will open and immediately the number of rows in the new_student table will increase to 5000 and the number of new_enrollments will be twice that value.
2) Describe what effect these two different scenarios would have on insert and update actions within your table data blocks.
3) In which scenarios are you likely to encounter possible row migration or row chaining? Why or why not?

C H A P T E R   7

REDO LOGS

CHAPTER OBJECTIVES

In this chapter, you will learn about:

- ✔ Redo Logs   Page 158
- ✔ Recovering Data with Redo Logs   Page 170

In the previous three chapters, you explored the logical database constructs, tablespaces, segments, and extents. Now you progress from logical database constructs to physical database constructs, to gain a better understanding of how the two types of constructs work together. Redo logs will be introduced first.

In Chapter 2, "Creating Your Database," you encounter the SGA (System Global Area) and its associated background processes. One of those processes is LGWR (Log Writer), the process that writes to redo logs. In the event of a media failure or instance failure, either of which can lead to loss of data, the only way to recover that data is to use the information that was written to the redo logs and archived redo logs (backup copies of redo logs). Recovering data using archived redo logs is discussed in Chapter 15, "Physical Backup and Recovery."

L A B   7 . 1

REDO LOGS

LAB OBJECTIVES

After this lab, you will:

✔ Understand Why Redo Logs Are Important
✔ Understand How **LGWR** Writes to Redo Logs

LAB 7.1 EXERCISES

7.1.1 UNDERSTAND WHY REDO LOGS ARE IMPORTANT

Committed transactions are not written immediately to the datafiles; they are first written to redo log files as redo entries via LGWR. Since the datafiles are not updated at the moment a transaction is committed, the action of writing to the redo logs first, then updating the datafiles at a later time, is known as an "asynchronous commit." Redo logs, then, are the files that store *redo entries*. Redo entries are the records of all changes made to the database.

> ### Redo Logs vs. Rollback Segments
>
> New DBAs often get confused with the difference between redo logs and rollback segments.
>
> The primary uses of rollback segments are:
>
> - To hold undo information, which is used to reconstruct data if a user or application issues the ROLLBACK command.
> - To provide a read-consistent view of the data. The mechanism for this is described in Chapter 12, "Rollback Segments."
>
> Redo logs are used for recovery since they store redo entries containing committed and uncommitted data changes, even before those changes are written to the datafiles.

Since DBWR only periodically writes information to the datafiles, the redo entries in the redo logs are very important. If a system failure occurs, committed transactions that have not yet been written to the datafiles can still be accessed and recovered because they were written to the redo logs, ensuring that the database can be restored to a consistent state.

One of several events must occur for DBWR to write data to the datafiles. These events include:

- A checkpoint (to be defined later) takes place.
- DBWR times out after three seconds of being idle.
- The area of the Database Buffer Cache in the SGA that contains modified data blocks is full and becomes needed.
- A log switch occurs.

Type the following query as user SYSTEM:

```
SELECT name, value
 FROM v$sysstat
 WHERE NAME LIKE 'redo%writes';
```

a) Write down the results of this query.

_____

_____

Now, connect as user PTH01 and enter the following DML statement. Do not enter the COMMIT command.

```
INSERT INTO orders
   VALUES (101, '01-OCT-99', '15-OCT-99',
           'PTH', '45.00', '45.00'
           );
```

Re-enter the query from Question a), remembering to re-connect as user SYSTEM.

    b) Write down the results of this query. What differences do you see between the results you receive now and the results you received in Question a)?

Now reconnect as user PTH01 and commit your inserted row.

```
COMMIT;
```

Re-enter the query from Question a), remembering to reconnect as user SYSTEM.

    c) Write down the results of this query. What differences do you see between the results you receive now and the results you received in Question b)?

---

    d) Based on your knowledge of redo logs thus far, explain the reason(s) for the values you've received.

7.1.2 UNDERSTAND HOW LGWR WRITES TO REDO LOGS

The Log Writer (LGWR) background process is responsible for writing *redo entries* (information from DML transactions and the DDL commands—CREATE, ALTER and DROP) from the Redo Log Buffer to the redo logs. Redo logs exist in groups. A group represents one or more redo log files. Every Oracle Database should contain at least two redo log groups. When redo entries are written to redo logs, they are written to one of the *groups* (set of multiple Oracle redo log files) defined for the database. In the db00 database, there are two redo log groups, each with two *members*. Each of those members is represented in the operating system by a file. Each member of a redo log group should be placed on a separate disk so that the loss of a disk storing redo information results in the loss of just one redo log member. The other members contain the same information and are used for backup and recovery.

As the db00 database exists at this point, there are two redo log groups. Creating a duplicate set of redo log files on another physical device results in four log files all together—two on one disk and an exact copy of the original two on another disk. Since these files resemble each other exactly, they are said to be "mirrored" and will be written to simultaneously.

Since the redo logs are critical for database recovery purposes, protecting them from damage such as accidental deletion, corruption, or media failures such as disk crashes is an essential job of every DBA. It is rare, but possible, that a redo log member could become corrupted. If a redo log group contains only one member, and that member is mirrored at the operating system level, it will be protected from being lost in case of disk failure. But, if that member were to become corrupted, that corruption would be mirrored as well. If there are two members in the group, and one of the members gets corrupted, the other member can be used to fill in any missing redo information. So, it is important for your redo log groups to contain multiple members, even if they are mirrored at the operating system level. Preferably, each member should be placed on a separate disk.

You already created a mirrored set of redo log files when you ran your CREATE DATABASE script, createdb00_01.sql.

Look at the log files now. Issue the following command as user SYSTEM through Server Manager in line mode or through SQL*Plus:

```
SELECT group#, member
  FROM v$logfile;
```

a) Write down the result set from this query.

_____

_____

_____

b) What do you think this result set represents?

_____

_____

Next, enter the following command—substituting your locations for the 'e:\oracle\ oradata\' values. This command creates new log files and may take a couple of minutes to run.

```
ALTER DATABASE
 ADD LOGFILE GROUP 3
  ('e:\oracle\oradata\db00\redo_03a.log',
   'e:\oracle\oradata\db00\redo03b.log'
  )
  SIZE 100K;
```

c) Issue the same query from V$LOGFILE as shown in Question a) and write down the new result set.

_____

_____

d) Compare the result set you received in Question a) with the result set you received in Question c). Explain the differences.

_____

_____

e) Why do you think a DBA should/should not create multiple members in redo log groups?

_____

_____

Here is an illustration of how LGWR interacts with the redo log groups. Assume that you have two online redo log groups, Group 1 and Group 2. As DML statements are issued and data is changed, the Redo Log Buffer (a memory area in the SGA used for temporarily storing redo entries) is filled. If that, or one of the events mentioned in Lab 7.1.1 occurs, the LGWR process writes redo entries from the Redo Log Buffer to one of the groups. For this scenario, say it writes to Group 1. When this happens, the LGWR assigns that particular *set* of entries a "log sequence number," perhaps 100. Once Group 1 is full, LGWR begins writing redo entries to Group 2 with a new log sequence number, this time maybe 101.

LGWR's action of beginning to write to a different redo log is known as a "log switch." A log switch will cause a "checkpoint" to occur, which causes DBWR to write the changed data blocks back to the datafiles.

f) What does the LGWR background process do?

_____

_____

_____

g) What is a log switch?

_____

_____

_____

Witness this activity by forcing a manual log switch.

Issue the following command as INTERNAL or SYS through Server Manager in line mode or through SQL*Plus:

```
SELECT MAX(sequence#)
   FROM v$log;
```

h) What is the most recent sequence number created for your redo logs?

_____

_____

Now issue the following DDL statement:

```
ALTER SYSTEM SWITCH LOGFILE;
```

Then re-issue the query executed in Question h):

```
SELECT MAX(sequence#)
  FROM v$log;
```

i) What is the value of your maximum sequence number this time? Why do you suppose you received this value?

If archiving has been enabled, then a log switch also invokes the ARCH background process. The result of the log switch is that the redo log just switched from is archived by ARCH. This means that as soon as one online redo log is full, ARCH copies it to an archived (or backup) version of the online redo log.

j) At this point in your learning, list the events you know a log switch can trigger.

LAB 7.1 EXERCISE ANSWERS

7.1.1 ANSWERS

a) Write down the results of this query.

Answer: Upon executing this query, you should have received a result similar to the following:

```
SQL> SELECT name, value
  2    FROM v$sysstat
  3    WHERE NAME LIKE 'redo%writes';
```

NAME	VALUE
redo synch writes	12
redo writes	76

Do not worry if your result set displays different values from the ones you see listed here.

b) Write down the results of this query. What differences do you see between the results you receive now and the results you received in Question a)?

Answer: Upon executing this query, you should have received a result similar to the following:

```
SQL> SELECT name, value
  2    FROM v$sysstat
  3    WHERE NAME LIKE 'redo%writes';
```

NAME	VALUE
redo synch writes	12
redo writes	77

The only difference you should see between the results you receive now and the results you received in Question a) is that the value for "redo writes" has increased by 1. The increase of 1 shows that the redo logs are written to when a DML statement is issued. This shows that the redo logs have kept track of all DML transactions executed thus far.

c) Write down the results of this query. What differences do you see between the results you receive now and the results you received in Question b)?

Answer: Upon executing this query, you should have received a result similar to the following:

```
SQL> SELECT name, value
  2    FROM v$sysstat
  3    WHERE NAME LIKE 'redo%writes';
```

NAME	VALUE
redo synch writes	13
redo writes	78

The differences you should see between the results you receive now and the results you received in Question b) are that the values for "redo synch writes" and "redo writes" have both changed. The value for "redo synch writes" keeps track of any committed transactions, while the value for "redo writes" shows that another transaction was initiated.

d) Based on your knowledge of redo logs thus far, explain the reason(s) for the values you've received.

Answer: V$SYSSTAT is keeping track of both DML transactions ("redo writes") and committed DML transactions ("redo synch writes").

7.1.2 ANSWERS

a) Write down the result set from this query.

```
SQL> SELECT group#, member
  2    FROM v$logfile;


GROUP#       MEMBER
----------   ----------------------------------
1            E:\ORACLE\ORADATA\DB00\REDO_01A.LOG
1            E:\ORACLE\ORADATA\DB00\REDO_01B.LOG
2            E:\ORACLE\ORADATA\DB00\REDO_02A.LOG
2            E:\ORACLE\ORADATA\DB00\REDO_02B.LOG
4 rows selected.
```

b) What do you think this result set represents?

Answer: This result set represents the fact that you have two sets of redo log files, in other words, two groups. These two groups each contain two redo log files, or members. For example, the files REDO_01A.LOG and REDO_01B.LOG are the two redo log members of Group 1. Note that all of the redo log members are listed as residing at the same location (E:\ORACLE\ORADATA\DB00). The members were created this way at database creation time (in Chapter 2, "Creating Your Database") to simplify the process of your first database creation. In a production environment, the members should be created on separate disks as discussed above.

c) Issue the same query from V$LOGFILE as shown in Question a) and write down the new result set.

```
SQL> SELECT group#, member
  2    FROM v$logfile;


GROUP#       MEMBER
----------   ----------------------------------
1            E:\ORACLE\ORADATA\DB00\REDO_01A.LOG
1            E:\ORACLE\ORADATA\DB00\REDO_01B.LOG
2            E:\ORACLE\ORADATA\DB00\REDO_02A.LOG
2            E:\ORACLE\ORADATA\DB00\REDO_02B.LOG
3            E:\ORACLE\ORADATA\DB00\REDO_03A.LOG
3            E:\ORACLE\ORADATA\DB00\REDO_03B.LOG
6 rows selected.
```

d) Compare the result set you received in Question a) with the result set you received in Question c). Explain the differences.

Answer: The result set you receive in Question c) should show you your additional group, Group 3, and your new additional duplicate members. REDO_03B.LOG is a duplicate of REDO_03A.LOG. You now have three online redo log groups. Each group consists of two members and each member is realized as a file on disk. Note that it is recommended that you create your log files on separate disks, even though the exercise of redo log file creation has been simplified here.

e) Why do you think a DBA should/should not create multiple members in redo log groups?

Answer: Since multiple members of redo log groups can be stored physically separate from one another, they help to ensure that redo information is available, even if one of the redo log file members gets corrupted or lost.

f) What does the LGWR background process do?

Answer: The LGWR background process writes redo entries from the Redo Log Buffer to the online redo logs.

g) What is a log switch?

Answer: A log switch is the moment that LGWR stops writing to one online redo log file and starts writing to another.

h) What is the most recent sequence number created for your redo logs?

Answer: Upon executing this query, you should have received a result similar to the following:

```
SQL> SELECT MAX(sequence#)
  2    FROM v$log;


MAX(SEQUENCE#)
--------------
           100
```

Do not worry if the value you received in your result set does not match the one you see here exactly.

i) What is the value of your maximum sequence number this time? Why do you suppose you received this value?

Answer: Upon executing these two statements, you should have received a result similar to the following:

```
SQL> ALTER SYSTEM SWITCH LOGFILE;

System altered.

SQL> SELECT MAX(sequence#)
  2     FROM v$log;

MAX(SEQUENCE#)
--------------
           101
```

You received this value because you forced a manual log switch. Each time a log switch takes place, a new log sequence number is generated.

j) At this point in your learning, list the events you know a log switch can trigger.

Answer: A log switch triggers a checkpoint, causing DBWR to write modified data blocks to the datafiles. Also, if archiving is enabled, a log switch can trigger the ARCH background process to write the full online redo log file being switched from to an archived redo log file.

LAB 7.1 SELF-REVIEW QUESTIONS

To test your progress, you should be able to answer the following questions.

1) Which process makes backup copies of redo log files after a log switch has occurred?

   a) _____ DBWR
   b) _____ LGWR
   c) _____ ARCH
   d) _____ SMON
   e) _____ PMON

2) Redo log groups are written to sequentially. They are never written to simultaneously.

   a) _____ True
   b) _____ False

**LAB
7.1**

3) Redo log members are written to sequentially. They are never written to simultaneously.

a) _____ True

b) _____ False

Quiz answers appear in Appendix A, Lab 7.1.

L A B   7 . 2

RECOVERING DATA
WITH REDO LOGS

LAB OBJECTIVE

After this lab, you will:

✔ Understand How Redo Logs Are Used In Recovering
Lost Data

LAB 7.2 EXERCISES

7.2. UNDERSTAND HOW REDO LOGS ARE USED IN RECOVERING LOST DATA

Here you explore how redo logs are used in recovering lost data. A more detailed discussion on this topic is found in Chapter 15, "Physical Backup and Recovery." To understand how redo logs are used in data recovery, it is important to understand not only how LGWR writes to the redo logs (Lab 7.1.2), but how often. See Figure 7.1 for an overview of how DBWR and LGWR read and write information.

Upon instance restart, the SMON (System Monitor) background process uses the redo logs and archived redo logs for database recovery.

Open your init.ora file and write down the setting and value for the LOG_CHECKPOINT_TIMEOUT parameter setting.

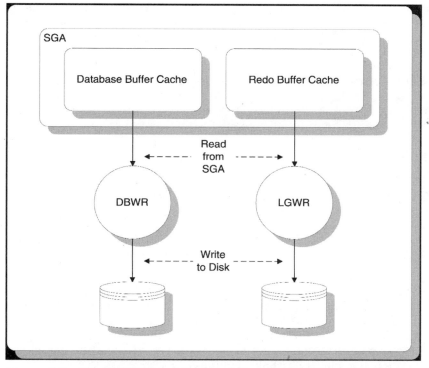

Figure 7.1 ■ **The DBWR background process reads modified data blocks from the Database Buffer Cache and writes them to the datafiles. The LGWR background process reads redo entries from the Redo Log Buffer and writes them to the redo logs.**

a) What do you think this value signifies?

_____

_____

Next write down the setting and value for the LOG_CHECKPOINT_INTER-VAL parameter setting.

b) What do you think this value means?

_____

_____

It is important to consider a couple of different types of problems that can occur in a database that may result in data inconsistency or data inaccuracy. These problems are often referred to as "failures." Two common failure types are "media" and "instance."

Instance failure occurs when the Instance suddenly dies. Examples of instance failures are power outages—a DBA shutting down the database using the SHUTDOWN ABORT option or an operating system crash. In a multi-user environment, such a failure could result in many incomplete transactions.

Media failure occurs when a datafile becomes corrupted or a disk gets lost.

> **c)** Based on your learning so far, what is a database system failure? Give examples.

_____

_____

Earlier, you saw that a checkpoint will take place during a log switch, which in turn causes DBWR to write all modified data blocks in the Database Buffer Cache to the datafiles. Once committed data is in a datafile, its associated redo log entries are needed only for the recovery of a lost or corrupted datafile. The only instance or process recovery now necessary is that which involves the changes to the data that are made after the last checkpoint occurs.

During a checkpoint, information is written to the headers of the datafiles and to the control files to indicate when the checkpoint occurred. However, if your database has many datafiles, LGWR may not be able to efficiently write committed transactions to redo logs if it must also update datafile headers with checkpoint information. Therefore, a special background process, CKPT (Checkpoint), may be started with the Instance. CKPT performs the checkpoint actions so that LGWR can concentrate on writing redo entries. In Oracle8x databases, this process is automatically started with the Instance. However, with pre-Oracle8x databases, this background process is optional, and is enabled by setting the parameter CHECKPOINT_PROCESS in your init.ora file equal to "TRUE":

```
checkpoint_process=true
```

and restarting your database.

CHECKPOINTS

There are different events that may cause a checkpoint to occur. Some of them are:

- A log switch has taken place.
- The timer set in the LOG_CHECKPOINT_TIMEOUT parameter of the init.ora file for seconds elapsed has been reached.
- The number of redo log blocks set in the LOG_CHECKPOINT_IN-TERVAL parameter of the init.ora file, that have been filled since the last checkpoint occurred, has been reached.
- The area of the Database Buffer Cache in the SGA, which contains modified data blocks, has been filled.
- The DBA has manually started a checkpoint by issuing the ALTER SYSTEM CHECKPOINT command.
- An instance has shut down via the SHUTDOWN NORMAL or SHUTDOWN IMMEDIATE options of the SHUTDOWN command.
- A tablespace or datafile has been taken offline.

In the case of instance failure, the Database is only consistent from the point when the last checkpoint took place (in other words, the last time all modified data blocks were written to disk). If instance failure occurs after transactions have been committed but before the modified data blocks have been written to the datafiles, then the redo entries will be needed for instance recovery.

d) What is a checkpoint and what are some of the events that can cause it to occur?

_____

_____

_____

e) When you execute the DDL statement ALTER SYSTEM SWITCH LOGFILE, what is taking place? Speak in terms of modified data, checkpoints, datafiles, and control files.

_____

_____

Type the following query as user SYSTEM:

```
SELECT name, value
  FROM v$sysstat
 WHERE name IN ('redo writes',
```

```
'redo synch writes',
'background checkpoints completed'
);
```

f) Write down the results of this query.

_____

_____

Now enter the following DDL command:

```
ALTER SYSTEM SWITCH LOGFILE;
```

Re-execute the query from Question f).

g) Write down the results of this query. Why do you think you received this result?

_____

_____

LAB 7.2 EXERCISE ANSWERS

7.2.1 ANSWERS

a) What do you think this value signifies?

Answer: LOG_CHECKPOINT_TIMEOUT = 1800. The number 1800 represents the number of seconds allowed to pass before a checkpoint takes place. If you want to recover your database more quickly, then you can set this value lower, to force checkpoints to occur more frequently. Of course, reducing this value also increases your amount of disk I/O and slows down system resources. Therefore, you should look at the history of the activity of your database when choosing this value. The goal is to discover a happy medium between the number of writes to disk and the number of redo entries held in memory and the online redo logs.

b) What do you think this value means?

Answer: LOG_CHECKPOINT_INTERVAL = 10000. The number 10000 represents the number of redo log blocks that are filled before a checkpoint occurs. If both the

LOG_CHECKPOINT_TIMEOUT and LOG_CHECKPOINT_INTERVAL parameters have values, then whichever timeout or interval occurs first will result in a checkpoint. The same principle applied in the answer to the previous question applies here as well. Choose your value for this parameter carefully.

c) Based on your learning so far, what is a database system failure? Give examples.

Answer: *A database system failure is a type of problem that can leave the database in an inconsistent or inaccurate state. Two examples of such failures are "media" failures and "instance" failures. "Instance" failures may occur when the Instance suddenly dies (like a power outage) and "media" failures may occur when a datafile becomes corrupted.*

d) What is a checkpoint and what are some of the events that can cause it to occur?

Answer: *A checkpoint is the moment when LGWR or CKPT (if it has been started with the Instance) writes checkpoint information to the headers of the datafiles and control files and DBWR writes changed data from the Database Buffer Cache in the SGA to the datafiles. Some of the events that can cause it to occur include a log switch, an instance shutdown, and/or a tablespace or datafile being taken offline.*

e) When you execute the DDL statement ALTER SYSTEM SWITCH LOGFILE, what is taking place? Speak in terms of modified data, checkpoints, datafiles, and control files.

Answer: *When you execute the DDL statement ALTER SYSTEM SWITCH LOGFILE, a checkpoint takes place, DBWR writes all modified data blocks in the Database Buffer Cache back to the datafiles, and LGWR (or CKPT, if it has been enabled) writes to the headers of both the datafiles and control files to indicate when the checkpoint occurred.*

f) Write down the results of this query.

Answer: *Upon executing this query, you should have received a result similar to the following:*

```
SQL> SELECT name, value
  2    FROM v$sysstat
  3   WHERE name IN ('redo writes',
  4                  'redo synch writes',
  5                  'background checkpoints completed'
  6                 );
```

NAME	VALUE
redo synch writes	13
redo writes	78
background checkpoints completed	3

Do not worry if your result set displays different values from the ones you see listed here.

g) Write down the results of this query. Why do you think you received this result?

Answer: Upon executing this query, you should have received a result similar to the following:

```
SQL> SELECT name, value
  2    FROM v$sysstat
  3   WHERE name IN ('redo writes',
  4                  'redo synch writes',
  5                  'background checkpoints completed'
  6                 );
```

NAME	VALUE
redo synch writes	13
redo writes	78
background checkpoints completed	4

Notice that the value for your "background checkpoints completed" row has now been incremented by one. The ALTER SYSTEM SWITCH LOGFILE command caused a checkpoint to occur and the value in the "background checkpoints completed" row to increase. Notice that the other two row values remain unchanged. Only when DML statements are being written does the "redo writes" row value increment, and only when DML statements are being committed do both the "redo writes" and "redo synch writes" row values increment. Also, a DML statement with a commit does not result in the "background checkpoints completed" row value being incremented.

LAB 7.2 SELF-REVIEW QUESTIONS

To test your progress, you should be able to answer the following questions.

1) Choose all of the situations below that will cause a checkpoint to occur: **HINT:** Do not choose those situations that take place as a result of a checkpoint occurring.

    a) _____ DBWR flushes modified data blocks to disk

    b) _____ A user changes some data and issues a COMMIT statement

    c) _____ A log switch occurs
    d) _____ LGWR flushes the Redo Log Buffer to disk
    e) _____ A user changes some data and issues a ROLLBACK statement

2) In Oracle versions 8.0 and above, the CKPT background process starts automatically at instance startup.

    a) _____ True
    b) _____ False

Quiz answers appear in Appendix A, Lab 7.2.

LAB
7.2

C H A P T E R 7

TEST YOUR THINKING

1) Write a query to find out how many members there are in your redo log groups. **HINT:** In addition to the familiar V$LOGFILE view, consider the V$LOG view.

2) Write a query to show the total amount of space used by all the members of your redo log groups.

3) Try to add an additional member to an existing redo log group where the new member has a different size than the existing members. What happens?

4) What do you think is the advantage(s) of employing the asynchronous commit method?

C H A P T E R 8

DATAFILES

CHAPTER OBJECTIVES

In this chapter, you will learn about:

- ✔ Datafiles   Page 180
- ✔ Manipulating Your Datafiles   Page 189

In Chapter 7, "Redo Logs," you begin exploring physical database constructs. That discussion is continued here with the datafile construct. Datafiles should already be familiar to you, especially in terms of the coverage in earlier chapters of this book on tablespaces and segments. The third construct (which is not given its own chapter in this book) is the control file. Control files store information about the state of the database. These three types of files: datafiles, redo log files, and control files, together comprise an Oracle Database.

The Oracle Database is affected by the activities of the DBWR and LGWR background processes, which are closely monitored by the DBA. In this chapter, you expand on the DBWR background process and its role in writing data to the datafiles. Your objective is to understand how all of the physical data associated with your database objects is maintained in datafiles.

LAB
8.1

L A B 8 . 1

DATAFILES

LAB OBJECTIVES

After this lab, you will be able to:

✔ Understand Datafiles
✔ Understand the Relationship Between Datafiles
and an Instance

LAB 8.1 EXERCISES

8.1.1 UNDERSTAND DATAFILES

Datafiles store the physical data for logical structures of a database, such as tables
and indexes.

 *Remember that one or more datafiles correspond(s) to a single tablespace
(refer back to Figure 4.2). Therefore, the data for one database object
(e.g., a table) may be stored in more than one datafile. However, even
though a database object may reside in more than one datafile, it will
always correspond to only one tablespace. See Figure 8.1 for an
illustration of this relationship.*

Figure 8.1 depicts the distribution of a table over multiple datafiles. The ORDERS
table is represented in the operating system by two datafiles: users01.dbf and

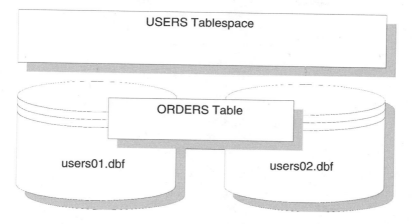

Figure 8.1 ■ The distribution of a table over multiple datafiles.

users02.dbf. However, the ORDERS table corresponds to only one tablespace, the USERS tablespace.

a) What is a datafile used for?

_____

_____

b) What is the relationship between datafiles, database objects (like tables and indexes), and tablespaces?

_____

_____

Type the following at the SQL*Plus command line while logged on as user SYSTEM:

```
SELECT a.table_name, b.file_name,
       c.tablespace_name
  FROM dba_tables a, dba_data_files b,
       dba_tablespaces c
 WHERE a.tablespace_name = b.tablespace_name
   AND b.tablespace_name = c.tablespace_name
   AND a.owner = 'PTH01'
   AND a.table_name = 'ORDERS';
```

c) Write down the results of this query.

_____

_____

d) How many datafiles did your result set return? Why do you
think you received this number?

_____

_____

One way of sizing your datafiles is to first determine how much data will be
stored in your database, then use that information to determine how many files
to keep the data in and how large the files should be. There are pros and cons to
creating large files. When you create a large file, you will have space available in
it for a longer period of time, thus eliminating the need to frequently add files.
However, those larger files will take longer to restore from their backup medium
(such as tape) when needed for recovery. As a DBA, you will constantly be making choices to balance these two issues.

e) How large should your datafiles be?

_____

_____

8.1.2 UNDERSTAND THE RELATIONSHIP BETWEEN DATAFILES AND AN INSTANCE

To understand the interaction between datafiles and an instance, it is important
to consider how DBWR interacts with the Database Buffer Cache. The buffers in
the Database Buffer Cache can be in three states:

- *Free*—These buffers contain unchanged data blocks—any buffer
  that does not contain data, or contains data in the same state as
  it exists in the datafiles. For example, blocks may have been
  brought into the Database Buffer Cache because a user issued a
  query. However, they can be overwritten (in the cache, that is)
  with new reads from disk because they have not been changed
  (i.e., updated).

- ***Dirty***—In contrast to free buffers, dirty buffers contain data blocks that have been changed in memory and are now no longer consistent with the data in the Database. They contain the most recent state of the data. "Dirty," in this sense, simply means "modified." Once DBWR writes the dirty/modified blocks to the datafiles, the Database Buffer Cache is considered "clean," since, at that moment, data in the Database Buffer Cache matches the data in the datafiles.

- ***Pinned***—Pinned buffers are those buffers that are currently being used, or accessed.
  - ***Pinned Dirty***—A pinned buffer becomes dirty if the data it contains is updated. A pinned dirty buffer then becomes a dirty buffer.
  - ***Pinned Clean/Free***—A pinned buffer is clean/free if the data it contains is merely read for a query.

a) In what different states can a buffer be in the Database Buffer Cache? What makes these states different from each other?

_____

_____

The buffers of the Database Buffer Cache are separated into two lists: the LRU (Least Recently Used) list and the LRUW (Dirty) list:

- ***LRUW/Dirty list***—Dirty buffer headers are stored in the dirty list. Data blocks listed in dirty lists are ultimately written to the datafiles by DBWR.

- ***LRU list***—This list contains pinned and free buffers, and some dirty buffers which eventually end up on the dirty list. Like the Least Recently Used algorithm from which it gets its name, the LRU list is employed to ensure that the newest (most recently used) buffers remain at the top or head of the list, while the older (least recently used) buffers move toward the tail or bottom of the list.

b) Describe the "lists" in the Database Buffer Cache. What kind of information do they contain?

_____

_____

When a user issues a database request, Oracle first checks to see if the data blocks associated with the request are already in the Database Buffer Cache. It uses this method because it is faster to retrieve data from memory than from disk. If the data is not already in memory, then Oracle reads the data from disk and searches for the first free buffer available, starting from the LRU end of the LRU list. The LRU end of the list is likely to list more free buffers since the buffers on that end are older than the buffers on the MRU (Most Recently Used) end. The buffers listed on the MRU end will more likely be pinned (vis-à-vis free), since they contain data that user requests currently need. Once a free buffer is found, Oracle copies the data block into that buffer and moves the buffer to the MRU end of the list, where it then becomes a pinned buffer.

As you can see, buffers are constantly being pushed from the MRU end to the LRU end of the list. As Oracle searches for a free buffer, it may encounter pinned buffers and dirty buffers. If it finds a pinned buffer, it ignores it. If it finds a dirty buffer, it knows that the dirty buffer contains data that must ultimately be written back to the datafiles, so it moves the dirty buffer to the dirty list and continues searching for a free buffer.

c) What happens to a free buffer once it has been overwritten with a new data block?

_____

_____

d) How does a dirty buffer get moved to the dirty list?

_____

_____

e) While searching for a free buffer, what does Oracle do when it encounters a pinned buffer?

_____

_____

Execute a query to find out how many data blocks in memory contain data that has not been modified. In other words, look at data blocks that are not *dirty*.

Type the following query while logged on as INTERNAL or SYS:

```
SELECT SUM(DECODE(BITAND(Flag,1),1,0,1))
       "Not Dirty"
  FROM SYS.X$BH;
```

X$ views are defined for the underlying dynamic performance tables against which many of the V$ views are defined. They are at this time undocumented and may change from version to version of the Oracle Server.

LAB 8.1

f) How many data blocks in memory are currently unchanged?

_____

_____

LAB 8.1 EXERCISE ANSWERS

8.1.1 ANSWERS

a) What is a datafile used for?

Answer: A datafile is used for physically storing data for all the logical structures of a database, such as tables and indexes.

b) What is the relationship between datafiles, database objects (like tables and indexes), and tablespaces?

Answer: One or more datafiles corresponds to a single tablespace. That tablespace may contain zero or more database objects. The data for one database object may then be stored in more than one datafile. However, like a datafile, a database object can correspond to only one tablespace.

c) Write down the results of this query.

Answer: Upon executing this query, you should have received a result similar to the following:

```
SQL> SELECT a.table_name, b.file_name,
  2          c.tablespace_name
  3     FROM dba_tables a, dba_data_files b,
  4          dba_tablespaces c
  5    WHERE a.tablespace_name = b.tablespace_name
  6      AND b.tablespace_name = c.tablespace_name
  7      AND a.owner = 'PTH01'
  8      AND a.table_name = 'ORDERS';
```

TABLE_NAME FILE_NAME

```
------------------------------------------------
TABLESPACE_NAME
------------------------------------------------
ORDERS        E:\ORACLE\ORADATA\DB00\USERS01.DBF
USERS
```

d) How many datafiles did your result set return? Why do you think you received this number?

Answer: The result set should have contained one datafile. You should have received this number because this tablespace was initially created with only one datafile.

e) How large should your datafiles be?

Answer: Determining the size of your datafiles depends on how much data you plan to store in your Database and how many files you'd like to use to store the data. This will impact how large your files will be and how much disk space your system will require.

8.1.2 ANSWERS

a) In what different states can a buffer be in the Database Buffer Cache? What makes these states different from each other?

Answer: Three types of buffers reside in the Database Buffer Cache: free, dirty, and pinned. Free buffers contain unchanged data blocks and can be overwritten with new reads from disk. Dirty buffers contain modified data blocks and therefore contain the most recent state of the data. Pinned buffers are those buffers currently being accessed. A pinned buffer's status may be changed to dirty if data was modified, or free if data was merely read for a query when the pinned buffer is no longer being accessed.

b) Describe the "lists" in the Database Buffer Cache. What kind of information do they contain?

Answer: There are two types of lists in the Database Buffer Cache: the "dirty" list and the "LRU" list. The dirty list contains modified data blocks, which eventually get written back to the datafiles by DBWR. The LRU list contains mainly pinned and free buffers, and a few dirty buffers, which eventually get moved to the dirty list.

c) What happens to a free buffer once it has been overwritten with a new data block?

Answer: Once a free buffer has been overwritten with a new data block, it is moved to the MRU end of the LRU list.

d) How does a dirty buffer get moved to the dirty list?

Answer: When Oracle is searching for a free buffer and comes across a dirty buffer, it moves the dirty buffer to the dirty list and continues searching for a free buffer.

e) While searching for a free buffer, what does Oracle do when it encounters a pinned buffer?

Answer: When Oracle encounters a pinned buffer, it ignores it.

f) How many data blocks in memory are currently unchanged?

Answer: Upon executing this query, you should have received a result similar to the following:

```
SQL> SELECT SUM(DECODE(BITAND(Flag,1),1,0,1))
  2         "Not Dirty"
  3    FROM SYS.X$BH;


Not Dirty
---------
      999
```

Of the data blocks currently in memory, 999 have not been altered.

LAB 8.1 SELF-REVIEW QUESTIONS

To test your progress, you should be able to answer the following questions.

1) Creating small datafiles will make your database more manageable.

    a) _____ True
    b) _____ False

2) There is no difference in the time it takes to recover small datafiles vs. large datafiles.

    a) _____ True
    b) _____ False

3) The three states buffers can be in inside the Database Buffer Cache are:

    a) _____ New, updated, and old
    b) _____ Pinned, free, and updated
    c) _____ Dirty, free, and old
    d) _____ Free, pinned, and dirty

4) A dirty buffer is one that contains incorrect data.

    a) _____ True
    b) _____ False

5) When a database request is issued, Oracle first checks to see if the data blocks associated with the request are already in the Database Buffer Cache before reading the data from disk.

    a) _____ True
    b) _____ False

6) The two lists into which the buffers in the Database Buffer Cache get separated are:

    a) _____ New and Old
    b) _____ Free and Updated
    c) _____ Dirty and LRU
    d) _____ LRU and MRU

7) When searching for a free buffer, Oracle begins its search from the MRU end of the LRU list.

    a) _____ True
    b) _____ False

Quiz answers appear in Appendix A, Lab 8.1.

LAB 8.2

MANIPULATING YOUR DATAFILES

LAB OBJECTIVE

After this lab, you will be able to:

✔ Create, Manipulate, and Delete a Datafile

LAB 8.2 EXERCISES

8.2 CREATE, MANIPULATE, AND DELETE A DATAFILE

This lab will give you some practice with physical database management in terms of manipulating datafiles. Remember that you created one datafile for each tablespace in your original CREATE DATABASE script (Chapter 2, "Creating Your Database"). You can also explicitly create datafiles online (as opposed to using a batch script, like you did in Chapter 2). Before you do so, however, refresh your memory about what you originally created, and find out the names of your existing files.

Type the following command in SQL*Plus while logged on as user SYSTEM:

```
SELECT file_name, tablespace_name
  FROM dba_data_files;
```

    a) Write down the names of your tablespaces and their associated datafiles.

_____

_____

LAB 8.2

Add the new tablespace using the command shown below. Note that when you create a tablespace, you must also create at least one datafile for it.

```
CREATE TABLESPACE myapp
    DATAFILE 'E:\ORACLE\ORADATA\DB00\MYAPP_01.DBF'
    SIZE 8K
    DEFAULT STORAGE (MAXEXTENTS UNLIMITED
                     PCTINCREASE 0
                     );
```

    b) Retype the query you executed in Question a) and verify whether you see your new tablespace and datafile in your result set.

_____

_____

Now alter the MYAPP tablespace and add another datafile by issuing the following command:

```
ALTER TABLESPACE myapp
    ADD DATAFILE 'E:\ORACLE\ORADATA\DB00\MYAPP_02.DBF'
    SIZE 8K;
```

    c) Retype the query you executed in Question a) and verify whether you see your new datafile in your result set.

_____

_____

Now type the following command:

```
SELECT tablespace_name
    FROM dba_tablespaces;
```

d) Write down the names of the tablespaces listed in your result set.

_____

_____

 The SELECT statements from DBA_DATA_FILES and DBA_TABLESPACES may be repeated throughout this lab. Though these actions may seem repetitive, they are useful in monitoring and verifying actions against the database.

Practice renaming an existing datafile by performing the following actions.

You need to shut down your database or take your tablespace offline before renaming a datafile. In this exercise, you will shut down the database. Issue the following command:

```
SHUTDOWN IMMEDIATE;
```

Now rename the datafile in the operating system.

- If you are in UNIX, you can use the mv command. For example, after navigating to the directory containing the myapp_01.dbf datafile, you can issue the following:

```
mv myapp_01.dbf myapp_01b.dbf
```

- If you are in NT, using Windows Explorer functionality, you can right-click on the file to bring up the menu, choose Rename and then change the name of the file from myapp_01.dbf to myapp_01b.dbf.

Now start the Instance by issuing the following command:

```
STARTUP MOUNT;
```

Issue an ALTER DATABASE command to rename the datafile in the database:

```
ALTER DATABASE RENAME FILE
  'E:\ORACLE\ORADATA\DB00\MYAPP_01.DBF' TO
  'E:\ORACLE\ORADATA\DB00\MYAPP_01B.DBF';
```

Now open the database by issuing the following command:

```
ALTER DATABASE OPEN;
```

e) Retype the query you executed in Question a) and verify whether you see your renamed datafile in your result set.

_____

_____

f) Write your observations about what just happened, noting the datafile that you moved/renamed.

_____

_____

Now resize an existing datafile. You will add an additional 2M to the USERS tablespace.

g) Using the DBA_DATA_FILES data dictionary view, write the statement you would type to obtain the size, in megabytes, of the MYAPP tablespace.

_____

_____

h) Write a query to find the name of the datafile associated with the USERS tablespace and that datafile's size in megabytes.

_____

_____

Figure out the size of that datafile + 2M and use that value for the *RESIZE* parameter in the following *ALTER DATABASE* statement. Resize the datafile by issuing the following command (remember to substitute the bracketed values with your own values):

```
ALTER DATABASE DATAFILE <filename> RESIZE <newsize>;
```

i) Re-issue the query you typed in Question h). What is the current size of the datafile associated with the USERS tablespace now?

_____

_____

Alternatively, it is possible to set up a datafile to extend automatically.

When setting up a datafile to extend automatically (using the AUTOEXTEND option), it is important to keep it in check by either using the MAXSIZE clause as in the statement shown below or through constant vigilance. An unchecked datafile that is set to AUTOEXTEND can grow until it has used up all the space on its disk.

Issue the following command using the filename you obtained in Question g):

```
ALTER DATABASE
    DATAFILE <filename> AUTOEXTEND ON MAXSIZE 25M;
```

This statement alters the filename specified with the sizing parameters "AUTOEXTEND" and "MAXSIZE." When more space is required, the Oracle Server will automatically extend the datafile with another area of disk space the same size as the datafile's current size. In other words, if the current size is 5M, then the size of the area of disk space made available to the datafile after the first 5M has been filled will be an additional 5M. The datafile will not, however, be allowed to extend beyond a maximum size of 25M.

LAB 8.2 EXERCISE ANSWERS

8.2 ANSWERS

a) Write down the names of your tablespaces and their associated datafiles.

Answer: Upon executing this query, you should have received a result set similar to the following:

```
SQL> SELECT file_name, tablespace_name
   2     FROM dba_data_files;
```

FILE_NAME	TABLESPACE_NAME
E:\ORACLE\ORADATA\DB00\USERS01.DBF	USERS
E:\ORACLE\ORADATA\DB00\INDX01.DBF	INDX
E:\ORACLE\ORADATA\DB00\RBS01.DBF	RBS
E:\ORACLE\ORADATA\DB00\TEMP01.DBF	TEMP
E:\ORACLE\ORADATA\DB00\SYSTEM01.DBF	SYSTEM

```
5 rows selected.
```

b) Retype the query you executed in Question a) and verify whether you see your new tablespace and datafile in your result set.

Answer: After creating the new tablespace, MYAPP, and retyping the query executed in Question a), you should have received a result similar to the following:

```
SQL> SELECT file_name, tablespace_name
  2     FROM dba_data_files;
```

FILE_NAME	TABLESPACE_NAME
E:\ORACLE\ORADATA\DB00\USERS01.DBF	USERS
E:\ORACLE\ORADATA\DB00\INDX01.DBF	INDX
E:\ORACLE\ORADATA\DB00\RBS01.DBF	RBS
E:\ORACLE\ORADATA\DB00\TEMP01.DBF	TEMP
E:\ORACLE\ORADATA\DB00\SYSTEM01.DBF	SYSTEM
E:\ORACLE\ORADATA\DB00\MYAPP_01.DBF	MYAPP

```
6 rows selected.
```

You should now be able to see your newly created tablespace, MYAPP, and its datafile, MYAPP_01.DBF.

c) Retype the query you executed in Question a) and verify whether you see your new datafile in your result set.

Answer: After adding another datafile to the MYAPP tablespace and retyping the query executed in Question a), you should have received a result similar to the following:

```
SQL> SELECT file_name, tablespace_name
  2     FROM dba_data_files;
```

FILE_NAME	TABLESPACE_NAME
E:\ORACLE\ORADATA\DB00\USERS01.DBF	USERS
E:\ORACLE\ORADATA\DB00\INDX01.DBF	INDX
E:\ORACLE\ORADATA\DB00\RBS01.DBF	RBS
E:\ORACLE\ORADATA\DB00\TEMP01.DBF	TEMP
E:\ORACLE\ORADATA\DB00\SYSTEM01.DBF	SYSTEM
E:\ORACLE\ORADATA\DB00\MYAPP_01.DBF	MYAPP
E:\ORACLE\ORADATA\DB00\MYAPP_02.DBF	MYAPP

7 rows selected.

You should be able to see your new datafile, MYAPP_02.DBF, in your result set.

d) Write down the names of the tablespaces listed in your result set.

Answer: Upon executing this query, you should have received a result similar to the following:

```
SQL> SELECT tablespace_name
  2    FROM dba_tablespaces;
```

```
TABLESPACE_NAME
----------------
SYSTEM
USERS
RBS
TEMP
INDX
MYAPP
```

6 rows selected.

e) Retype the query you executed in Question a) and verify whether you see your renamed datafile in your result set.

Answer: After renaming the path for the MYAPP_01.DBF datafile and retyping the query you executed in Question a), you should have received a result similar to the following:

```
SQL> SELECT file_name, tablespace_name
  2    FROM dba_data_files;
```

```
FILE_NAME                             TABLESPACE_NAME
----------------------------------    ---------------
E:\ORACLE\ORADATA\DB00\USERS01.DBF    USERS
E:\ORACLE\ORADATA\DB00\INDX01.DBF     INDX
E:\ORACLE\ORADATA\DB00\RBS01.DBF      RBS
E:\ORACLE\ORADATA\DB00\TEMP01.DBF     TEMP
E:\ORACLE\ORADATA\DB00\SYSTEM01.DBF   SYSTEM
E:\ORACLE\ORADATA\DB00\MYAPP_01B.DBF  MYAPP
E:\ORACLE\ORADATA\DB00\MYAPP_02.DBF   MYAPP

7 rows selected.
```

You should now see your tablespace, MYAPP, and its two associated datafiles, MYAPP_01B.DBF and MYAPP_02.DBF. Note that you no longer see a listing for MYAPP_01.DBF.

f) Write your observations about what just happened, noting the datafile that you moved/renamed.

Answer: Had you not renamed the MYAPP_01.DBF file with an ALTER DATABASE statement, you would not have been able to receive the file as part of your result set with the new name of MYAPP_01B.DBF. But more importantly, you would not have been able to open the file again at the restart of the database. The control files would, at that point, not have contained location information for the MYAPP_01B.DBF datafile.

g) Using the DBA_DATA_FILES data dictionary view, write the statement you would type to obtain the current size, in megabytes, of the MYAPP tablespace.

Answer: Here is one solution:

```
SELECT tablespace_name,
       SUM(bytes)/1024/1024 "SIZE IN MEGABYTES"
  FROM dba_data_files
 WHERE tablespace_name = 'MYAPP'
 GROUP BY tablespace_name;
```

h) Write a query to find the name of the datafile associated with the USERS tablespace and that datafile's size in megabytes.

Answer: Upon issuing the query you wrote, you should receive a result set similar to the following:

```
SQL> SELECT file_name,
  2          bytes/1024/1024 "SIZE IN MEGABYTES"
  3      FROM dba_data_files
```

```
    4   WHERE tablespace_name = 'USERS';
FILE_NAME                                SIZE IN MEGABYTES
----------------------------------- -----------------
E:\ORACLE\ORADATA\DB00\USERS01.DBF                13
```

*The name of the datafile associated with the USERS tablespace is
E:\ORACLE\ORADATA\DB00\USERS01.DBF, and its current size is 13M.*

i) Re-issue the query you typed in Question h). What is the current size of the
datafile associated with the USERS tablespace now?

*Answer: After resizing your datafile and re-issuing the query you wrote in Question h),
you should receive a result set similar to the following:*

```
SQL> SELECT file_name,
  2           bytes/1024/1024 "SIZE IN MEGABYTES"
  3     FROM dba_data_files
  4    WHERE tablespace_name = 'USERS';

FILE_NAME                                SIZE IN MEGABYTES
----------------------------------- -----------------
E:\ORACLE\ORADATA\DB00\USERS01.DBF                15
```

*Now you can see that the current size of the datafile associated with the USERS
tablespace is 15M, or (13M + 2M).*

LAB 8.2 SELF-REVIEW QUESTIONS

To test your progress, you should be able to answer the following questions:

1) If you move a datafile, it is not really necessary to issue an ALTER DATABASE
command to inform the control files of the new location for the file since Oracle
automatically knows where to look for its datafiles upon database startup.

   a) _____ True
   b) _____ False

2) Which data dictionary views can be used to verify actions affecting tablespaces
and datafiles? Check all that apply.

   a) _____ DBA_DATAFILES
   b) _____ DBA_DATABASE
   c) _____ DBA_FILES
   d) _____ DBA_TABLESPACES

e) _____   DBA_DATA_FILES

3) For this question, please choose the best answer. Based on the knowledge you've gained thus far, the steps for renaming a datafile in Oracle are:

   a) _____   Rename the datafile in the operating system, rename the datafile in Oracle, shut down the database, mount the database, and open the database.

   b) _____   Shut down the database, rename the datafile in the operating system, mount the database, rename the datafile in Oracle, and open the database.

   c) _____   Shut down the database, mount the database, rename the datafile in the operating system, rename the datafile in Oracle, and open the database.

   d) _____   Shut down the database, rename the datafile in Oracle, rename the datafile in the operating system, mount the database, and open the database.

   e) _____   Both b) and c) are correct in that the datafile can be renamed in the operating system any time after the database is shut down as long as the datafile is renamed in Oracle after the database is mounted and before the database is opened.

   f) _____   The three options b), c), and d) are all correct in that as long as the database is shut down first, it is safe to then rename the datafile in the operating system and rename the datafile in Oracle before mounting and then opening the database.

Quiz answers appear in Appendix A, Lab 8.2.

CHAPTER 8

TEST YOUR THINKING

1) Discuss the different options for increasing space in your database by manipulating datafiles. **HINT:** At this point in your learning about datafiles, you should be able to discuss at least two options.

2) Based on the knowledge you've gained thus far, which "STARTUP" mode do you think you should be in to recover a lost datafile? Based on your learning of datafiles so far, just speak generally about what state you think the database should be in when you plan to manipulate datafiles. Why?

3) Based on your current knowledge, briefly discuss the differences between control files, datafiles, and redo log files and how the three types of files work together.

C H A P T E R   9

USER CREATION

CHAPTER OBJECTIVE	
In this chapter, you will learn about:	
✔ Creating and Manipulating Users	Page 202

U p to this point, you have been executing queries and DDL statements after connecting as one of the following: PTH01, SYSTEM, SYS, and occasionally, INTERNAL. In this chapter, you learn how to create and manipulate users. You also learn how these actions are relevant to database security and maintenance.

Oracle has stated that the ability to connect as INTERNAL will be discontinued starting with Oracle8.2.x. INTERNAL is actually an alias for connecting as SYS AS SYSDBA, so this is not a significant loss. Connecting as SYS AS SYSDBA explicitly will provide you the same type of access and privileges (such as the ability to start and stop the database) as the INTERNAL account.

There is a subtle difference between the terms *"user"* and *"schema"*. A *schema* is the set of objects associated with a user. That is, a user owns all the objects contained within its associated schema. For example, the name of the schema associated with the user PTH01 is also PTH01. Hence, you can connect to the database as user PTH01. Note, however, that the fully-qualified name of the STUDENT table owned by PTH01 would be PTH01.STUDENT (schemaname.objectname).

L A B   9 . 1

CREATING AND
MANIPULATING USERS

LAB OBJECTIVE

After this lab, you will be able to:

✔ Create and Manipulate Users

LAB 9.1 EXERCISES

9.1 CREATE AND MANIPULATE USERS

In creating a user, the goal is to create a secure account with the appropriate privileges and default settings. The CREATE USER statement accomplishes this task, and provides the options listed in Table 9.1.

 To be able to create user accounts, you must have the CREATE USER system privilege. All DBA user accounts have this privilege.

The following listing shows a sample CREATE USER command:

```
CREATE USER cat IDENTIFIED BY meow
    DEFAULT TABLESPACE users
    TEMPORARY TABLESPACE temp;
```

Table 9.1 ■ Options for Creating a User

Option	Purpose
User	Account or schema name.
Identified By	The account password immediately follows this option.
Default Tablespace	The tablespace where objects created by this user will be stored by default.
Temporary Tablespace	The tablespace used by this user for sort operations. In Oracle8i, temporary LOBs and temporary tables are also stored in this tablespace.
Quota	The amount of space in the default tablespace that the user may claim for storing objects. A user must be given resource quotas to create objects in the database.
Profile	A set of resource limits assigned to a user. If this option is not specified, then the user is assigned a default profile. Profiles are discussed in Chapter 10, "Privilege and Resource Groups."

If you do not specify a default tablespace for a new user, it will automatically be set to SYSTEM. It is recommended that you always specify a default tablespace other than SYSTEM when you create users. Also, the default tablespace for a user should never be the same as its temporary tablespace.

After you create an account, you must grant *privileges* to it. A *privilege* is simply the right to perform some type of action in the database. Named groups of privileges are called *roles*. Oracle provides standard roles that are commonly assigned to new users. Roles are discussed further in Chapter 10, "Privilege and Resource Groups." Table 9.2 outlines some common privileges and roles granted to new users.

To illustrate the process of user creation, log into SQL*Plus as SYSTEM and execute the following two commands:

```
CREATE USER student IDENTIFIED BY learn;
GRANT CONNECT, RESOURCE TO student;
```

Table 9.2 ■ Privileges and Roles Granted to New Users

Permission	Type	Type of Permission Granted
CREATE SESSION	Privilege	This privilege merely allows a user to log on to Oracle. Most application end-users, i.e., non-developers and non-DBAs, receive this privilege only. These users should then be given the privileges necessary for performing the appropriate operations on objects in other schemas.
CONNECT	Role	This role gives the user the CREATE SESSION and ALTER SESSION privileges, and the ability to create tables, views, sequences, clusters, synonyms, and links to other databases.
RESOURCE	Role	This role is usually provided to developers and other sophisticated users, and permits them to perform many of the same actions allowed with the CONNECT role. It also includes the ability to create procedures, functions, packages, triggers, and indexes, and gives a user unlimited tablespace quotas on every tablespace in the database. In Oracle8, this role also gives a user the ability to create types. Furthermore, this role in Oracle8i provides a user the ability to create indextypes and operators.
DBA	Role	The DBA role includes all system privileges, as well as the ability to grant all privileges to other users. Like the RESOURCE role, the DBA role also gives a user unlimited space quotas on every tablespace in the database.

The text immediately following the keywords IDENTIFIED BY indicates the password for the user being created. In this case, the new user, STUDENT, is being assigned the password *learn*.

Type the following command:

```
CONNECT student/learn
```

Now type the following DDL statement:

```
CREATE TABLE mytab1 (id INTEGER);
```

Now query the data dictionary to find out where your new table has been stored:

```
SELECT table_name, tablespace_name
  FROM user_tables;
```

a) In which tablespace did the table get created? Why?

_____

_____

b) Is it desirable for the table to be in this tablespace? Why?

_____

_____

c) Write the query you would use to find out whether a primary key constraint was created for this table.

_____

_____

d) Execute this query. Was a primary key constraint created? Why or why not?

_____

_____

Type the following two commands:

```
CONNECT system/manager

DROP USER student;
```

e) What happens when you try to drop user STUDENT?

_____

_____

f) What do you think this response means?

_____

_____

g) Write the query you would use to check whether user
STUDENT was dropped. Execute it and compare your result
with the result received in Question e).

_____

_____

Now type the following:

```
DROP USER student CASCADE;
```

The CASCADE keyword is included in this DROP USER statement so that you are
able to drop all objects in the STUDENT schema (in this case, the MYTAB1 table),
before dropping user STUDENT. Since this user owns objects, you must specify
the CASCADE option to drop the user.

**Now re-create user STUDENT. This time, specify its default and temporary ta-
blespaces. Do not grant any privileges yet.**

```
CREATE USER student IDENTIFIED BY learn
    DEFAULT TABLESPACE users
    TEMPORARY TABLESPACE temp;
```

Type the following two commands:

```
GRANT CREATE SESSION TO student;

CONNECT student/learn
```

h) What happens when you try to connect to the database as user STUDENT?

Now type the following DDL statement:

```
CREATE TABLE mytab2
    (id INTEGER, constraint mytab2_pk primary key (id));
```

i) What happens when you try to create this new table?

j) What do you think this response means? Why?

Type the following two commands:

```
CONNECT system/manager

GRANT CONNECT TO student;
```

Now type the following:

```
CONNECT student/learn

CREATE TABLE mytab2
    (id INTEGER, constraint mytab2_pk primary key (id));
```

k) What happens upon attempting to create this table again?

l) What do you think needs to be corrected?

_____

_____

Correct the problem by typing the following:

```
CONNECT system/manager

ALTER USER student QUOTA UNLIMITED ON users;
```

Now reconnect as user STUDENT and try to re-create the MYTAB2 table:

```
CONNECT student/learn

CREATE TABLE mytab2
     (id INTEGER, constraint mytab2_pk primary key (id));
```

m) Upon your third attempt to create the MYTAB2 table, what response do you receive?

_____

_____

Now query the data dictionary to find out where your new table has been
stored:

```
SELECT table_name, tablespace_name
  FROM user_tables;
```

n) In which tablespace did the table get created? Why?

_____

_____

o) Is it desirable for the table to be in this tablespace? Why?

_____

_____

Now create another user by typing the following:

```
CONNECT system/manager

CREATE USER teacher IDENTIFIED BY classroom
    DEFAULT TABLESPACE users
    TEMPORARY TABLESPACE temp
    QUOTA 10K ON users;

CONNECT teacher/classroom
```

p) What happens when you try to connect to the database as user TEACHER?

_____

_____

q) What will you need to do to correct the problem? Just state your answer. Do not take corrective action at this time.

_____

_____

LAB 9.1 EXERCISE ANSWERS

9.1 ANSWERS

a) In which tablespace did the table get created? Why?

Answer: Upon executing this query, you should have received a result similar to the following:

```
SQL> SELECT table_name, tablespace_name
  2    FROM user_tables;
```

TABLE_NAME	TABLESPACE_NAME
MYTAB1	SYSTEM

The table was created in this tablespace because a default tablespace was not specified in the CREATE TABLE statement.

b) Is it desirable for the table to be in this tablespace? Why?

Answer: It is not desirable for the table to be in this tablespace. The SYSTEM tablespace should be reserved for the data dictionary, the SYSTEM rollback segment, and other objects that the Oracle Server specifies for storage there.

c) Write the query you would use to find out whether a primary key constraint was created for this table.

Answer: The following query may be used to find out whether a primary key constraint was created for this table:

```
SELECT constraint_name, constraint_type
  FROM user_constraints
 WHERE constraint_type = 'P';
```

d) Execute this query. Was a primary key constraint created? Why or why not?

Answer: Upon executing this query, you should have received a result similar to the following:

```
SQL> SELECT constraint_name, constraint_type
  2    FROM user_constraints
  3   WHERE constraint_type = 'P';
```

no rows selected

A primary key constraint was not created because the table was created with no constraints.

e) What happens when you try to drop user STUDENT?

Answer: Upon executing this statement, you should have received a result similar to the following:

```
SQL> DROP USER student;
DROP USER student
*
ERROR at line 1:
ORA-01922: CASCADE must be specified to drop 'STUDENT'
```

f) What do you think this response means?

Answer: This response means that the STUDENT account cannot be dropped with the DROP USER student; *statement because objects exist within the user*

STUDENT's schema. The error message tells you that the keyword CASCADE must be included to successfully drop user STUDENT. Note that using CASCADE will not only drop the user, but also all of the objects in its schema.

g) Write the query you would use to check whether user STUDENT was dropped. Execute it and compare your result with the result received in Question e).

Answer: The following query may be used to find out whether user STUDENT was dropped:

```
CONNECT student/learn

SELECT username
  FROM user_users;
```

Upon executing this query, you should have received a result similar to the following:

```
SQL> SELECT username
  2    FROM user_users;
```

USERNAME

STUDENT

The result received in this query confirms the result received from the query executed in Question e). User STUDENT still exists in the system.

h) What happens when you try to connect to the database as user STUDENT?

Answer: Upon executing this statement, you should have received a result similar to the following:

```
SQL> CONNECT student/learn
```
Connected.

i) What happens when you try to create this new table?

Answer: Upon executing this CREATE TABLE statement, you should have received a result similar to the following:

```
SQL> CREATE TABLE mytab2
  2    (id INTEGER,
  3     constraint mytab2_pk primary key (id)
  4    );
```
CREATE TABLE mytab2
 *

```
ERROR at line 1:
ORA-01031: insufficient privileges
```

j) What do you think this response means? Why?

Answer: This response means that user STUDENT has not been granted the privilege to create objects in the database. The only privilege granted to user STUDENT so far is the ability to connect to the database.

k) What happens upon attempting to create this table again?

Answer: Upon attempting to create this table again, you should have received a result similar to the following:

```
SQL> CREATE TABLE mytab2
  2  (id INTEGER, constraint mytab2_pk primary key (id));
CREATE TABLE mytab2
*
ERROR at line 1:
ORA-01950: no privileges on tablespace 'USERS'
```

l) What do you think needs to be corrected?

Answer: User STUDENT must be given a resource quota on the USERS tablespace to be able to create and store objects within it.

m) Upon your third attempt to create the MYTAB2 table, what response do you receive?

Answer: Upon your third attempt to create the MYTAB2 table, you should have received a result similar to the following:

```
SQL> CREATE TABLE mytab2
  2  (id INTEGER, constraint mytab2_pk primary key (id));

Table created.
```

n) In which tablespace did the table get created? Why?

Answer: Upon executing this query, you should have received a result similar to the following:

```
SQL> SELECT table_name, tablespace_name
  2     FROM user_tables;
```

TABLE_NAME	TABLESPACE_NAME
MYTAB2	USERS

This time, the table was created in the USERS tablespace. This happened because the default tablespace of USERS was specified in the CREATE USER statement for user STUDENT.

o) Is it desirable for the table to be in this tablespace? Why?

Answer: It is desirable for the table to be in this tablespace. The table is being stored in user STUDENT's default tablespace, USERS, which is allowable since it is a tablespace other than SYSTEM or TEMP.

p) What happens when you try to connect to the database as user TEACHER?

Answer: Upon executing this statement, you should have received a result similar to the following:

```
SQL> CONNECT teacher/classroom
ERROR:
ORA-01045: user TEACHER lacks CREATE SESSION privilege;
logon denied

Warning: You are no longer connected to ORACLE.
```

q) What will you need to do to correct the problem? Just state your answer. Do not take corrective action at this time.

Answer: You must grant user TEACHER either the CREATE SESSION privilege or the CONNECT role. Only then will this user be able to successfully connect to the database.

LAB 9.1 SELF-REVIEW QUESTIONS

To test your progress, you should be able to answer the following questions.

1) If you do not specify a default tablespace when creating a user, Oracle will automatically store the user's objects in the USERS tablespace.

    a) _____ True
    b) _____ False

2) The difference between granting a user a quota on a tablespace and granting a user the RESOURCE role is:

   a) _____ The RESOURCE role does not give unlimited quotas.
   b) _____ There is no difference. The two actions are exactly the same.
   c) _____ The RESOURCE role gives unlimited quotas for all tablespaces in the system.
   d) _____ Even when granting the RESOURCE role, you must explicitly specify a quota for a particular tablespace.

3) The set of objects associated with a user account is called a schema.

   a) _____ True
   b) _____ False

4) If you issue the following two statements, the user will be able to create objects in his/her default tablespace?

   a) _____ True
   b) _____ False

```
CREATE USER brown IDENTIFIED BY crayon
   DEFAULT TABLESPACE users
   TEMPORARY TABLESPACE temp;

GRANT CONNECT TO brown;
```

5) When you create a new user, the following action(s) should be performed if the user wants to be able to connect to the database and create objects:

   a) _____ Specify a default tablespace
   b) _____ Give a resource quota on the default tablespace
   c) _____ Grant the user the CREATE SESSION privilege
   d) _____ Grant the user the CONNECT role
   e) _____ All of the above
   f) _____ Answers a), b), and d)

6) What keyword must be included in a DROP USER statement if you want to drop a user that owns objects?

   a) _____ ALL
   b) _____ DELETE CONSTRAINTS
   c) _____ BYPASSING REFERENTIAL INTEGRITY
   d) _____ CASCADE

Quiz answers appear in Appendix A, Lab 9.1.

CHAPTER 9

TEST YOUR THINKING

1) If you want to create users within a company with different levels of access and capabilities to manipulate the database, what issues must you keep in mind, based on your knowledge of creating users thus far?

2) Suppose you need to create the following three new users:

- An administrative assistant who queries the database and reports on data result sets.
- A systems analyst who suggests and implements system enhancements, such as database views.
- An applications developer who redesigns certain business processes.

Write the DDL statements you would execute to give each user proper access and appropriate privileges. Assume that, for business reasons, you must give each user only the minimum privileges necessary to complete his or her respective tasks.

CHAPTER 10

PRIVILEGE AND RESOURCE GROUPS

CHAPTER OBJECTIVES

In this chapter, you will learn about:

✔ Creating and Manipulating Privileges   Page 218
✔ Creating and Manipulating Roles   Page 230
✔ Creating and Manipulating Profiles   Page 237

After a user has been created in the database, he or she automatically has access to any objects in his or her own schema. For example, user STUDENT can access any objects in the STUDENT schema. However, user STUDENT must be given privileges to access objects in any other schema. A *privilege* is simply the right to perform some type of action in the database.

Through privileges, the Oracle Server controls everything, from the ability to create users to allowing those users to grant privileges of their own. A set of privileges granted to a user is called the user's *security domain*. This security domain is composed of privileges explicitly granted to the user as well as privileges obtained through *roles*. *Roles* are simply named groups of privileges that can be granted to either users or to other roles.

In this chapter, you also learn about groups of resource limits, known as *profiles*. Resource limits can control, for example, how many sessions a user can have open at one time, and the length of time that a particular user's session can stay connected to a database.

LAB 10.1

CREATING AND MANIPULATING PRIVILEGES

LAB OBJECTIVE

After this lab, you will be able to:

✔ Create and Manipulate Privileges

LAB 10.1 EXERCISES

10.1 CREATE AND MANIPULATE PRIVILEGES

There are two types of Oracle Server privileges: *system* privileges and *object privileges*. *System* privileges include rights to perform system-wide database actions, whereas *object* privileges consist of rights to perform specific actions on specific schema objects.

The following are examples of system privileges:

- GRANT ANY PRIVILEGE
- CREATE ROLE
- CREATE USER
- ALTER ANY INDEX
- DROP ANY TRIGGER
- SELECT ANY TABLE

- ALTER SESSION
- ALTER PROFILE

The owner of a particular object grants object privileges to other users who should be allowed access to it. For example, if there's a user named GARDENER that owns a table named ORDERS, then GARDENER is the only account with the ability to view or manipulate data in this table unless he or she explicitly grants access to other users. This is done by granting object privileges, which may include, for example, the ability to select records from or insert records into the ORDERS table, or even the ability to alter the table itself. Therefore, user STUDENT cannot perform any action on the ORDERS table unless he or she is granted specific privileges to do so by user GARDENER.

Granting a privilege is merely the act of giving the privilege to another user.

Type the following at the SQL*Plus command line while logged on as user STUDENT:

```
INSERT INTO mytab2
        (id)
   VALUES (7);

COMMIT;

GRANT SELECT ON mytab2 TO pth01;

CONNECT pth01/books

SELECT * FROM mytab2;
```

a) What happens when you try to retrieve data from the MYTAB2 table?

_____

_____

b) What do you think needs to be corrected?

_____

_____

c) Write the new query you would use to select information from the MYTAB2 table.

_____

_____

You can usually only grant privileges for objects you own, unless you've been given the GRANT OPTION privilege for other objects. The WITH GRANT OPTION clause can be included in an object privilege granted to you, allowing you to grant that privilege to others, even though you do not own the object. To give a user the privilege to not only select data from or perform DML statements on an object, but also to grant the same privilege(s) to others, you must include the WITH GRANT OPTION clause in your GRANT statement.

Type the following at the SQL*Plus command line:

```
CONNECT student/learn

GRANT SELECT ON mytab2 TO pth01 WITH GRANT OPTION;

CONNECT system/manager

CREATE USER gardener IDENTIFIED BY flowers;

GRANT CREATE SESSION TO gardener;

CONNECT pth01/books
```

d) Write the statement that user PTH01 would use to give user GARDENER the ability to query the MYTAB2 table. Execute the statement. What result do you receive?

_____

_____

e) Connect as user GARDENER and try to query the MYTAB2 table. What is the result of this action?

_____

_____

To grant a system privilege, you must have either the GRANT ANY PRIVILEGE system privilege, or the system privilege that you are attempting to grant must have been granted to you with the ADMIN OPTION.

Type the following at the SQL*Plus command line:

```
CONNECT system/manager

GRANT CREATE USER TO pth01 WITH ADMIN OPTION;

CONNECT pth01/books

CREATE USER test1 IDENTIFIED BY blue;

CONNECT system/manager

GRANT CREATE SESSION TO test1;

CONNECT pth01/books

GRANT CREATE USER TO test1;

CONNECT test1/blue

CREATE USER test2 IDENTIFIED BY red;
```

f) Describe what happens as a result of executing this set of commands where users perform actions with system privileges.

_____

_____

Just as users can grant privileges to others, they can also *revoke* them. Note that, to revoke an object privilege, you must be the user who originally granted that privilege.

Type the following at the SQL*Plus command line:

```
CONNECT student/learn

REVOKE SELECT ON mytab2 FROM pth01;
```

g) Connect as user PTH01 and attempt to query the MYTAB2 table. What is the response from the system?

_____

_____

h) Why do you think you received this response?

_____

_____

i) Connect as user GARDENER and attempt to query the MYTAB2 table. What do you think has taken place in the system?

_____

_____

Unlike revoking object privileges, to revoke a system privilege from a user, you do not need to have granted that system privilege to that user in the first place. If you want to revoke a system privilege from another user, you only need to have that privilege with the ADMIN OPTION. For example, if user SYSTEM grants the CREATE TABLE system privilege to user TEACHER, then grants the same privilege to user STUDENT with the ADMIN OPTION, user STUDENT can revoke this privilege from user TEACHER even though user STUDENT is not the original grantor.

User STUDENT would not be able to revoke any system privilege from user SYSTEM since SYSTEM has the DBA role.

Now type the following:

```
CONNECT system/manager

REVOKE CREATE USER FROM pth01;
```

j) Connect as user PTH01 and try to create a new user. What is the response from the system? Why?

_____

_____

k) Connect as user TEST1 and try to create a new user. What is the response from the system? Why do you think you received this response?

_____

_____

To obtain information about privileges granted to users and roles, you can query the data dictionary views DBA_SYS_PRIVS, DBA_TAB_PRIVS, and DBA_COL_PRIVS. DBA_SYS_PRIVS stores information about granted system privileges, and both DBA_TAB_PRIVS and DBA_COL_PRIVS store information about granted object privileges.

Type the following at the SQL*Plus command line while logged on as user SYSTEM:

```
SELECT *
  FROM dba_sys_privs
 WHERE grantee = 'TEST1';
```

l) What information do you receive about the system privileges granted to TEST1? Why do you receive this result?

_____

_____

Now type the following:

```
SELECT table_name, column_name, privilege, grantable
  FROM dba_col_privs;
```

m) Which object privileges are displayed? Why do you receive this result?

_____

_____

LAB 10.1 EXERCISE ANSWERS

10.1 ANSWERS

a) What happens when you try to retrieve data from the MYTAB2 table?

Answer: Upon executing this query, you should have received a result similar to the following:

```
SQL> SELECT * FROM mytab2;
SELECT * FROM mytab2
              *
ERROR at line 1:
ORA-00942: table or view does not exist
```

b) What do you think needs to be corrected?

Answer: Although user PTH01 has been granted the SELECT object privilege on the MYTAB2 table, PTH01 does not own the table.

c) Write the new query you would use to select information from the MYTAB2 table.

Answer: The query should be amended as follows:

```
SELECT * FROM student.mytab2;
```

That is, the table name should be prefixed with the owner name.

d) Write the statement that user PTH01 would use to give user GARDENER the ability to query the MYTAB2 table. Execute the statement. What result do you receive?

Answer: The following statement will accomplish this:

```
GRANT SELECT ON student.mytab2 TO gardener;
```

Upon executing this statement, you should have received a result similar to the following:

```
SQL> GRANT SELECT ON student.mytab2 TO gardener;

Grant succeeded.
```

e) Connect as user GARDENER and try to query the MYTAB2 table. What is the result of this action?

Answer: Upon executing this query, you should have received a result similar to the following:

```
SQL> CONNECT gardener/flowers
Connected.
SQL> SELECT * FROM student.mytab2;

       ID
---------
        7
```

User GARDENER is able to select data from the MYTAB2 table because the SELECT object privilege was granted by a user who was given this privilege with the GRANT OPTION.

f) Describe what happens as a result of executing this set of commands where users perform actions with system privileges.

Answer: Upon executing the final command, you should have received a result similar to the following:

```
SQL> CREATE USER test2 IDENTIFIED BY red;

User created.
```

You received this response because the CREATE USER system privilege was granted by a user who was given this privilege with the ADMIN OPTION. In other words, user TEST1 was able to create user TEST2 because user PTH01 granted user TEST1 the CREATE USER system privilege, and user PTH01 has this system privilege with the ADMIN OPTION.

g) Connect as user PTH01 and attempt to query the MYTAB2 table. What is the response from the system?

Answer: Upon executing this query, you should have received a result similar to the following:

```
SQL> SELECT * FROM student.mytab2;
SELECT * FROM student.mytab2
                     *
ERROR at line 1:
ORA-00942: table or view does not exist
```

h) Why do you think you received this response?

Answer: You received this response because the privilege to select data from the MYTAB2 table was revoked from user PTH01 by user STUDENT. User STUDENT granted the privilege to user PTH01 in the first place, therefore user STUDENT is the only user who can revoke the privilege from user PTH01.

i) Connect as user GARDENER and attempt to query the MYTAB2 table. What do you think has taken place in the system?

Answer: Upon executing this query, you should have received a result similar to the following:

```
SQL> SELECT * FROM student.mytab2;
SELECT * FROM student.mytab2
                      *
ERROR at line 1:
ORA-00942: table or view does not exist
```

Revoking an object privilege from a user who was granted the privilege with the GRANT OPTION has a cascading effect. Those users were granted the privilege by the user whose privilege(s) you are revoking will automatically have their privilege(s) revoked as well.

j) Connect as user PTH01 and try to create a new user. What is the response from the system? Why?

Answer: Upon executing this statement, you should have received a result similar to the following:

```
SQL> CREATE USER test3 IDENTIFIED BY green;
CREATE USER test3 IDENTIFIED BY green
                      *
ERROR at line 1:
ORA-01031: insufficient privileges
```

User SYSTEM has revoked the CREATE USER system privilege from user PTH01, so any attempt by user PTH01 to create a new user now returns a result similar to that shown above.

k) Connect as user TEST1 and try to create a new user. What is the response from the system? Why do you think you received this response?

Answer: Upon executing this query, you should have received a result similar to the following:

```
SQL> CREATE USER test3 IDENTIFIED BY green;
```

User created.

Unlike the rules for object privileges, revoking a system privilege from a user does not have a cascading effect. Users who have been granted a system privilege by a user who has that privilege with the ADMIN OPTION retain that privilege, even if the grantor's privilege is revoked. Table 10.1 illustrates the differences between revoking the two types of privileges and whether the revoke action has a cascading effect.

I) What information do you receive about the system privileges granted to TEST1? Why do you receive this result?

Answer: Upon executing this query, you should have received a result similar to the following:

```
SQL> SELECT *
  2    FROM dba_sys_privs
  3    WHERE grantee = 'TEST1';
```

Table 10.1 ■ Revoking Privileges

Privilege	Revoke Criteria	Cascading Effect?
Object	Only the original grantor can revoke an object privilege from a user.	Yes, revoking an object privilege from a user who was granted the privilege with the GRANT OPTION has a cascading effect. Those users who have been granted the privilege by the user whose privilege(s) are being revoked automatically have their privilege(s) revoked as well.
System	Any user who has a particular system privilege with the ADMIN OPTION may revoke that system privilege from another user. The user performing the revoking action does not necessarily have to be the original grantor of that system privilege.	No, revoking a system privilege from a user does not have a cascading effect. Users who have been granted a system privilege by a user who has that privilege with ADMIN OPTION retain that privilege, even if the grantor's privilege is revoked.

GRANTEE	PRIVILEGE	ADM
TEST1	CREATE SESSION	NO
TEST1	CREATE USER	NO

You received this result because the two system privileges currently granted to user TEST1 are: CREATE SESSION and CREATE USER. The last column, 'ADM', denotes whether the listed grantee has the ADMIN OPTION for the associated system privilege.

m) Which object privileges are displayed? Why do you receive this result?

Answer: Upon executing this query, you should have received a result similar to the following:

```
SQL> SELECT table_name, column_name, privilege,
  2          grantable
  3     FROM dba_col_privs;
```

no rows selected

You received this result because currently no object privileges exist. They have been revoked.

LAB 10.1 SELF-REVIEW QUESTIONS

To test your progress, you should be able to answer the following questions.

1) The two types of Oracle Server privileges are:

    a) _____ Table and DBA
    b) _____ Item and system
    c) _____ Object and DBA
    d) _____ Object and system

2) Examples of system privileges are: Check all that apply.

    a) _____ The ability to select data from the table MYTAB2
    b) _____ The ability to create a user
    c) _____ The ability to alter a user
    d) _____ The ability to update a column in table MYTAB2

3) To grant object privileges for objects you do not own, you must have the privileges with the following option:

    a) _____ CASCADE
    b) _____ ADMIN

c) _____ GRANT
d) _____ EXTERNAL

4) To revoke an object privilege, you must have granted the privilege you are revoking.

   a) _____ True
   b) _____ False

5) To grant a system privilege, you must have the privilege with the following option:

   a) _____ CASCADE
   b) _____ ADMIN
   c) _____ GRANT
   d) _____ EXTERNAL

6) To revoke a system privilege, you must have granted the privilege you are revoking.

   a) _____ True
   b) _____ False

7) Revoking a system privilege from a user has a cascading effect. All users who were granted the system privilege from the user whose privilege has been revoked subsequently lose the privilege as well.

   a) _____ True
   b) _____ False

8) Prefixing a table name with an owner in a SELECT or DML statement allows for the following action to take place:

   a) _____ The user issuing the query is given a more complete result set.
   b) _____ The user inherits all object privileges from the owner listed in the prefix.
   c) _____ If you have been granted an object privilege for an object you do not own and no public synonym currently exists for the object, you cannot take advantage of that privilege without specifying the owner of the object in your statement.
   d) _____ It does nothing. It is simply a style convention.

Quiz answers appear in Appendix A, Lab 10.1.

L A B 1 0 . 2

CREATING AND
MANIPULATING ROLES

LAB OBJECTIVE

After this lab, you will be able to:

✔ Create and Manipulate Roles

LAB 10.2 EXERCISES

10.2 CREATE AND MANIPULATE ROLES

A *role* is a named set of privileges that can be given to users and other roles. Using roles makes the task of managing security easier than granting privileges to individual users. This is especially true when groups of users require the same privileges.

Granting a role to all of the users in one particular department, for example, takes fewer commands than granting the necessary privileges to each user in that department individually. In addition, privileges granted through roles are easier to maintain. To continue our example: If the requirements for the department change, and all of the users in the department were granted their privileges through a role, then you only need to change the privileges granted to the role. This eliminates the need for revoking and granting privileges for the users in the department one by one.

A DBA, or any other user with the CREATE ROLE privilege, can create roles, assign various privileges to roles, and grant roles to users or to other roles. A user who has been granted a role has implicitly been granted all privileges associated with that role. A role can be created with a statement similar to the following:

```
CREATE ROLE colors;
```

After you create a role, you can assign privileges to it. You assign privileges to roles the same way you assign privileges to users. You GRANT them. The following GRANT statements illustrate granting privileges to a role.

```
GRANT SELECT, INSERT, UPDATE, DELETE
    ON mytab2 TO colors;

GRANT CONNECT TO colors;
```

 You cannot grant system and object privileges in the same command.

Once a role has been created, it can be granted to users and/or to other roles.

Type the following at the SQL*Plus command line while logged on as user SYSTEM:

```
CREATE ROLE school;

GRANT CREATE SESSION TO school;

GRANT school TO teacher;

CONNECT teacher/classroom
```

a) What happens when user TEACHER attempts to connect to the database?

_____

_____

b) You have not granted the CONNECT role to user TEACHER. Did user TEACHER get the CONNECT role from somewhere else (yes or no)?

_____

_____

c) How was user TEACHER able to connect to the database?

_____

_____

Now type the following:

```
SELECT * FROM student.mytab2;
```

d) What happens when user TEACHER attempts to query the MYTAB2 table? Why do you think you received this response?

_____

_____

Now type the following:

```
CONNECT student/learn

GRANT SELECT ON mytab2 TO school;

CONNECT teacher/classroom

SELECT * FROM student.mytab2;
```

e) What happens when user TEACHER attempts to query the MYTAB2 table this time? Why do you think you received this response?

_____

_____

Now type the following:

```
INSERT INTO student.mytab2
          (id)
     VALUES (3);
```

f) What happens when user TEACHER attempts to insert into the MYTAB2 table? Why do you think you received this response?

_____

_____

Now type the following:

```
CONNECT student/learn

GRANT INSERT, UPDATE, DELETE ON mytab2 TO school;

CONNECT teacher/classroom

INSERT INTO student.mytab2
          (id)
     VALUES (3);
```

It can be quite tedious to prefix the table name with the owner name each time you want to select or manipulate data from a table you do not own. To avoid repetitive typing and the chore of having to remember which users own which objects, you can create *synonyms* for those objects. Using the MYTAB2 table as an example, creating a synonym would create a name that stands for STUDENT.MYTAB2. If you create a *public* synonym, then the synonym name is accessible to all users.

Type the following while logged on as user SYSTEM:

```
CREATE PUBLIC SYNONYM mytab2 FOR student.mytab2;

CONNECT teacher/classroom

SELECT * FROM mytab2;
```

g) What response do you receive upon attempting to query the MYTAB2 table without first prefixing the table name with the name of the owner? Why do you think you received this response?

_____

_____

10.2 ANSWERS

a) What happens when user TEACHER attempts to connect to the database?

Answer: Upon executing this statement, you should have received a result similar to the following:

```
SQL> CONNECT teacher/classroom;
Connected.
```

b) You have not granted the CONNECT role to user TEACHER. Did user TEACHER get the CONNECT role from somewhere else (yes or no)?

Answer: No, user TEACHER did not get the CONNECT role from somewhere else. User TEACHER does not have the CONNECT role.

c) How was user TEACHER able to connect to the database?

Answer: User TEACHER was able to connect to the database because he or she had been granted the SCHOOL role, which has the CREATE SESSION system privilege.

d) What happens when user TEACHER attempts to query the MYTAB2 table? Why do you think you received this response?

Answer: Upon executing this statement, you should have received a result similar to the following:

```
SQL> SELECT * FROM student.mytab2;
SELECT * FROM student.mytab2
                        *
ERROR at line 1:
ORA-00942: table or view does not exist
```

You received this response because the only privilege that user TEACHER has been granted through the SCHOOL role is the ability to create a session (i.e., to connect to the database).

e) What happens when user TEACHER attempts to query the MYTAB2 table this time? Why do you think you received this response?

Answer: Upon executing this statement, you should have received a result similar to the following:

```
SQL> SELECT * FROM student.mytab2;

      ID
---------
       7
```

You received this response because user STUDENT granted the SELECT object privilege on table MYTAB2 to the SCHOOL role. Since user TEACHER has the SCHOOL role, any privileges granted to the SCHOOL role have now also been granted to user TEACHER.

f) What happens when user TEACHER attempts to insert into the MYTAB2 table? Why do you think you received this response?

Answer: Upon executing this statement, you should have received a result similar to the following:

```
SQL> INSERT INTO student.mytab2
  2              (id)
  3         VALUES (3);
INSERT INTO student.mytab2
                  *
ERROR at line 1:
ORA-01031: insufficient privileges
```

You received this response because the only object privilege the SCHOOL role has been granted so far is the ability to select data from the MYTAB2 table.

g) What response do you receive upon attempting to query the MYTAB2 table without first prefixing the table name with the name of the owner? Why do you think you received this response?

Answer: Upon executing this statement, you should have received a result similar to the following:

```
SQL> SELECT * FROM mytab2;

      ID
---------
       7
       3
```

You received this response because the table STUDENT.MYTAB2 is now being accessed via the public synonym MYTAB2. The public synonym has alleviated the need for typing a prefix.

LAB 10.2 SELF-REVIEW QUESTIONS

To test your progress, you should be able to answer the following questions.

1) A role is simply a named set of privileges.

    a) _____ True
    b) _____ False

2) Roles are useful for:

    a) _____ Maintaining privileges for groups of similar users
    b) _____ Cutting down on the number of commands necessary to grant privileges
    c) _____ Assuring that a group of users is able to smoothly transition from one set of privileges to another
    d) _____ All of the above

3) If you are granted a role, it does not necessarily mean that you inherit all of the privileges associated with that role.

    a) _____ True
    b) _____ False

4) A synonym is

    a) _____ A way to enable a role without using a password
    b) _____ Another name for an object that would otherwise need to be identified as <owner_name>.<object_name>
    c) _____ A name that can only be used by its creator
    d) _____ Just another name for a role
    e) _____ The name for a system or object privilege within a role

Quiz answers appear in Appendix A, Lab 10.2.

LAB 10.3

CREATING AND MANIPULATING PROFILES

LAB OBJECTIVE

After this lab, you will be able to:

✔ Create and Manipulate Profiles

LAB 10.3 EXERCISES

10.3 CREATE AND MANIPULATE PROFILES

A *profile* is a set of resource limits. Profiles are used to limit users' system and database resources and to maintain password restrictions. If you do not create custom profiles, then the Oracle Server assigns its default profile, called DEFAULT, to users. This profile specifies unlimited resources for each of its parameters. Table 10.2 lists some of the available resources that can be restricted through profiles.

Only one of the two resource parameters, PASSWORD_REUSE_MAX and PASSWORD_REUSE_TIME, can be set to a value other than UNLIMITED.

To make the Oracle Server enforce resource limits, you must set the value of the initialization parameter RESOURCE_LIMIT in your init.ora file to TRUE.

Table 10.2 ■ System and database resources

Resource	As of Oracle Version	Description
CONNECT_TIME	7x	The maximum number of minutes that a user can retain a session connected to a database.
CPU_PER_SESSION	7x	The CPU time, in hundredths of seconds, that can be used by a session.
FAILED_LOGIN_ATTEMPTS	8x	The number of consecutive failed login attempts that will lock an account.
IDLE_TIME	7x	The maximum number of minutes a session can remain connected to the database without being active, i.e., idle.
LOGICAL_READS_PER_SESSION	7x	The maximum number of data blocks that can be read by the user within a session.
PASSWORD_LIFE_TIME	8x	The maximum number of days a password can be used before it expires.
PASSWORD_GRACE_TIME	8x	The number of days during which a user's password can still be changed once it has reached its PASSWORD_LIFE_TIME setting.
PASSWORD_LOCK_TIME	8x	The number of days an account will be locked if the FAILED_LOGIN_ATTEMPTS setting is exceeded.
PASSWORD_REUSE_MAX	8x	The number of times a user must change his or her password before he or she is able to reuse an old password.
PASSWORD_REUSE_TIME	8x	The number of days that must pass before an old password can be reused.
SESSIONS_PER_USER	7x	The number of concurrent sessions a user can have open at once.

LAB
10.3

Make a backup copy of your init.ora file in your pfile directory. The name of your backup file should be init.ora.03, or whatever the next highest version number is. Open your init.ora file for editing and check to see whether the RESOURCE_LIMIT parameter is specified. If it is, then ensure its value is set to TRUE. Otherwise, add the following line to your init.ora file:

```
resource_limit = TRUE
```

IMPORTANT: If you had to add or change the parameter, then you must restart your database for the change to take effect.

To create a profile, you must have the CREATE PROFILE system privilege. With this privilege, you can create a new profile using the CREATE PROFILE command, as the following exercise illustrates.

Log into SQL*Plus as user SYSTEM and type the following command:

```
CREATE PROFILE student_profile LIMIT
        FAILED_LOGIN_ATTEMPTS 2
        SESSIONS_PER_USER 1
        CONNECT_TIME 50
        IDLE_TIME 10;

ALTER USER student PROFILE student_profile;

CONNECT student/classroom
```

a) What happens when you attempt to connect to the database as user STUDENT with the password CLASSROOM? Why do you think you received this response?

_____

_____

b) Try to connect to the database as user STUDENT with the password CLASSROOM twice more. Then, try to connect to the database as user STUDENT with the password LEARN. Now what is the response from the system? Why do you think you received this response?

_____

_____

To unlock the account, use the ACCOUNT UNLOCK clause of the ALTER USER command. Now type the following:

```
CONNECT system/manager

ALTER USER student ACCOUNT UNLOCK;

CONNECT student/learn
```

    c) What happens when you attempt to connect to the database as user STUDENT with the password LEARN this time? Were you able to successfully connect?

To alter a profile, you must have the ALTER PROFILE system privilege.

    d) Write the statement you would use to alter the STUDENT_PROFILE profile and add the PASSWORD_ LOCK_TIME resource parameter set to a value of one.

    e) Execute your statement. (Remember that you must be logged in as a user with the appropriate privileges.) What is the response from the system? Did you receive the result you expected to receive? Why or why not?

When an account becomes locked due to repeated failed login attempts, it will automatically become unlocked when its profile's PASSWORD_LOCK_TIME value is exceeded. For example, with a PASSWORD_LOCK_TIME value of 1, if you had not been able to unlock the STUDENT account, it would have remained locked for one day, then it would have been automatically unlocked.

The maximum lifetime for a password can be set via the PASSWORD_LIFE_TIME resource parameter.

f) Write the statement you would use to alter the STUDENT_PROFILE profile and add the PASSWORD_LIFE_TIME resource parameter set to a value of 60.

_____

_____

g) Execute your statement. (Remember that you must be logged in as a user with the appropriate privileges.) What is the response from the system?

_____

_____

Unlike a *locked* account, which may be re-enabled, for instance, with the passage of one day, an *expired* account must be re-enabled by a user with DBA privileges using the ALTER USER command.

Now type the following while logged on as user SYSTEM:

```
ALTER USER student PASSWORD EXPIRE;

CONNECT student/learn
```

h) What happened when you attempted to connect as STUDENT/LEARN? What did you have to do? Which new password did you choose? Remember your new password.

_____

_____

To see the expiration date of the STUDENT account, you can query the Expiry_Date column of the DBA_USERS data dictionary view.

Type the following while logged on as user SYSTEM:

```
SELECT username, expiry_date
  FROM dba_users
 WHERE username = 'STUDENT';
```

i) What is the result of this query?

j) Write the statement you would use to alter the STUDENT_PROFILE profile, adding the PASSWORD_REUSE_MAX resource parameter set to a value of three and the PASSWORD_REUSE_TIME resource parameter set to a value of UNLIMITED.

k) Execute your statement. (Remember that you must be logged in as a user with the appropriate privileges.) What is the response from the system?

Type the following while logged on as user SYSTEM:

```
ALTER USER student IDENTIFIED BY learn;

ALTER USER student IDENTIFIED BY reading;

ALTER USER student IDENTIFIED BY learn;
```

l) What happens when you attempt to change user STUDENT's password back to LEARN? Why do you think you received this response?

m) What do you think you will need to do? Create the statement, execute the statement, and remember to write down your final password for user STUDENT.

_____

_____

10.3 ANSWERS

a) What happens when you attempt to connect to the database as user STUDENT with the password CLASSROOM? Why do you think you received this response?

Answer: Upon executing this statement, you should have received a result similar to the following:

```
SQL> CONNECT student/classroom
ERROR:
ORA-01017: invalid username/password; logon denied


Warning: You are no longer connected to ORACLE.
```

You received this response because the password for user STUDENT is not CLASSROOM.

b) Try to connect to the database as user STUDENT with the password CLASSROOM twice more. Then, try to connect to the database as user STUDENT with the password LEARN. Now what is the response from the system? Why do you think you received this response?

Answer: Upon executing this statement, you should have received a result similar to the following:

```
SQL> CONNECT student/learn
ERROR:
ORA-28000: the account is locked
```

You received this response because, in attempting to connect to the database with an incorrect password for user STUDENT, you exceeded the limit specified in the FAILED_LOGIN_ATTEMPTS parameter in the STUDENT_PROFILE profile.

c) What happens when you attempt to connect to the database as user STUDENT with the password LEARN this time? Were you able to successfully connect?

Answer: Upon executing this statement, you should have received a result similar to the following:

```
SQL> CONNECT student/learn
Connected.
```

Yes. Now that the account has been unlocked and the correct password has been entered, you should have been able to successfully connect.

d) Write the statement you would use to alter the STUDENT_PROFILE profile and add the PASSWORD_LOCK_TIME resource parameter set to a value of one.

Answer: An example of the statement you might use to alter the STUDENT_PROFILE profile to include the above specification is:

```
CONNECT system/manager

ALTER PROFILE student_profile
        LIMIT PASSWORD_LOCK_TIME 1;
```

e) Execute your statement. (Remember that you must be logged in as a user with the appropriate privileges.) What is the response from the system? Did you receive the result you expected to receive? Why or why not?

Answer: Upon executing this statement, you should have received a result similar to the following:

```
SQL> ALTER PROFILE student_profile
            LIMIT PASSWORD_LOCK_TIME 1;

Profile altered.
```

Yes. With this statement, the STUDENT_PROFILE profile was successfully altered.

f) Write the statement you would use to alter the STUDENT_PROFILE profile and add the PASSWORD_LIFE_TIME resource parameter set to a value of 60.

Answer: An example of the statement you might use to alter the STUDENT_PROFILE profile to include the above specification is:

```
ALTER PROFILE student_profile
   LIMIT PASSWORD_LIFE_TIME 60;
```

g) Execute your statement. (Remember that you must be logged in as a user with the appropriate privileges.) What is the response from the system?

Answer: Upon executing this statement, you should have received a result similar to the following:

```
SQL> ALTER PROFILE student_profile
  2              LIMIT PASSWORD_LIFE_TIME 60;

Profile altered.
```

h) What happened when you attempted to connect as STUDENT/LEARN? What did you have to do? Which new password did you choose? Remember your new password.

Answer: Upon executing this statement, you should have received a result similar to the following:

```
SQL> CONNECT student/learn
ERROR:
ORA-28001: the password has expired


Changing password for student
Old password: ********
New password: *****
Retype new password: *****
Password changed
Connected.
```

Acting as the DBA, you manually forced user STUDENT's password to expire. When you attempted to connect as STUDENT/LEARN, you should have been prompted by SQL*Plus to change the password. Alternatively, you could have changed user STUDENT's password via the ALTER USER command while connected as a user with DBA privileges. In this example, the new password chosen for user STUDENT was STUDY.

i) What is the result of this query?

Answer: Upon executing this query, you should have received a result similar to the following:

```
SQL> SELECT username, expiry_date
  2    FROM dba_users
  3   WHERE username = 'STUDENT';
```

USERNAME	EXPIRY_DA
STUDENT	06-APR-00

Depending on when you add the PASSWORD_LIFE_TIME resource parameter to the STUDENT_PROFILE profile and subsequently change the password for user STUDENT, the result you receive from the above query should be <the number specified in the PASSWORD_LIFE_TIME resource parameter> days greater than the date of the password change.

j) Write the statement you would use to alter the STUDENT_PROFILE profile, adding the PASSWORD_REUSE_MAX resource parameter set to a value of three and the PASSWORD_REUSE_TIME resource parameter set to a value of UNLIMITED.

Answer: An example of the statement you might use to alter the STUDENT_PROFILE profile to include the above specifications is:

```
ALTER PROFILE student_profile
   LIMIT PASSWORD_REUSE_MAX 3
   PASSWORD_REUSE_TIME UNLIMITED;
```

k) Execute your statement. (Remember that you must be logged in as a user with the appropriate privileges.) What is the response from the system?

Answer: Upon executing this statement, you should have received a result similar to the following:

```
SQL> ALTER PROFILE student_profile
  2    LIMIT PASSWORD_REUSE_MAX
  3    PASSWORD_REUSE_TIME UNLIMITED;
```

Profile altered.

l) What happens when you attempt to change user STUDENT's password back to LEARN? Why do you think you received this response?

Answer: Upon executing this series of statements, you should have received a result similar to the following:

```
SQL> ALTER USER student IDENTIFIED BY learn;
ALTER USER student IDENTIFIED BY learn
*
ERROR at line 1:
ORA-28007: the password cannot be reused
```

You received this response because the PASSWORD_REUSE_MAX resource parameter in the STUDENT_PROFILE profile is set to a value of 3. In other words, the password has not yet been changed a sufficient number of times to allow you to reuse the LEARN password.

m) What do you think you will need to do? Create the statement, execute the statement, and remember to write down your final password for user STUDENT.

Answer: You need to alter user STUDENT and give him or her a password other than LEARN. An example of the statement you might use is:

```
ALTER USER student IDENTIFIED BY study;
```

Upon executing this statement, you should have received a result similar to the following:

```
SQL> ALTER USER student IDENTIFIED BY study;
```

User altered.

In this example, the new password chosen for user STUDENT is STUDY.

 Navigate to the Web site http:\\www.phptr.com/Caffrey for important additional information about user STUDENT.

LAB 10.3 SELF-REVIEW QUESTIONS

To test your progress, you should be able to answer the following questions.

1) A profile is

    a) _____ A named set of privileges
    b) _____ A list of storage parameters for a schema object
    c) _____ A set of resource limits
    d) _____ The directory location of your init.ora file

2) Examples of system and database resources include the following:

    a) _____ IDLE_TIME
    b) _____ LOGON_TIME
    c) _____ SESSIONS_PER_USER
    e) _____ CONNECT_TIME

**LAB
10.3**

f) _____ Only a), b), and c)

g) _____ Only a), c), and e)

3) An expired account is the same as a locked account since you cannot connect to the database using either one.

a) _____ True

b) _____ False

4) What is missing from the following CREATE PROFILE statement?

```
CREATE PROFILE student_profile FAILED_LOGIN_ATTEMPTS 2;
```

a) _____ The IDENTIFIED BY clause

b) _____ All necessary resource parameters must be specified in the CREATE PROFILE statement

c) _____ An "=" sign between the resource parameter and the assigned value

d) _____ The LIMIT keyword

e) _____ All of the above

5) To unlock a locked account, you must

a) _____ Alter the profile

b) _____ Alter the user

c) _____ Drop the associated account and alter the profile

d) _____ Drop the associated account and re-create the account

e) _____ None of the above

6) The PASSWORD_REUSE_MAX and PASSWORD_REUSE_TIME resource parameters are mutually exclusive.

a) _____ True

b) _____ False

7) If you don't create any profiles, then the Oracle Server uses the DEFAULT profile. This profile specifies

a) _____ Unlimited tablespace quotas

b) _____ Lowest possible values for all resource limits

c) _____ That all schema objects will be stored permanently

d) _____ Unlimited resources for each of its parameters

Quiz answers appear in Appendix A, Lab 10.3.

CHAPTER 10

TEST YOUR THINKING

1) Suppose that you have been given the task of granting privileges to users in a payroll department. There are three levels of users within the department: administrative and support staff, supervisory staff, and client account managers. Create the statements you would use to grant each level of user his or her proper amount of authority. Be sure to set up these authorities using roles for ease of maintenance.

2) Suppose that you must also set the resource limits for the users in this department. Using profiles, create the statements you would use to restrict the system and database resources for these users.

3) Study the various data dictionary views that provide information about privileges, roles, and profiles. **HINT:** You are already familiar with the views DBA_SYS_PRIVS, DBA_COL_PRIVS, and DBA_USERS. Additionally, you should consider the views DBA_ROLES, DBA_ROLE_PRIVS, and DBA_TAB_PRIVS. In querying the views DBA_COL_PRIVS and DBA_TAB_PRIVS, what kinds of privileges are you able to obtain information about? Would you be able to see if a user has been granted SELECT object privileges on objects he or she does not own?

C H A P T E R   1 1

AUDITING

CHAPTER OBJECTIVES

In this chapter, you will learn about:

✔ Auditing Sessions, Auditing Database Actions,
  and Auditing Objects   Page 252

Chapter 10, "Privilege and Resource Groups," discusses how security can be managed through the creation of roles and profiles. However, even with these in place, security problems may still occur. If a DBA suspects that database security is being compromised, he or she can audit certain database activities. *Auditing* involves capturing information about operations performed by database users.

The Oracle Server provides several auditing options. For example, you can choose to audit certain types of SQL statements, such as INSERT or UPDATE statements. You can audit statements that use specific system privileges, such as CREATE TABLE or ALTER TABLE. You can also audit the unsuccessful attempts to perform some type of action in the database, such as failed login attempts. Auditing can be limited to a specific user or group of users, or can even be limited to actions performed on a specific schema object on a "by session" or "by access" basis. The following three types of audits are discussed in this chapter:

- Session audits.
- Database action audits.
- Object audits.

L A B   1 1 . 1

AUDITING SESSIONS, AUDITING DATABASE ACTIONS, AND AUDITING OBJECTS

LAB OBJECTIVES

After this lab, you will be able to :

✔ Audit Sessions, Audit Database Actions, and Audit Objects

LAB 11.1 EXERCISES

11.1 AUDIT SESSIONS, AUDIT DATABASE ACTIONS, AND AUDIT OBJECTS

To enable auditing within an Oracle database, you must first specify the destination for the audit trail. Audit records may be written to either the SYS.AUD$ table or to an operating system file. (Note that the latter option is not available for all operating systems.) If an operating system destination is chosen, the resulting files will be written to the "adump" directory and will have ".aud" filename extensions.

To enable database auditing, you must provide a value for the AUDIT_TRAIL parameter in the init.ora file. Table 11.1 lists the possible values for this parameter.

Table 11.1 ■ AUDIT_TRAIL

Value	Description
DB	Auditing is enabled. Audit records will be written to the SYS.AUD$ table.
OS	Auditing is enabled. Audit records will be written to an audit trail in the operating system (subject to availability within your operating system).
NONE	Auditing is disabled (default).
TRUE	This value is supported for backward-compatibility with versions of Oracle prior to 8.x. It is equivalent to the DB value.
FALSE	This value is supported for backward-compatibility with versions of Oracle prior to 8.x. It is equivalent to the NONE value.

Make a backup copy of your init.ora file in your pfile directory. The name of your backup file should be init.ora.04, or whatever the next highest version number is. Open your init.ora file for editing and check to see whether the AUDIT_TRAIL parameter is specified. If it is, ensure its value is set to DB; otherwise, add the following lines to your init.ora file:

```
audit_trail = DB
```

Also, if you are using an operating system other than NT, you must add a line for the path statement for your adump directory. This line specifies in which directory the Oracle Server will store your audit files. In UNIX, an example of the line you might add to your init.ora file is:

```
audit_file_dest = /u01/export/home/db00/admin/db00/adump
```

IMPORTANT: If you had to add or change any of these parameters, then you must restart your database. Each time the Instance is restarted, the Instance reads the init.ora file. If you make a change to the init.ora file, the only way the Instance can read the change is through the act of refreshing (restarting the database).

The command to begin auditing connect (login) attempts is:

```
AUDIT SESSION;
```

L AB
11.1

You must either have the DBA role or have been granted the AUDIT SYSTEM privilege to begin auditing CONNECT attempts. Also note that issuing the AUDIT command with the SESSION option does not cause current sessions to be audited.

When auditing has been enabled, the database, by default, records both success-ful and unsuccessful attempts to perform some type of action. However, if you want to audit only the attempts that succeed or the attempts that fail, you can use additional syntax with the AUDIT command:

```
AUDIT SESSION WHENEVER SUCCESSFUL; or
AUDIT SESSION WHENEVER NOT SUCCESSFUL;
```

Type the following at the SQL*Plus command line while logged on as user SYSTEM:

```
AUDIT SESSION;

CONNECT system/manager

CONNECT student/study

CONNECT teacher/classroom

CONNECT gardener/flowers

CONNECT test1/blue
```

Create the following SQL*Plus script and place it in our adhoc directory. Save it with the name audit01.sql.

```
COLUMN os_username FORMAT a15
COLUMN username FORMAT a15
COLUMN terminal FORMAT a15
COLUMN LOGON_TIME FORMAT a22
COLUMN LOGOFF_TIME FORMAT a22
SELECT os_username, username, terminal, returncode,
       TO_CHAR(timestamp, 'DD-MON-YYYY HH24:MI:SS')
       LOGON_TIME,
       TO_CHAR(logoff_time, 'DD-MON-YYYY HH24:MI:SS')
       LOGOFF_TIME
  FROM dba_audit_session;
```

While logged on as user SYSTEM, run the audit01.sql script.

a) What results did you receive?

_____

_____

b) Analyze the results and describe the differences you see. What is different about, for example, the usernames and logon/logoff times?

_____

_____

Now type the following while logged on as user SYSTEM:

```
NOAUDIT SESSION;
```

This command halts the session-level auditing that you enabled earlier.

Any system-level action affecting a database object can be audited.

To illustrate this type of auditing, execute the following commands while logged on as user SYSTEM:

```
AUDIT CREATE TABLE BY student;

CONNECT student/study

CREATE TABLE mytab3
    (id INTEGER, constraint mytab3_pk primary key (id));
```

Note that the following repeated attempts to create the MYTAB3 table are intentional for purposes of this exercise. Continue by executing the following statement:

```
CREATE TABLE mytab3
    (id INTEGER, constraint mytab3_pk primary key (id));
```

The data dictionary view DBA_AUDIT_OBJECT can be queried to determine how a schema object is affected by a database action.

Create the following SQL*Plus script and place it in your adhoc directory. Save it with the name audit02.sql.

```
COLUMN os_username FORMAT a15
COLUMN username FORMAT a15
COLUMN terminal FORMAT a15
COLUMN owner FORMAT a15
COLUMN obj_name FORMAT a15
COLUMN TIME FORMAT a22
SELECT os_username, username, terminal, owner, obj_name,
       action_name, returncode,
       TO_CHAR(timestamp, 'DD-MON-YYYY HH24:MI:SS') TIME
  FROM dba_audit_object;
```

While logged on as user SYSTEM, run the audit02.sql script.

c) What results did you receive?

_____

_____

d) Analyze the results and describe the information that was returned. What happened as a result of your attempt to create the same table twice?

_____

_____

Now type the following, while logged on as user SYSTEM, to turn off this type of auditing:

```
NOAUDIT CREATE TABLE BY student;
```

It is also possible to audit SELECT, INSERT, UPDATE, and DELETE operations on specific database tables. Depending on the type of audit you wish to conduct, you can include either the BY SESSION or BY ACCESS clause in the AUDIT command. This clause is available for both object audits and system-level action audits. It denotes whether an audit record will be written once for each session (BY SESSION) or once for each time a schema object is accessed (BY ACCESS).

Type the following while logged on as user SYSTEM:

```
AUDIT INSERT ON student.mytab2 BY SESSION;
```

```
AUDIT INSERT ON student.mytab3 BY ACCESS;
```

```
CONNECT student/study

INSERT INTO mytab2 (id) VALUES (1);

INSERT INTO mytab2 (id) VALUES (2);

INSERT INTO mytab2 (id) VALUES (4);

INSERT INTO mytab2 (id) VALUES (5);

INSERT INTO mytab3 (id) VALUES (1);

INSERT INTO mytab3 (id) VALUES (2);

INSERT INTO mytab3 (id) VALUES (3);

INSERT INTO mytab3 (id) VALUES (4);
```

e) While logged on as user SYSTEM, run the audit02.sql script. What results did you receive?

_____

_____

f) Analyze the results and describe the information that was returned. How many records are written for an audit issued on a BY SESSION basis compared to those written on a BY ACCESS basis?

_____

_____

Issue the following commands while logged on as user SYSTEM:

```
NOAUDIT INSERT ON student.mytab2;

NOAUDIT INSERT ON student.mytab3;
```

As an alternative to storing audit records in the SYS.AUD$ table, you can write them to operating system files. Note that the availability of this option is operating system-dependent.

You will now repeat the previous exercises (Questions a) through f)), but will direct the output to operating system files and use new methods of accessing the audit records within these files.

If you are running a widely used operating system, such as UNIX or NT, then your operating system most likely allows auditing. In this case, you may continue to practice auditing by completing the following exercises.

Make a backup copy of your init.ora file in your pfile directory. The name of your backup file should be init.ora.05, or whatever the next highest version number is. Open your init.ora file for editing and change the value of the AUDIT_TRAIL parameter to OS. After the change, the parameter in your init.ora file should read:

```
audit_trail = OS
```

IMPORTANT: Remember to restart your database now to allow the change to take effect.

Type the following at the SQL*Plus command line while logged on as user SYSTEM:

```
AUDIT SESSION;

CONNECT system/manager

CONNECT student/study

CONNECT teacher/classroom

CONNECT gardener/flowers

CONNECT test1/blue

NOAUDIT SESSION;
```

The init.ora parameter, AUDIT_FILE_DEST, may be specified to write audit records to a specific location. However, this parameter is not supported in Windows NT environments. If you are running Windows NT, your results are always written to the NT Event Viewer.

g) Open your init.ora file and check the AUDIT_FILE_DEST parameter for the location of your operating system audit trail files. Open the file. (If you are using Windows NT, go to Start ⇒ Programs ⇒ Administrative Tools ⇒ Event Viewer. In the menu bar of the Event Viewer, choose Log ⇒ Application. Double-click on the events listed.) What results did you receive?

_____

_____

h) Analyze the results and describe the differences you see. You should notice quite a few differences from the results you received in Questions b), d) and f).

_____

_____

You may be wondering what the numeric codes in the audit records mean. These are codes reflecting the type of database action that was performed and the privilege that was used to perform it. For example, the value returned to you in the "ACTION" column of your audit records is 100. Coincidentally, the value returned to you in the "PRIV$USED" column is five. These are not very useful unless you are already familiar with their meanings. Information about these values is available in several data dictionary views.

To find out the name of the database action that corresponds to the numeric code of 100, query the AUDIT_ACTIONS data dictionary view. Type the following at the SQL*Plus command line while logged on as user SYSTEM:

```
SELECT action, name
  FROM audit_actions
 WHERE action = 100;
```

Similarly, to discover the name of the privilege used to allow you to perform this database action, query the STMT_AUDIT_OPTION_MAP data dictionary view. While still logged on as user SYSTEM, issue the following query:

```
SELECT option#, name
  FROM stmt_audit_option_map
 WHERE option# = 5;
```

i) What results did you receive? What is the name of the database action attempted? What is the name of the system privilege used to attempt the database action?

LAB 11.1 EXERCISE ANSWERS

11.1 ANSWERS

a) What results did you receive?

Answer: Upon executing this series of statements and running the audit01.sql script, you should have received a result similar to the following:

```
SQL> @audit01
```

OS_USERNAME	USERNAME	TERMINAL	RETURNCODE	LOGON_TIME	LOGOFF_TIME
db00	SYSTEM	JEROMY	0	12-FEB-2000 15:35:59	2-FEB-2000 15:36:09
db00	STUDENT	JEROMY	0	12-FEB-2000 15:36:09	12-FEB-2000 15:36:20
db00	TEACHER	JEROMY	0	12-FEB-2000 15:36:20	12-FEB-2000 15:36:21
db00	GARDENER	JEROMY	0	12-FEB-2000 15:36:21	12-FEB-2000 15:36:21
db00	TEST1	JEROMY	0	12-FEB-2000 15:36:21	12-FEB-2000 15:38:38
db00	SYSTEM	JEROMY	0	12-FEB-2000 15:38:39	

```
6 rows selected.
```

The columns in your result set correspond to the following:

OS_USERNAME—*The operating system username. In this example, the operating system username is "db00".*

USERNAME—*The account attempting to log on to the Oracle database. In this example, the username is different for each logon attempt.*

TERMINAL—*The name of the computer terminal you are executing your statements from. In this example, the name of the computer terminal is "JEROMY".*

RETURNCODE—*The return code for the success or failure of your attempted action. A return code of zero indicates a successful action.*

LOGON_TIME—*The time that the account logged on, or attempted to log on, to the Oracle database.*

LOGOFF_TIME—*The time that the account logged off from the Oracle database.*

b) Analyze the results and describe the differences you see. What is different about, for example, the usernames and logon/logoff times?

Answer: The only differences between the rows in the result set returned in Question a) are the usernames and the corresponding logon and logoff times. If you mistyped any passwords, you may see a return code of 1017, instead of zero for that particular user. A return code of 1017 signifies that an invalid account or password was used to connect to the database. Additionally, you would not see a logoff time for that account. Notice that you also do not see a logoff time for the last row returned in the result set from Question a). If you do not see a logoff time for a user, (and the return code for that user is zero), then that user is currently logged on.

c) What results did you receive?

Answer: Upon executing this series of statements and running the audit02.sql script, you should have received a result similar to the following:

```
SQL> @audit02
```

OS_USERNAME	USERNAME	TERMINAL	OWNER	OBJ_NAME	ACTION_NAME	RETURNCODE	TIME
db00	STUDENT	JEROMY	STUDENT	MYTAB3	CREATE TABLE	0	12-FEB-2000 17:09:07
db00	STUDENT	JEROMY	STUDENT	MYTAB3	CREATE TABLE	955	12-FEB-2000 17:09:18

The columns in your result set correspond to the following:

OS_USERNAME—*The operating system username. In this example, the operating system username is "db00".*

USERNAME—*The account attempting to perform a database action against the Oracle database. The username will be different for each record in this example.*

TERMINAL—*The name of the computer terminal you are executing your statements from. In this example, the name of the computer terminal is "JEROMY".*

OWNER—*The name of the owner of the schema object upon which an action is being performed. In this example, tables are being created by user STUDENT, so the owner of these objects is also user STUDENT.*

OBJ_NAME—*The name of the schema object upon which an action is being performed. In this example, the name of the schema object in both rows returned is "MYTAB3".*

ACTION_NAME—*The name of the action being performed or attempted. In this example, the name of the action in both rows returned is "CREATE TABLE".*

RETURNCODE—*The return code for the success or failure of your attempted action. A return code of zero indicates a successful action.*

TIME—*The time that a particular action was performed or attempted.*

d) Analyze the results and describe the information that was returned. What happened as a result of your attempt to create the same table twice?

Answer: As expected, the timestamps were different for each record. More importantly, the return codes were different: zero for the first row, and 955 for the second. The first row's return code of zero confirms that the table MYTAB3 was created successfully. The second row's return code of 955 shows that, while attempting to create the table, the Oracle Server found that the given name was already being used by an existing object. Therefore, the action was unsuccessful.

e) While logged on as user SYSTEM, run the audit02.sql script. What results did you receive?

Answer: Upon executing this series of statements and running the audit02.sql script, you should have received a result similar to the following:

```
SQL> @audit02

OS_USERNAME   USERNAME   TERMINAL  OWNER    OBJ_NAME    ACTION_NAME   RETURNCODE TIME
-----------   --------   --------  -------  --------    -----------   --------------
db00          STUDENT    JEROMY    STUDENT  MYTAB3      CREATE TABLE 0 12-FEB-2000
                                                                     17:09:07
```

db00	STUDENT	JEROMY	STUDENT	MYTAB3	CREATE TABLE	955	12-FEB-2000 17:09:18
db00	STUDENT	JEROMY	STUDENT	MYTAB2	SESSION REC	0	12-FEB-2000 17:59:22
db00	STUDENT	JEROMY	STUDENT	MYTAB3	INSERT	0	12-FEB-2000 17:59:23
db00	STUDENT	JEROMY	STUDENT	MYTAB3	INSERT	0	12-FEB-2000 17:59:23
db00	STUDENT	JEROMY	STUDENT	MYTAB3	INSERT	0	12-FEB-2000 17:59:23
db00	STUDENT	JEROMY	STUDENT	MYTAB3	INSERT	0	12-FEB-2000 17:59:24

7 rows selected.

f) Analyze the results and describe the information that was returned. How many records are written for an audit issued on a BY SESSION basis compared to those written on a BY ACCESS basis?

Answer: Since you audited INSERT attempts BY SESSION for MYTAB2, the audit shows only one record for this type of action. In contrast, since you audited INSERT attempts BY ACTION for MYTAB3, the audit shows one record for each INSERT attempt that was performed on this table.

g) Open your init.ora file and check the AUDIT_FILE_DEST parameter for the location of your operating system audit trail files. Open the file. (If you are using Windows NT, go to Start ⇒ Programs ⇒ Administrative Tools ⇒ Event Viewer. In the menu bar of the Event Viewer, choose Log ⇒ Application. Double-click on the events listed.) What results did you receive?

Answer: If you performed this exercise in a UNIX environment, then you should see that each session audit was written to a separate, numbered file. In this case, your audit file directory should look similar to the following:

```
ora_14164.aud   ora_14169.aud   ora_14171.aud
ora_14165.aud   ora_14170.aud   ora_14172.aud
```

When you execute this same series of statements and write the session audits to the database table SYS.AUD$, six records are created. Similarly, six audit files are written to the operating system audit trail or, if you are using Windows NT, each session audit will appear as an entry in the NT Event Viewer. The contents of these files or Event Viewer entries should look similar to the following:

```
Mon Feb  7 22:23:23 2000
SESSIONID: "25" ENTRYID: "1" STATEMENT: "1" USERID: "SYSTEM"
TERMINAL: "JEROMY"
ACTION: "100" RETURNCODE: "0" COMMENT$TEXT: "Authenticated
by: DATABASE" OS$USER
ID: "db00" PRIV$USED: 5


Mon Feb  7 22:23:37 2000
SESSIO


"ora_14164.aud"


Mon Feb  7 22:23:38 2000
SESSIONID: "26" ENTRYID: "1" STATEMENT: "1" USERID:
"STUDENT" TERMINAL: "JEROMY"
 ACTION: "100" RETURNCODE: "0" COMMENT$TEXT: "Authenticated
by: DATABASE" OS$USE
RID: "db00" PRIV$USED: 5


Mon Feb  7 22:24:23 2000
SESSIO


"ora_14165.aud"


Mon Feb  7 22:24:23 2000
SESSIONID: "27" ENTRYID: "1" STATEMENT: "1" USERID:
"TEACHER" TERMINAL: "JEROMY"
 ACTION: "100" RETURNCODE: "0" COMMENT$TEXT: "Authenticated
by: DATABASE" OS$USE
RID: "db00" PRIV$USED: 5


Mon Feb  7 22:25:20 2000
SESSIO


"ora_14169.aud"
```

```
Mon Feb  7 22:25:20 2000
SESSIONID: "28" ENTRYID: "1" STATEMENT: "1" USERID:
"GARDENER" TERMINAL: "JEROMY"
ACTION: "100" RETURNCODE: "0" COMMENT$TEXT: "Authenticated
by: DATABASE" OS$US
ERID: "db00" PRIV$USED: 5


Mon Feb  7 22:25:45 2000
SESSIO


"ora_14170.aud"


Mon Feb  7 22:25:45 2000
SESSIONID: "29" ENTRYID: "1" STATEMENT: "1" USERID: "TEST1"
TERMINAL: "JEROMY"
ACTION: "100" RETURNCODE: "0" COMMENT$TEXT: "Authenticated
by: DATABASE" OS$USERI
D: "db00" PRIV$USED: 5


Mon Feb  7 22:26:05 2000
SESSIO


"ora_14171.aud"


Mon Feb  7 22:26:05 2000
SESSIONID: "30" ENTRYID: "1" STATEMENT: "1" USERID: "SYSTEM"
TERMINAL: "JEROMY"
ACTION: "100" RETURNCODE: "0" COMMENT$TEXT: "Authenticated
by: DATABASE" OS$USER
ID: "db00" PRIV$USED: 5


Mon Feb  7 22:26:47 2000
SESSI


"ora_14172.aud"
```

The meaning of each labeled field of information is as follows:

SESSIONID—Unique ID number given to each session (applies to both successful and unsuccessful logon attempts).

ENTRYID—Unique ID number assigned to each audit trail entry per session. Since only one logon attempt is made per session, in this example, only one audit trail entry per session is written.

STATEMENT—*Unique ID number assigned to each statement executed.* **Note:** *A statement may cause many actions.*

USERID—*Identifier for the account attempting to log on to the Oracle database. Each user ID in the above example is different per session logon attempt.*

TERMINAL—*The name of the computer terminal you are executing your statements from. In this example, the name of the computer terminal is "JEROMY".*

ACTION—*A numeric code indicating the type of database action.*

RETURNCODE—*A numeric code indicating the success or failure of the attempted action. A return code of zero indicates a successful action.*

COMMENT$TEXT—*A text comment on the audit trail entry. This also indicates how the user was authenticated. The method of authentication can be one of the following:*

1. *"DATABASE"—Authentication was done by password.*

2. *"NETWORK"—Authentication was done by Net8 or the Advanced Networking Option.*

3. *"PROXY"—The client was authenticated by another user. The name of the proxy user follows the method type.*

In the above example, the user was authenticated by password.

OS$USERID—*The operating system username or ID. In this example, the operating system user ID is "db00".*

PRIV$USED—*The numeric ID for the system privilege used to execute the action.*

h) Analyze the results and describe the differences you see. You should notice quite a few differences from the results you received in Questions b), d), and f).

Answer: One difference between the records received in Question g) is that the session IDs are different for each record. Each session ID is numbered sequentially. Another difference is that the user ID is different for each record. Each logon attempt received its own separate record. If all accounts were valid, then you should have received a return code of zero within each record.

i) What results did you receive? What is the name of the database action attempted? What is the name of the system privilege used to attempt the database action?

Answer: Upon executing this series of statements, you should have received a result similar to the following:

```
SQL> SELECT action, name
  2     FROM audit_actions
  3    WHERE action = 100;


   ACTION NAME
   -------- ----------------------------
       100 LOGON

SQL> SELECT option#, name
  2     FROM stmt_audit_option_map
  3    WHERE option# = 5;


   OPTION# NAME
   -------- ------------------------------------
         5 CREATE SESSION
```

The name of the database action attempted is "LOGON", and the name of the system privilege used to attempt this database action is "CREATE SESSION".

LAB 11.1 SELF-REVIEW QUESTIONS

To test your progress, you should be able to answer the following questions.

1) The three different types of actions which may be audited are:

    a) _____ INSERT, UPDATE, and LOGON
    b) _____ SESSION, DATABASE ACTION, and DELETE
    c) _____ OBJECT ACCESS, CREATE TABLE, and LOGON
    d) _____ SESSION, DATABASE ACTION, and OBJECT ACCESS

2) Which of the following values for the AUDIT_TRAIL parameter in the init.ora file are valid? Check all that apply.

    a) _____ NONE
    b) _____ ENABLED
    c) _____ OS
    d) _____ TRUE

3) When auditing has been enabled, the database, by default, will record only successful attempts to perform some type of action.

    a) _____ True
    b) _____ False

4) Depending on the type of audit you would like to conduct, the following two clauses in the AUDIT command are available, and will affect the number of audit records ultimately written:

   a) _____ BY SESSION and BY ACTION
   b) _____ BY ACCESS and BY OBJECT
   c) _____ BY SESSION and BY OBJECT
   d) _____ BY SESSION and BY ACCESS

Quiz answers appear in Appendix A, Lab 11.1.

CHAPTER 11

TEST YOUR THINKING

1) For what reasons might you enable auditing for your database? Discuss the reasons in terms of security issues, user privileges, day-to-day database activity (such as access), and database growth.

2) Discuss the pros and cons of storing audit records in a database table or in an operating system file. Which do you think is more secure? What limitations might you encounter in each case?

3) Study the various data dictionary views that provide information about the different types of audits that you can perform. **HINT:** You are already familiar with the data dictionary views DBA_AUDIT_SESSION and DBA_AUDIT_OBJECT. Also consider SYSTEM_PRIVILEGE_MAP, AUDIT_ACTIONS, and STMT_AUDIT_OPTION_MAP. If your operating system allows operating system audit trails, compare the information stored in these data dictionary views to the information stored in audit trails written to the operating system.

CHAPTER 12

ROLLBACK SEGMENTS

CHAPTER OBJECTIVES

In this chapter, you will learn about:

✔ Rollback Segment Management   Page 272

The information in a rollback segment is used for query read consistency, canceling (*rolling back*) a transaction, and recovering a transaction. Rollback segments store *before-image* information of data whenever a transaction modifies data. This before-image information is referred to as a "snapshot." It is the image of the data as it existed before the start of a transaction, and it is the image that remains consistent and available to the user throughout the life of a transaction. (The use of the term, snapshot, in this chapter, is not to be confused with the Oracle snapshot object that is used in distributed transaction processing. Distributed transaction processing is not discussed in this book).

The System Change Number (SCN) is the unique number assigned to each new transaction by the Oracle Server. It serves as a relative timestamp that defines the state of the database at a precise moment in time. When data is modified through a transaction, the previous values of the data (along with their SCNs) get stored in rollback segments. This way, the Server can obtain values that correspond to the SCN noted when a query began. If a row has been modified since the query began, the Server obtains the data for the query from the rollback segment.

L A B 1 2 . 1

ROLLBACK SEGMENT MANAGEMENT

LAB OBJECTIVES

After this lab, you will be able to:

✔ Configure and Maintain Rollback Segments

LAB 12.1 EXERCISES

12.1 CONFIGURE AND MAINTAIN ROLLBACK SEGMENTS

UNDERSTANDING TRANSACTIONS

Rollback segments are very important in terms of transactions. A *transaction* is often referred to as a logical unit of work. This logical unit of work is an SQL statement or related set of statements that Oracle treats as a single unit. Modified data is written permanently to the redo logs when a user issues the COMMIT statement. And part or all of a transaction can be canceled, or *undone*, when a user issues the ROLLBACK statement.

Transactions are managed by ORACLE with locking (discussed in Chapter 13, "Locking") and by use of the *multi-version consistency model*. In short, this model allows the Oracle Server to act as though each transaction has its own copy of the data. In other words, at any given time, there exist multiple, overlapping versions of the database. A transaction begins with the first SQL statement in the transaction and completes with a COMMIT or ROLLBACK statement.

For querying, ORACLE guarantees a transaction *statement-level read consistency*. Statement-level read consistency means that when a user executes a query, the current view of the data remains the same while ORACLE is fetching and returning the result set. However, if a transaction consists of multiple queries, each individual query is internally consistent, but not with any other query. For a multiple-query transaction to have data consistency, it must be started with the command SET TRANSACTION READ ONLY. This command guarantees the transaction *transaction-level read consistency*, which means that the transaction does not see the results of the changes brought about by other transactions.

WHAT GETS STORED IN A ROLLBACK SEGMENT

When a transaction modifies data, it modifies the data in the data blocks associated with the changed rows. To understand the significance of the rollback segment, one must understand what is stored in the rollback segment when a transaction modifies data. The rollback segment only stores the before-image snapshot of the row(s) within a particular data block if it was modified. For example, if a transaction modifies a data block by changing a value in one of the columns of one of its rows from 200 to 100, then the old value of 200 is stored in the rollback segment and the original data block contains the new value of 100. If the transaction is rolled back, then the value of 200 is copied from the rollback segment back to the data block.

Part of the information in rollback segments consists of *undo* entries. If a row is inserted into a table, the undo created by that transaction would include, among other information, the rowid of that row so that an undo operation only needs the rowid to restore the row back to its original state. For update transactions, rollback segments store the old values of the updated columns.

Every rollback segment header has a *transaction table*. Every data block has a *transaction directory* in its header. When a transaction modifies data, it updates the transaction directory in the data block header of the data block that contains the data's row or set of rows. This header, in turn, points to the rollback segment containing the undo information for the transaction. Concurrently, the transaction places an entry in the transaction table of the header of the rollback segment. Along with other information, the transaction table entry contains the address of the modified data block, the status of the transaction (*commit*—the transaction is complete and the space used for its undo entries is now available to be overwritten by new transaction undo entries, or *active*—the transaction has not yet completed with the issuance by the user of either a COMMIT or ROLLBACK command), and the location within the rollback segment where the undo entries for the particular transaction are stored.

HOW ROLLBACK SEGMENTS EXTEND

Rollback segments consist of multiple extents. Unlike other segments, a rollback segment is ring-shaped and writes to its extents in an ordered, circular fashion, moving from one extent to the next, after the current extent is full. The current extent being written to is called the *head* of the rollback segment. The extent that contains the oldest active undo information (the first undo entry of the oldest transaction) is called the *tail*. The undo information created by a transaction is guaranteed to remain in the rollback segment until the transaction commits or rolls back. Figure 12.1 illustrates how rollback segments extend.

A few important rules to keep in mind when allocating space for rollback segments are:

- One rollback segment extent may have multiple transactions written to it.
- The head of the rollback segment never moves into a rollback extent currently occupied by the tail. (The exception to this rule is the *ORA-1555: snapshot too old (rollback segment too small)* error

Segment Head
(Current extent
being written to)

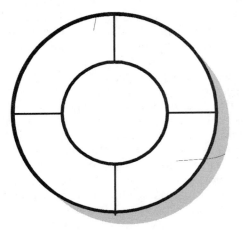

Segment Tail
(First extent of the
oldest active
transaction in the
rollback segment)

Figure 12.1 ■ How rollback segments extend.

message. Please see the sidebar entitled "ORA-1555: snapshot too old".)

- If the head cannot use the next extent, it allocates another extent and inserts it into the ring-shaped rollback segment.

- A rollback segment block contains only one active transaction at a time. This way, contention on the rollback segment block is reduced.

- A transaction cannot span multiple rollback segments. All of its undo entries can be stored in only one rollback segment.

- As the head tries to advance, extents cannot be skipped or used out of order.

ORA-1555: snapshot too old

This error message occurs when data manipulation transactions are performed simultaneously with long-running queries. Both online transaction processing and batch processing are being executed in the database at the same time. Long-running queries, therefore, may receive the "snapshot too old" error message. The occurrence of this error has to do with the definitions of "active" and "inactive" data.

While a transaction is executing, the data being modified by the transaction is considered "active." Once a transaction is complete, its data continues to remain in the rollback segment to support the queries and transactions that began executing before it was committed. So, if a query accesses the same table as a transaction, it will need to use the data stored by the transaction's rollback segment entry. However, once the transaction is complete, its data is then "inactive."

This means that the transaction's data blocks are now available to be overwritten by new transactions, regardless of the fact that the long-running query is still using the data from those blocks. Therefore, when the query attempts to read the blocks that have been overwritten, it will fail. The solution is to schedule batch processing to take place during a time period when you expect the least amount of online transaction processing.

HOW ROLLBACK SEGMENTS USE SPACE

When a transaction begins, ORACLE begins writing an undo entry to a rollback segment. The entry cannot expand into another rollback segment and it cannot switch to another rollback segment. ORACLE begins writing its undo entry to the first available extent. When an entry requires space in more than one extent, the rollback segment tries to locate the next available extent for the entry.

It tries to extend into the next sequential extent within the rollback segment. If the current extent is the last extent in the rollback segment, ORACLE attempts to extend the entry for the current transaction into the first extent. In essence, it attempts to overwrite old undo entries in the first extent with the continuing undo entry for the current transaction. However, that extent may currently be in use (*active*). If so, the rollback segment is forced to extend and acquire a new extent. The entry is then continued in this new extent.

CREATING AND TESTING ROLLBACK SEGMENTS

A few tests should be conducted by the DBA to find out how large and how numerous the rollback segments must be to handle normal database processing.

Type the following at the SQL*Plus command line while logged on as user SYSTEM:

```
SELECT segment_name, tablespace_name, status
  FROM dba_rollback_segs;
```

a) Write down the names of your rollback segments as well as their associated tablespaces. What resulting statuses do you see, and what do you think those statuses indicate?

_____

_____

Choose the first rollback segment that does not begin with 'SYS' (it is most likely 'RB01'), and execute the following query:

```
SELECT initial_extent, next_extent, min_extents,
       max_extents, pct_increase
  FROM dba_rollback_segs
 WHERE segment_name = 'RB01';
```

Oracle strongly recommends that DBAs create rollback segments with initial and next extents that are all the same size.

b) Write down the results of this query. Are the initial and next extent parameter values the same or different? What is the value specified for the PCTINCREASE parameter? Why do you think Oracle recommends that DBAs create rollback segments with initial and next extents of the same size?

_____

_____

Each rollback segment must have a minimum of two extents. Therefore, the MINEXTENTS parameter for a rollback segment should never be set to a value less than two.

During this lab, you are selecting from the dynamic performance views (i.e., the ones that begin with V$). Do not shut down the database unless you are instructed to do so, since the statistics in the V$ views are reset when you restart the database.

Type the following while logged on as user SYSTEM:

```
DESC v$rollstat
```

c) Write down at least three types of information that can be obtained from this view.

_____

_____

To find out how the values in this table change, type the following two statements:

```
ALTER ROLLBACK SEGMENT RB04 OFFLINE;

SELECT DISTINCT status FROM v$rollstat;
```

d) Compare the results you receive here with the action you performed in Question c). What can you deduce about the information that is represented in V$ROLLSTAT?

_____

_____

Now take a look at another related dynamic performance view by typing the following:

```
DESC v$rollname
```

e) What kind of information does V$ROLLNAME contain?

_____

_____

f) Using V$ROLLNAME and V$ROLLSTAT, write a query to display the names and statuses of your rollback segments and execute it. What are the names and statuses of your rollback segments? Of the rollback segments listed, how many are offline? Why?

_____

_____

You need an adequate number of rollback segments to prevent contention between transactions.

Determine whether your system is running into contention by issuing the following query:

```
SELECT n.name,
       ROUND(100 * s.waits/s.gets) "%Contention"
  FROM v$rollname n, v$rollstat s
 WHERE n.usn = s.usn;
```

If "%Contention" is greater than 1%, you will need to add more rollback segments.

g) Do you see any value for "%Contention" greater than 1? Why do you think it is necessary to perform this test?

_____

_____

Determine the amount of undo information that has been created in each of the rollback segments since the database was started by issuing the following query:

```
SELECT n.name, s.writes "Bytes written to date"
  FROM v$rollname n, v$rollstat s
 WHERE n.usn = s.usn;
```

h) Write down the results. Do you see all of your rollback segments listed with corresponding results? Why or why not? Note that the information you gather in this question will be used in Question i) below.

_____

_____

Determine the amount of undo information created for a particular transaction (i.e., a rollback segment entry). Open another SQL*Plus session and connect to your database as user SCOTT. The password for user SCOTT is TIGER.

If you are unable to connect as user SCOTT, create this user while logged into SQL*Plus as user SYSTEM by executing the following set of statements:

```
CREATE USER scott IDENTIFIED BY tiger
DEFAULT TABLESPACE tools
TEMPORARY TABLESPACE temp
QUOTA UNLIMITED ON tools;

GRANT CONNECT TO scott;
```

Run the demobld.sql script to create user SCOTT's schema. If you are using UNIX, this script can be found in a directory structure similar to the following:

```
$ORACLE_HOME/sqlplus/demo/demobld.sql
```

If you are using NT, this script can be found in a directory structure similar to the following:

```
e:\oracle\ora81\sqlplus\demo\demobld.sql
```

Force a rollback segment selection by issuing the following statement:

```
SET TRANSACTION USE ROLLBACK SEGMENT RB03;
```

Now create some undo entries by typing the following DML statements.

```
INSERT INTO DEPT (deptno, dname, loc)
          VALUES (50, 'PAYROLL', 'SAN FRANCISCO');
COMMIT;
```

In your SQL*Plus session where you are already logged on as user SYSTEM, re-issue the query listed just before Question h).

> **i)** Write down the results. For rollback segment RB03, subtract the "Bytes written to date" value received in your result set for Question h) from the "Bytes written to date" value received in your result set for this question and write down the result.

_____

_____

The value you receive as a result of this subtraction is roughly the number of bytes of undo information that was created in the rollback segment for this transaction.

> **j)** What do you think this information is useful for?

_____

_____

Determine the number of rollback segments needed in your system with the aid of the following chart from the *Oracle Database Administrator's Guide* of the Oracle documentation set.

Number of Concurrent Transactions (n)	Recommended Number of Rollback Segments
n < 16	4
16 <= n <= 32	8
32 <= n	n/4, but no more than 50

Given: There is an average of five concurrent transactions for each table in user SCOTT's schema at any one moment. Determine the total number of expected concurrent transactions. *HINT:* You need to look at SCOTT's USER_TABLES data dictionary view or the DBA_TABLES data dictionary view, using the appropriate WHERE clause, to find out how many tables are in user SCOTT's schema.

k) Write down the query you used to find out the number of tables contained in user SCOTT's schema. Issue the query. How many tables are listed?

_____

_____

l) Multiply the result you receive in Question k) by the average number of concurrent transactions for each table in user SCOTT's schema. How many concurrent transactions can you expect in user SCOTT's schema at any one moment? Compare this product with the values in the "Number of Concurrent Transactions" column in the chart above. How many rollback segments are needed to support the expected transactions?

_____

_____

If you do not have enough rollback segments, add additional ones as needed. Size them the same as the other rollback segments already in the database. Use the DBA_ROLLBACK_SEGS data dictionary view to obtain the name of the tablespace and segment/extent information supporting your non-system rollback segments. Use this information to fill in the blanks in Question m).

m) Fill in the blanks in the following CREATE ROLLBACK SEGMENT statement:

```
CREATE ROLLBACK SEGMENT RB05
    TABLESPACE _____
    STORAGE (INITIAL _____ NEXT _____
             MINEXTENTS _____ MAXEXTENTS _____
             OPTIMAL _____
                [HINT: This OPTIMAL value is typically
                       obtained with the following
                       formula: INITIAL + (NEXT *
                                MINEXTENTS)
                ]
        );
```

Notice the last storage clause, OPTIMAL. Remember that rollback segments dynamically extend when necessary. Without specifying the OPTIMAL storage clause for a rollback segment, once the transaction requiring the rollback segment to extend completes, the rollback segment simply keeps the extra space it has acquired. This phenomenon can cause rollback segment space management problems. One single large transaction can potentially use all of the space available in the rollback segment tablespace.

The OPTIMAL storage clause allows DBAs to specify an optimal size for a rollback segment. When a rollback segment extends beyond the length specified in the OPTIMAL clause, it later dynamically *shrinks* itself back to this length specification. It performs this shrinking action by eliminating its oldest inactive extent.

Create rollback segment RB05 using the above CREATE ROLLBACK SEGMENT statement with your sizing values. Create any necessary additional rollback segments with the same statement, ensuring that the rollback segment name contains the appropriate next sequential number (for example, RB06, RB07, etc.).

You now know how many rollback segments there are and how many concurrent transactions there will be. Assume that all of the transactions are the same size (the same number of bytes) as the transaction investigated in Question i).

n) If the space usage is evenly distributed across the rollback segments, how much space is needed in each rollback segment?

Ensure that all of your rollback segments are online by issuing the following five commands:

```
ALTER ROLLBACK SEGMENT RB04 ONLINE;
ALTER ROLLBACK SEGMENT RB05 ONLINE;
ALTER ROLLBACK SEGMENT RB06 ONLINE;
ALTER ROLLBACK SEGMENT RB07 ONLINE;
ALTER ROLLBACK SEGMENT RB08 ONLINE;
```

Ensure that your new rollback segments are listed in your init.ora file by completing the following instructions. Make a backup copy of your init.ora file in your pfile directory. The name of your backup file should be init.ora.06, or whatever the next highest version number is. Open your init.ora file for editing and change the value of the ROLLBACK_SEGMENTS parameter to include all newly created rollback segments.

o) Why do you think this step is necessary?

IMPORTANT: You must restart your database before continuing.

LAB 12.1 EXERCISE ANSWERS

12.1 ANSWERS

a) Write down the names of your rollback segments as well as their associated tablespaces. What resulting statuses do you see, and what do you think those statuses indicate?

Answer: Upon executing this query, you should have received a result similar to the following:

```
SQL> SELECT segment_name, tablespace_name, status
  2      FROM dba_rollback_segs;
```

SEGMENT_NAME	TABLESPACE_NAME	STATUS
SYSTEM	SYSTEM	ONLINE
SYSROL	SYSTEM	OFFLINE
RB01	RBS	ONLINE
RB02	RBS	ONLINE
RB03	RBS	ONLINE
RB04	RBS	ONLINE

```
6 rows selected.
```

The status "ONLINE" means that a rollback segment has been "activated," or made available to the database users. If a rollback segment's status shows that it is "OFFLINE," then it has been "deactivated."

"Deactivated" does not have the same meaning as "dropped." If a rollback segment has been deactivated as a result of being taken offline, it still exists as a database object. It is just not currently available.

b) Write down the results of this query. Are the INITIAL and NEXT extent parameter values the same or different? What is the value specified for the PCTINCREASE parameter? Why do you think Oracle recommends that DBAs create rollback segments with initial and next extents of the same size?

Answer: Upon executing this query, you should have received a result similar to the following:

```
SQL> SELECT initial_extent, next_extent, min_extents,
  2          max_extents, pct_increase
  3      FROM dba_rollback_segs
  4    WHERE segment_name = 'RB01';
```

INITIAL_EXTENT	NEXT_EXTENT	MIN_EXTENTS	MAX_EXTENTS	PCT_INCREASE
102400	102400	2	2.147E+09	0

The INITIAL and NEXT extent parameters are the same size (as they should be), 100 kilobytes. The PCTINCREASE parameter value is zero. Oracle recommends that DBAs create rollback segments with initial and next extents of the same size so that, without the possibility of extents growing exponentially, expansion and shrinkage can be manageable and predictable.

c) Write down at least three types of information that can be obtained from this view.

Answer: Upon issuing this command, you should have received a result similar to the following:

```
SQL> DESC v$rollstat
```

Name	Null?	Type
USN		NUMBER
EXTENTS		NUMBER
RSSIZE		NUMBER
WRITES		NUMBER
XACTS		NUMBER
GETS		NUMBER
WAITS		NUMBER
OPTSIZE		NUMBER
HWMSIZE		NUMBER
SHRINKS		NUMBER
WRAPS		NUMBER
EXTENDS		NUMBER
AVESHRINK		NUMBER
AVEACTIVE		NUMBER
STATUS		VARCHAR2(15)
CUREXT		NUMBER
CURBLK		NUMBER

Some of the types of information that can be obtained from this view include:

USN—The rollback segment number.

EXTENTS—The number of current extents in the rollback segment.

RSSIZE—The current size of the rollback segment, in bytes.

WRITES—*The number of bytes of undo entries written to the rollback segment.*

XACTS—*The number of active transactions.*

GETS—*The number of requests for the rollback segment header.*

WAITS—*The number of requests for the rollback segment header that were not imme-diately serviced.*

SHRINKS—*The number of shrinks that the rollback segment has been made to perform to stay at the size specified with the OPTIMAL parameter.*

WRAPS—*The number of times an undo entry has wrapped from one extent into another.*

EXTENDS—*The number of times the rollback segment had to acquire a new extent.*

STATUS—*The status of the rollback segment.*

d) Compare the results you receive here with the action you perform in Question c). What can you deduce about the information that is represented in V$ROLLSTAT?

Answer: Upon executing this series of statements you should have received a result similar to the following:

```
SQL> ALTER ROLLBACK SEGMENT RB04 OFFLINE;

Rollback segment altered.

SQL> SELECT DISTINCT status FROM v$rollstat;

STATUS
---------------
ONLINE
```

The dynamic performance table, V$ROLLSTAT, contains information about only those rollback segments whose status is not currently "OFFLINE."

e) What kind of information does V$ROLLNAME contain?

Answer: Upon issuing this command, you should have received a result similar to the following:

```
SQL> DESC v$rollname
```

Name	Null?	Type
USN		NUMBER
NAME	NOT NULL	VARCHAR2(30)

The information contained in *V$ROLLNAME* includes:

USN—The rollback segment number.

NAME—The name of the rollback segments that are currently online.

f) Using V$ROLLNAME and V$ROLLSTAT, write a query to display the names and statuses of your rollback segments and execute it. What are the names and statuses of your rollback segments? Of the rollback segments listed, how many are offline? Why?

Answer: One possible solution for this query is:

```
SELECT name, status
  FROM v$rollstat s, v$rollname n
 WHERE s.usn = n.usn;
```

Upon executing this query, you should receive a result similar to the following:

```
SQL> SELECT name, status
  2    FROM v$rollstat s, v$rollname n
  3   WHERE s.usn = n.usn;
```

NAME	STATUS
SYSTEM	ONLINE
RB01	ONLINE
RB02	ONLINE
RB03	ONLINE
RB04	ONLINE

None of the rollback segments listed are offline. Remember, V$ROLLSTAT contains information about only those rollback segments that are online. If you want to see status information about both online and offline rollback segments, you should query the DBA_ROLLBACK_SEGS data dictionary view.

g) Do you see any value for "%Contention" greater than 1? Why do you think it is necessary to perform this test?

Answer: Upon executing this query, you should have received a result similar to the following:

```
SQL> SELECT n.name, ROUND(100 * s.waits/s.gets)
  2          "%Contention"
  3    FROM v$rollname n, v$rollstat s
  4    WHERE n.usn = s.usn;
```

NAME	%Contention
SYSTEM	0
RB01	0
RB02	0
RB03	0

In this example, the value of "%Contention" for all the online rollback segments is 0. A "%Contention" value <=1 means that there is no contention. A "%Contention" value >1, indicates that contention exists, and therefore corrective action is required.

The existence of contention means that at some point in the rollback segment's history, there was not enough room for transaction undo entries in the header of the rollback segment. The percentage value indicates approximately how often (i.e., what percentage of time during which the rollback segment was being used) this happened. New transactions will be forced to wait for space to become free in the rollback segment header. Users will experience this situation in the form of system performance degradation. If contention is indicated, a corrective action such as the creation of additional rollback segments should be performed.

h) Write down the results. Do you see all of your rollback segments listed with corresponding results? Why or why not? Note that the information you gather in this question will be used in Question i) below.

Answer: Upon executing this query, you should have received a result similar to the following:

```
SQL> SELECT n.name, s.writes "Bytes written to date"
  2    FROM v$rollname n, v$rollstat s
  3    WHERE n.usn = s.usn;
```

NAME	Bytes written to date
SYSTEM	9660
RB01	268
RB02	54
RB03	54

You will not see ALL of your rollback segments listed with current results. Notice that rollback segment RB04 is not listed. This is because, like V$ROLLSTAT, V$ROLLNAME provides information for only those rollback segments whose status is not currently "OFFLINE".

i) Write down the results. For rollback segment RB03, subtract the "Bytes written to date" value received in your result set for Question h) from the "Bytes written to date" value received in your result set for this question and write down the result.

Answer: Upon executing this query again, your new result set should look similar to the following:

```
SQL> SELECT n.name, s.writes "Bytes written to date"
  2    FROM v$rollname n, v$rollstat s
  3    WHERE n.usn = s.usn;
```

NAME	Bytes written to date
SYSTEM	9660
RB01	268
RB02	54
RB03	250

For rollback segment RB03, 250 – 54 = 196. 196 bytes of undo information were created in rollback segment RB03 after user SCOTT inserted a row in the DEPT table. Do not worry if the values you receive do not exactly match the values you see listed here. The point of this exercise is that after you force the rollback segment selection of RB03 and issue a transaction in user SCOTT's schema, you should notice an increase in the value for the "Bytes written to date" column upon reissuing the query above. The values for all other listed rollback segments should remain the same for both query result sets.

j) What do you think this information is useful for?

Answer: This information is useful for predicting how large your transactions will be so that you may size your rollback segments appropriately.

k) Write down the query you used to find out the number of tables contained in user SCOTT'S schema. Issue the query. How many tables are listed?

*Answer: One possible query to find out the number of tables contained in user SCOTT's schema is (using your SQL*Plus session where you are already logged on as user SCOTT):*

```
SELECT COUNT(*)
  FROM user_tables;
```

Upon issuing this query, you should receive a result similar to the following:

```
SQL> SELECT COUNT(*)
  2     FROM user_tables;

COUNT(*)
----------
         6
```

There are six tables in user SCOTT's schema.

l) Multiply the result you receive in Question k) by the average number of concurrent transactions for each table in user SCOTT's schema. How many concurrent transactions can you expect in user SCOTT's schema at any one moment? Compare this product with the values in the "Number of Concurrent Transactions" column in the chart above. How many rollback segments are needed to support the expected transactions?

Answer: Since user SCOTT has an average number of five concurrent transactions for each of the six tables in his schema, he can expect 30 concurrent transactions at any one moment. According to the chart above, eight non-system rollback segments are needed to support the expected transactions.

m) Fill in the blanks in the following CREATE ROLLBACK SEGMENT statement.

Answer: After filling in the blanks, your CREATE ROLLBACK SEGMENT statement should appear similar to the following:

```
CREATE ROLLBACK SEGMENT RB05
    TABLESPACE _____RBS_____
    STORAGE (INITIAL __100K_____ NEXT ___100K____
         MINEXTENTS ____2_____ MAXEXTENTS UNLIMITED
                     OPTIMAL _____300K_____
        ) ;
```

Except for the value for the OPTIMAL storage parameter, the rest of these values can be obtained by querying the DBA_ROLLBACK_SEGS data dictionary view as follows:

```
SQL> SELECT tablespace_name, initial_extent,
  2         next_extent, min_extents,
  3         max_extents
  4    FROM dba_rollback_segs
  5   WHERE segment_name = 'RB01';
```

TABLESPACE_NAME	INITIAL_EXTENT	NEXT_EXTENT	MIN_EXTENTS	MAX_EXTENTS
RBS	102400	102400	2	2.147E+09

n) If the space usage is evenly distributed across the rollback segments, how much space is needed in each rollback segment?

*Answer: Assuming that all of the transactions are the same size (the same number of bytes) as the transaction investigated in Question i), then 196 (the expected number of bytes of undo information per transaction) * 30 (the number of concurrent transactions at any one moment) = 5880. 5880 / 8 (the number of non-system rollback segments) = 735. Therefore, if the space usage is evenly distributed across the rollback segments, 735 bytes of space are needed in each rollback segment.*

o) Why do you think this step is necessary?

Answer: This step is necessary because, although you bring your new rollback segments online manually in this exercise, once the database is shut down, the rollback segments are automatically taken offline. Upon database startup, the only way to ensure that your rollback segments are brought back online (without your having to explicitly set each of them online with an ALTER ROLLBACK SEGMENT statement) is to include their names in the list of rollback segment names following the ROLLBACK_ SEGMENTS parameter in your init.ora configuration file.

LAB 12.1 SELF-REVIEW QUESTIONS

To test your progress, you should be able to answer the following questions.

1) A transaction is often referred to as:

a) _____ an SQL statement or set of SQL statements
b) _____ a logical unit of work
c) _____ any DML statement that modifies data
d) _____ all of the above

2) *Statement-level read consistency* means that:

a) _____ this type of consistency refers to multiple-query transactions
b) _____ the data remains the same while ORACLE is fetching and returning it
c) _____ if you execute a query once, then re-execute it, the data returned in both result sets is exactly the same
d) _____ you receive your result set in a textual ASCII format

3) Rollback segments, like other types of segments, should be created with a minimum of one extent.

a) _____ True
b) _____ False

4) The transaction table in a rollback segment header contains which of the following: (Check all that apply.)

a) _____ rowids for inserted or deleted rows
b) _____ the location in the rollback segment where a transaction's undo entries may be found
c) _____ the address of the modified data block
d) _____ the status of the transaction
e) _____ old values for updated columns

5) Which of the following descriptions for the way rollback segments operate is NOT true?

a) _____ a rollback segment block contains only one active transaction at a time

b) _____ as the head tries to advance, the extents cannot be skipped or used out of order

c) _____ one rollback segment extent may have multiple transactions written to it

d) _____ a transaction can span multiple rollback segments for purposes of load balancing

e) _____ the head of the rollback segment never moves into an extent currently occupied by the tail

6) Once a transaction is complete, its data is deleted from the rollback segment.

a) _____ True

b) _____ False

7) A transaction in a rollback segment always has one of the two following statuses:

a) _____ ACTIVE or COMPLETE

b) _____ COMMIT or ROLLBACK

c) _____ COMMIT or ONLINE

d) _____ ACTIVE or INACTIVE

e) _____ ACTIVE or COMMIT

Quiz answers appear in Appendix A, Lab 12.1.

CHAPTER 12

TEST YOUR THINKING

1) If you create a rollback segment with the OPTIMAL clause, in which data dictionary view(s) can that value be found? Write a query to show the names and storage parameters of your non-system rollback segments, including the OPTIMAL clause values.

2) Open your create script 'createdb00_02.sql' for viewing. Notice that when creating the first four non-system rollback segments, RB01, RB02, RB03 and RB04, there are no specifications for either the MINEXTENTS or MAXEXTENTS storage parameter. From where do these rollback segments obtain the values for these parameters?

3) Starting with Oracle 7.x, the value for PCTINCREASE may not be specified when creating or altering rollback segments. The value is fixed at PCTINCREASE 0. Why do you think this restriction has been introduced?

C H A P T E R   1 3

LOCKING

CHAPTER OBJECTIVES

In this chapter, you will learn about:

✔ Locking and Data Consistency and Concurrency   Page 000

While most examples in this book provide a scenario where you are the only user in the database, the more common *real-world* scenario is one in which multiple users *concurrently* (simultaneously) access one database. Potential problems of a multi-user environment are loss of data consistency (discussed in Chapter 12, "Rollback Segments") or reduction in data access concurrency.

If a group of schoolchildren raising money for a class field trip were to begin processing cookie orders electronically, quite easily two or more of them might make a simultaneous sales transaction. Since the number of boxes of chocolate mint cookies is limited, how do you ensure that several of the schoolchildren don't sell the same box?

It is important to discuss how the Oracle Server keeps data consistent while multiple users are concurrently writing to the same database. One other issue of equal importance is when some users read from a database while other users write to it. The ultimate goal in addressing each of these problems is to achieve maximum concurrency (a large number of simultaneous users accessing a single database) while maintaining flawless data consistency and integrity.

Problems may certainly stem from two or more processes trying to modify the same piece of information. To prevent one process from interfering with the work of another, the Oracle Server uses *locks*. Typically, a lock is some form of mechanism that controls access. Regarding databases, a *lock* prevents some type of access to a database resource that is currently being accessed by another process.

LAB 13.1

LOCKING AND DATA CONSISTENCY AND CONCURRENCY

LAB OBJECTIVES

After this lab, you will be able to:

✔ Create, Review, and Eliminate Locks

LAB 13.1 EXERCISES

13.1 CREATE, REVIEW, AND ELIMINATE LOCKS

STATEMENTS VS. TRANSACTIONS

A *statement* is merely a single SQL command like a simple SELECT, INSERT, UPDATE, or DELETE statement (possibly including multiple clauses such as WHERE and ORDER BY) that ends with a semicolon. An example of a statement is:

```
DELETE FROM math_class
 WHERE student_id = 170;
```

On the other hand, a *transaction* consists of one or more SQL statements issued by a single user or application. A transaction is only complete when the user or application issues a COMMIT or ROLLBACK statement. An example of a transaction is:

```
DELETE FROM math_class
  WHERE student_id = 170;
INSERT INTO math_class
       (student_id, last_name, first_name)
VALUES (175, 'Eckhardt', 'Emily');
COMMIT;
```

 A statement typically simply ends with a semicolon, while a transaction ends with a COMMIT or ROLLBACK statement as well as a semicolon.

If two transactions are said to be *concurrent*, it does not necessarily mean they begin and end at the same time. They are said to be concurrent because the potential exists for them to overlap and possibly interfere with one another. Therefore, true concurrency poses potential problems such as the one described in the example with the schoolchildren selling boxes of chocolate mint cookies.

The Oracle Server gets around these problems by treating concurrent processes vying for the same resource as if they were happening sequentially—one after the other. To test data consistency during concurrent processing, the data returned to each of two or more SQL statements should be the same as it would be if the two or more statements occurred one after the other. To sequentially process actions while achieving data consistency and providing access to multiple concurrent users, the Oracle Server divides these actions into manageable pieces such as SQL statements and transactions.

THE LOST-UPDATE PROBLEM

If there were no locking mechanism in place, you could run into the lost-update problem. Referring to the example regarding the schoolchildren sales staff, the danger of having multiple users write to the same database is that one user could possibly interfere with the work of another user. Say the database begins with 10 boxes of chocolate mint cookies remaining for the day's sales. The first salesperson, Michael, sells four boxes and updates the database. Before the update is committed, however, another salesperson, Matthew, sells three boxes. Matthew's process subtracts three from the current value (10) in the database. The resulting value, of course, is seven. In the meantime, Michael's value, six, is written to the database. A fraction of a second later, Matthew's value, seven, is written to the database. Therefore, Michael's sale has been overwritten. Even though there are only six boxes of chocolate mint cookies left, the database says that there are still seven boxes available.

Clearly, this result is undesirable. In the example, it would lead to more boxes sold than are currently available. This problem is very similar to other situations in the real world. If many users have uncontrolled access to the same items in a database at the same time, it will not be long before data becomes corrupted. It is therefore quite necessary to have some sort of mechanism in place to prevent process interference and possible data destruction.

WHAT IS A LOCK?

As stated in the chapter overview, a *lock* is a mechanism put in place by the Oracle Server to prevent processes from interfering with, and possibly overriding, each other. This task is accomplished by preventing access to a resource requested by one process when the resource is already currently being accessed by another process.

For example, suppose you and a co-worker, Ram, both have permission to write to a text file. If Ram is currently editing the file and you open the file to make your own changes, you will receive a message that the file is locked by user RAM. You cannot edit the file because either the operating system or the editor has placed a lock on the file. Depending on the operating system and/or editor, you may not even be able to view the file if it is currently locked by another user. However, this latter situation is less common.

The Oracle Server has its own system for managing locks, irrespective of the lock manager provided with the operating system in which Oracle may be running. The reason for this is that Oracle's lock manager is more sophisticated than that of most single operating systems and chooses the optimal level of restrictiveness (type of lock) and amount of information locked (row vs. table).

HOW ARE LOCKS USED?

Consider again the example where you and your co-worker, Ram, are both trying to access the same text file. Say you are not interested in changing the file, but merely want to view it. If the application does not allow you to view the file while Ram is changing it, then data consistency is being provided at the cost of concurrency.

The goal of a good lock manager is to discover the optimal balance between maintaining data consistency while providing maximum concurrent data access. It achieves this goal by using different types of locks for different situation requirements. These locks vary by both their level of restrictiveness (exclusive or shared) and by the amount of information locked (row or table).

The restrictiveness of a lock refers to the number of users or processes allowed concurrent access to and the types of operations that may be performed on a locked resource.

Locks can be either *exclusive* or *shared*. An *exclusive* lock on a resource (such as a row) prevents all other transactions from locking that resource. This does not mean that other transactions cannot access the row. It means that other transactions cannot modify the row at the same time any transaction holds an exclusive lock. Each transaction must wait to obtain an exclusive lock to be able to modify a row's data. In Oracle, any lock on a row is always an exclusive lock.

If a transaction consists of only SELECT statements, it can access any rows that have exclusive locks placed on them since a SELECT statement does not alter the row's data, and therefore never locks it.

A *shared* lock is one that allows other transactions to lock a resource with another shared lock; however, it prevents locking with an exclusive lock. In the example of the text file that you and your co-worker are both trying to access, if Ram is currently modifying the file, the operating system may place a shared lock on the file so that you and other users can obtain access to the file. This access is read-only, since you are not able to write to the file until Ram's exclusive lock on the file has been released.

Shared locks obviously allow more concurrent transactions. The more restrictive any lock is, the less concurrency available to users and applications. To maximize concurrency, the Oracle Server automatically uses the least restrictive lock necessary to prevent interference and data destruction among processes.

THE AMOUNT OF INFORMATION LOCKED

A *row* lock locks only the row being modified. This type of locking is important because when many users are accessing the same table, row-level locking allows rows in the rest of the table to be modified. In contrast to row-level locking, another type of locking is *block-level* locking.

Oracle does not use block-level locking.

In block-level locking, the entire data block containing the row being modified gets locked. Therefore, if a block contains more than one row, however only one row is currently being modified, the block-level lock would prevent all rows in the block from being modified by another user. If a row is spread over multiple blocks, say four, and each block contains other rows, then block-level locking would keep all rows in all four blocks from being modified.

A *table* lock, on the other hand, when obtained by a transaction, ensures that no other transaction can perform actions that affect any part of the rest of the table. A transaction obtains a table lock when a table is being changed. Actually, whenever a transaction obtains a row lock, it also obtains a table lock, although the table lock is shared while the row lock is exclusive.

To understand why Oracle enables a table lock when it has already obtained a row lock, it is important to look at the purposes behind each type of lock. A row lock is acquired whenever a DML statement such as INSERT, UPDATE, or DELETE is issued for a row. This row lock prevents other similar statements from being issued against the locked row until its current modification is complete and its current row lock is released. Conversely, a table lock is acquired to ensure that the definition of the table cannot be changed—for example, with DDL alterations—until the DML transaction has been committed.

Even though Oracle does use table locks, these locks do not prevent users from issuing DML or SELECT statements.

The only way that an Oracle table lock can prevent a DML operation is if manual locking has been activated by a user explicitly issuing a LOCK command with a very restrictive mode. An example of this kind of command is:

```
LOCK TABLE math_class IN EXCLUSIVE MODE;
```

The Oracle Server's automatic locking behavior is not that restrictive. Each transaction acquires a lock with the minimum restriction necessary to prevent other transaction impedance. This way, data access concurrency is maximized and the waiting time for locks to be released for users entering data is minimized.

DEADLOCKS

A *deadlock* is a situation in which two or more transactions cannot complete because each is waiting for the other to release a lock.

For example, suppose two banking co-workers, Varun and Ernie, are accessing two separate funds for the same customer. Ernie is required to transfer $100,000 from the customer's stock fund to his education fund. Meanwhile, Varun is fulfilling a request from the customer's wife to transfer $50,000 from the education fund to the stock fund. Each worker's transaction consists of two statements. The transaction for each co-worker is outlined below with the corresponding times that indicate when each statement begins.

Ernie's statements:
UPDATE stock fund time = 1:00:00
UPDATE education fund time = 1:00:02

Varun's statements:
UPDATE education fund time = 1:00:01
UPDATE stock fund time = 1:00:03

Ernie's transaction begins first. His transaction locks the row in the stock fund and will not release the lock until the education fund has been updated accordingly. Concurrently, however, the education fund's row has been locked because Varun began his transaction after Ernie's began, but before it completed. He cannot end the transaction and release the lock on the education fund because of Ernie's lock on the stock fund. Therefore, the result of Ernie's and Varun's actions is a deadlock.

The Oracle Server gets out of this situation by using rollbacks. As soon as it notices a deadlock, it rolls back the transaction that detected the deadlock. This is usually the first transaction; therefore, the first lock is released. This action allows the second transaction to proceed (in our example, Varun's transaction may now commit). Once Varun has committed, then Ernie may proceed with his transaction and commit as well.

Oracle's design makes deadlocks a rarity. The potential for a deadlock is low because Oracle uses row-level locking and because SELECT statements (or any statements that simply read data) do not acquire any locks.

To illustrate how Oracle handles locks, create and review a lock situation by completing the following exercise.

Log into SQL*Plus as user SCOTT (the password is TIGER) and enter the following command:

```
GRANT INSERT, UPDATE, DELETE, SELECT ON dept TO pth01;
```

In a separate SQL*Plus session, log on as user PTH01 (the password is BOOKS) and minimize all application windows you may have running except for these two SQL*Plus sessions.

In user SCOTT's session, update the DEPT table with the following DML statement. (Do not issue a COMMIT statement until instructed to do so):

```
UPDATE scott.dept
   SET loc = 'LOS ANGELES'
 WHERE deptno = 40;
```

In user PTH01's session, issue the same UPDATE statement as above, substituting the value 'LOS ANGELES' with the value 'PHOENIX'.

a) What happened to user PTH01's session when you executed this second UPDATE statement? What do you think is the reason for this result?

_____

_____

b) What two commands may be issued in user SCOTT's session to undo the situation noted in Question a)? (Do not issue either of them at this time.)

_____

_____

This is a typical situation for the DBA to resolve. A user will come to your desk and say, "I think the database is broken because my screen is frozen." Or, they may say, "I think someone is locking the row I'm trying to update."

Now open a third SQL*Plus session and log on as user SYSTEM. Find out which user is waiting for a lock to be released by issuing the following statement:

```
SELECT sid, username, lockwait, row_wait_obj#,
       row_wait_row#
  FROM v$session
 WHERE username IS NOT NULL;
```

The dynamic performance view V$SESSION provides Instance-specific information about all currently active sessions. If there is a value in the LOCKWAIT column, it indicates that the corresponding user is waiting for a lock to be released.

c) Write down the results of this query. Based on the results, which user is waiting for a lock to be released?

_____

_____

d) Write a query joining the query in Question c) to the DBA_OBJECTS data dictionary view to include in the result set the name and owner of the object involved in the lock. *HINT:* Your WHERE clause should include the following condition:

```
v$session.row_wait_obj# = dba_objects.object_id
```

Write down this query.

_____

_____

e) Execute this query and write down the results. What is the name of and who is the owner of the locked object?

_____

_____

f) Add the block number and file number to the query you constructed in Question d). Write down this query and execute it. What is the row number, block number, and file

number for the row involved in the lock? You will need these
values in Question g) to obtain the exact row in contention.

In Oracle8.x, the PL/SQL package DBMS_ROWID is available to assist you in
converting the information obtained in Question f) to the row's ROWID.
Among other functions available in the DBMS_ROWID package, useful conversion functions are

- ROWID_ROW_NUMBER
- ROWID_BLOCK_NUMBER
- ROWID_TO_ABSOLUTE_FNO

g) Using the row number, block number, and file number obtained
in Question f), write the query you would use to select the
exact row from the DEPT table that is currently in contention.
Execute this query and write down the results.

Minimize the SQL*Plus session for user SYSTEM. Tile the sessions for user
SCOTT and user PTH01 so that both are visible on your screen at the same
time. While keeping an eye on both, issue the following command in user
SCOTT's session:

```
ROLLBACK;
```

h) What happened in the session for user PTH01? Why do you
think you received this result?

Issue the ROLLBACK command in user PTH01's session.

LAB 13.1 EXERCISE ANSWERS

13.1 ANSWERS

a) What happened to user PTH01's session when you executed this second UPDATE statement? What do you think is the reason for this result?

Answer: Upon executing this second UPDATE statement, you will notice that user PTH01's session ended up hanging. The reason for this result is that two processes are attempting to update the same row at the same time, and the first transaction must complete before the second transaction will be allowed to proceed.

b) What two commands may be issued in user SCOTT's session to undo the situation noted in Question a)? (Do not issue either of them at this time.)

Answer: Either of the following two commands, COMMIT or ROLLBACK, may be issued in user SCOTT's session to undo the situation noted in Question a).

c) Write down the results of this query. Based on the results, which user is waiting for a lock to be released?

Answer: Upon issuing this query, you should have received a result similar to the following:

```
SQL> SELECT sid, username, lockwait, row_wait_obj#,
  2         row_wait_row#
  3    FROM v$session;
```

SID	USERNAME	LOCKWAIT	ROW_WAIT_OBJ#	ROW_WAIT_ROW#
1	PTH01	03CDCDA8	10920	3
2	SYSTEM		-1	0
3	SCOTT		-1	0

Based on the results, user PTH01 is waiting for a lock to be released. The value received for the column ROW_WAIT_OBJ# is the numerical identifier for the entity upon which a lock has been placed; in this example, that entity is the DEPT table.

d) Write a query joining the query in Question c) to the DBA_OBJECTS data dictionary view to include in the result set the name and owner of the object involved in the lock. *HINT: Your WHERE clause should include the following condition:*

```
v$session.row_wait_obj# = dba_objects.object_id
```

Write down this query.

Answer: An example of one possible solution in writing this query is:

```
SELECT sid, username, lockwait, row_wait_obj#,
       row_wait_row#, owner, object_name
  FROM v$session, dba_objects
 WHERE v$session.row_wait_obj# = dba_objects.object_id;
```

e) Execute this query and write down the results. What is the name of and who is the owner of the locked object?

Answer: Upon executing this query, you should have received a result similar to the following:

```
SQL> SELECT sid, username, lockwait, row_wait_obj#,
  2         row_wait_row#, owner, object_name
  3    FROM v$session, dba_objects
  4   WHERE v$session.row_wait_obj# =
  5         dba_objects.object_id;
```

SID	USERNAME	LOCKWAIT	ROW_WAIT_OBJ#	ROW_WAIT_ROW#	OWNER	OBJECT_NAME
9	PTH01	03CDCDA8	10920	3	SCOTT	DEPT

The name of the locked object is "DEPT" and user SCOTT is its owner.

f) Add the block number and file number to the query you constructed in Question d). Write down this query and execute it. What is the row number, block number, and file number for the row involved in the lock? You will need these values in Question g) to obtain the exact row in contention.

Answer: One example of the query you would use to obtain the ROWID for the row that is currently in contention should be similar to the following:

```
SELECT sid, username, lockwait, row_wait_obj#,
       row_wait_row#, row_wait_block#,
       row_wait_file#, owner, object_name
  FROM v$session, dba_objects
 WHERE v$session.row_wait_obj# = dba_objects.object_id;
```

Upon executing this query, you should receive a result set similar to the following:

```
SQL> SELECT sid, username, lockwait, row_wait_obj#,
  2          row_wait_row#, row_wait_block#,
  3          row_wait_file#, owner, object_name
  4     FROM v$session, dba_objects
  5    WHERE v$session.row_wait_obj# =
          dba_objects.object_id;
```

SID	USERNAME	LOCKWAIT	ROW_WAIT_OBJ#	ROW_WAIT_ROW#
8	SCOTT	02DA4EE0	21205	3

ROW_WAIT_BLOCK#	ROW_WAIT_FILE#	OWNER	OBJECT_NAME
5916	2	SCOTT	DEPT

The row number is 3, the block number is 5916, and the file number is 2.

g) Using the row number, block number, and file number obtained in Question f), write the query you would use to select the exact row from the DEPT table that is currently in contention. Execute this query and write down the results.

Answer: One example of the query you would use to select the exact row from the DEPT table that is currently in contention is:

```
SELECT * FROM scott.dept
  WHERE DBMS_ROWID.ROWID_ROW_NUMBER(ROWID)= 3
    AND DBMS_ROWID.ROWID_BLOCK_NUMBER(ROWID) = 5916
    AND DBMS_ROWID.ROWID_TO_ABSOLUTE_FNO
        (ROWID, 'SCOTT', 'DEPT') = 2;
```

Upon executing this query, you should receive a result set similar to the following:

```
SQL> SELECT * FROM scott.dept
  2    WHERE DBMS_ROWID.ROWID_ROW_NUMBER(ROWID)= 3
  3      AND DBMS_ROWID.ROWID_BLOCK_NUMBER(ROWID) = 5916
  4      AND DBMS_ROWID.ROWID_TO_ABSOLUTE_FNO
  5          (ROWID, 'SCOTT', 'DEPT') = 2;
```

DEPTNO	DNAME	LOC
40	OPERATIONS	LOS ANGELES

h) What happened in the session for user PTH01? Why do you think you received this result?

Answer: In the session for user PTH01, the UPDATE operation finally completed. You received this result because the ROLLBACK operation performed in the session for user SCOTT released the row lock for this row, meaning that user PTH01's transaction could then proceed.

LAB 13.1 SELF-REVIEW QUESTIONS

To test your progress, you should be able to answer the following questions.

1) Which of the following commands may be referred to as a statement:

    a) _____ An UPDATE operation
    b) _____ A DELETE operation
    c) _____ An INSERT operation
    d) _____ A SELECT operation
    e) _____ All of the above

2) Which of the following is TRUE about transactions:

    a) _____ They begin and end at the same time
    b) _____ They never overlap
    c) _____ The Oracle Server treats them as if they occur sequentially
    d) _____ They never include more than one DML statement

3) A table lock is the same thing as a row lock—you're simply locking that many more rows.

    a) _____ True
    b) _____ False

4) The commands that mark the end of a transaction are

    a) _____ INSERT or END
    b) _____ UPDATE or COMMIT
    c) _____ DELETE or ROLLBACK
    d) _____ COMMIT or ROLLBACK
    e) _____ SELECT or COMMIT

5) Which of the following is NOT TRUE about locks?

a) _____ A lock can be either *exclusive* or *shared*.

b) _____ When an exclusive lock is obtained, a simultaneous shared lock is also obtained.

c) _____ An exclusive lock provides the same amount of data concurrency that a shared lock provides.

d) _____ A transaction acquires a lock with the minimum allowed restrictiveness in favor of higher concurrency.

e) _____ An exclusive row lock prevents other DML operations from taking place on a row, while a shared lock prevents DDL operations from taking place on the row's table.

6) Oracle uses block-level locking.

a) _____ True

b) _____ False

7) A situation in which two or more transactions cannot proceed because each is waiting for the other to release a lock is known as:

a) _____ Complete lock

b) _____ Deadlock

c) _____ Exclusive lock

d) _____ Deferred lock

Quiz answers appear in Appendix A, Lab 13.1.

C H A P T E R   1 3

TEST YOUR THINKING

1) If you are writing batch scripts that contain multiple transactions, discuss a method to ensure that the transactions within your scripts will be committed to the database without failing or being held up by other concurrent processes?

2) Manual locking can be invoked by means of a SELECT ... FOR UPDATE statement. An example of this statement may look like the following:

```
SELECT *
  FROM dept
 WHERE dname = 'SALES'
 FOR UPDATE;
```

This kind of statement locks any rows whose values meet the criteria in the WHERE clause of the SELECT statement. These rows are locked so that a user or application may see the values before updating them, or before deleting the rows they are contained in. Also, they are locked so that while a user or application is viewing the values, another user or application cannot change these values. In which real-world scenarios do you suppose you might want to invoke manual locking?

3) Since SELECT statements do not acquire locks, how does Oracle guarantee query read consistency? *HINT:* You may want to refer to Chapter 12, "Rollback Segments," for assistance.

CHAPTER 14

LOGICAL BACKUP AND RECOVERY

CHAPTER OBJECTIVES

In this chapter, you will learn about:

✔ Backup and Recovery Using the Import
and Export Utilities   Page 312

Data backups are absolutely essential to optimal database planning and maintenance. Backups are not only used for recovery in emergency situations, but also in situations where you are simply reorganizing a database, for example. Since data loss is always possible, it is important to develop a backup and recovery strategy. There are two types of data loss: *logical* and *physical*. Chapter 15, "Physical Backup and Recovery," discusses backup and recovery strategies in terms of physical data loss. Physical data loss involves the loss of database components at the operating system level, such as datafiles and redo log files. This chapter discusses backup and recovery strategies in terms of logical data loss, which is the loss of database components such as tables, indexes, and rows (table records).

Logical data loss can occur, for example, when someone is not careful about how they've constructed a WHERE clause in a DELETE statement, or when someone accidentally drops the wrong table. Physical data loss can occur, for example, when a critical database file is accidentally overwritten, or a disk drive crashes, or a datafile is accidentally deleted. A sound strategy for backup and recovery includes both physical data and logical data backups.

LAB 14.1

BACKUP AND RECOVERY USING THE IMPORT AND EXPORT UTILITIES

LAB OBJECTIVES

After this lab, you will be able to :

✔ Perform a Logical Backup Using the Export Utility
✔ Perform a Logical Recovery Using the Import Utility

LAB 14.1 EXERCISES

14.1.1 PERFORM A LOGICAL BACKUP USING THE EXPORT UTILITY

A logical data backup usually consists of SQL statements to re-create the Database objects (tables, indexes, views, synonyms, roles, grants, and so forth), along with the row data. This type of backup should be used when, for instance, you are switching machines, if you need to move data between instances or between schemas, or if you are copying data between different hardware architectures, operating system versions, or versions of Oracle. Whenever you create logical backups in Oracle, you use the EXP (for Export) utility supplied by Oracle. Because the export is in Oracle's proprietary format, you can only use the IMP (for Import) utility to import the data.

IMP cannot import data from other database systems. To perform this kind of import, you should use the SQL*Loader utility.

To practice using Oracle's EXP utility, perform the following exercise.

You create the STUDENT user in Chapter 9, "User Creation." Now you need to import the data for the STUDENT schema.

IMPORTANT: If the password for user STUDENT is still set to STUDY, you must alter the user STUDENT and assign the password LEARN.

Navigate to the Web site for this book (accessible through www.phptr.com) and download the files required to create and install the STUDENT schema. Read the instructions supplied in the README.TXT file and carefully follow the directions. Once all the scripts have completed successfully and you have loaded all the STUDENT schema objects into your database, you can create an export file with the following exercise.

Create a text file in your exp directory called student_data_exp.par. This file will be used to provide parameters to the EXP utility when you run the utility. In that file, write the following parameters and corresponding values:

```
userid = student/learn
file = student_data.dmp
direct = y
log = student_data_exp.log
```

Save and exit the file.

a) What do you think these particular parameters provide information for?

_____

_____

The parameter options for the EXP utility provide information about, for instance, which user ID/password EXP should use to log in to the database to perform the export, the name of the export file (the backup), and the name of a file where you would like the output of your actions to be logged. This output is usually sent to the terminal screen; however, you can additionally save this output to later check for any errors that may have occurred in the process. The "direct" parameter improves exporting performance by reading the data blocks directly (as opposed to going through the normal database engine). Your exports will run much faster if you use this option.

There are three EXPORT modes:

- *Full*—Creates a backup of all objects in the database.
- *User*—Creates a backup of all objects owned by a specific user.
- *Table*—Creates a backup of only specific tables owned by a specific user.

To set the *full* export mode in the export command, you specify the parameter FULL=Yes (or simply, FULL=Y). The *user* export mode is set using the OWNER parameter followed by a list of usernames whose objects are exported, e.g., OWNER=PTH01. If this parameter is not specified, the default value is the current user. The EXP parameter file shown in Question a) creates an export file in user export mode. Since neither the FULL nor OWNER parameter is specified, objects are exported for the user performing the export; in this case, the user STUDENT. You can set the *table* export mode by specifying the TABLES parameter to export selected tables only, e.g., TABLES=course.

Also, you can perform an export at three different levels of data accumulation: complete, cumulative, and incremental. A *complete* export backs up all of the data in a database. An *incremental* export backs up only data that has changed since the last time an incremental export was performed. Finally, a *cumulative* export backs up only data that has changed since the last time a cumulative export was performed. This type of export is used to create an amalgamation of incremental exports already performed.

You can only perform a CUMULATIVE or INCREMENTAL export if you are in the FULL export mode. Furthermore, to perform an INCREMENTAL or CUMULATIVE export, you must be logged on as a user with DBA privileges or have been granted the EXP_FULL_DATABASE system privilege. SYS and SYSTEM can both perform these types of exports.

Check your ORACLE.HOME/bin directory for the export utility version you have installed. This will affect how you run the EXP utility. For the example listed here, the export utility application is called Exp. Hence, when you invoke this application, you invoke it with the same name, exp. You will need to perform this same check for your version of the IMP utility. From the UNIX command line or the MS-DOS command line, navigate to your exp directory and run the EXP utility by typing the following command:

```
exp parfile = student_data_exp.par
```

Open the log file created in your exp directory and check it for errors.

b) What result do you receive after running your export? What do you think this result means?

_____

_____

14.1.2 PERFORM A LOGICAL RECOVERY USING THE IMPORT UTILITY

To practice using Oracle's IMP utility, perform the following exercise.

Create a text file in your exp directory called student_data_imp.par. This file will be used to provide parameters to the IMP utility when you run the utility. In that file, write the following parameters and corresponding values:

```
userid = system/manager
fromuser = student
touser = pth01
file = student_data.dmp
log = student_data_imp.log
```

Save and exit the file.

a) What do you think these particular parameters provide information for?

_____

_____

The parameter options for the IMP utility provide information about, for instance, which user ID/password IMP should use to log in to the database to perform the import, the name of the export file (the backup), and the name of the file where you would like the output of your actions to be logged.

 To use IMP, you must at least have the CREATE SESSION privilege. If your export file contains a full database export, you must have the IMP_FULL_DATABASE privilege to import it. Of course, a DBA user has this privilege.

From the UNIX or MS-DOS command line, navigate to your exp directory and run the IMP utility by typing the following command:

```
imp parfile = student_data_imp.par
```

Open the log file created in your exp directory and check it for errors.

> **b)** What result do you receive after running your import? What do you think this result means?

_____

_____

Log into SQL*Plus as user STUDENT and create a table called NEW_TABLE with one column, NAME, of data type VARCHAR2. Insert a few values into this table.

Re-export the STUDENT schema data using the same parameter file and EXP utility command you execute in Lab 14.1.1.

Edit your student_data_imp.par parameter file and add the following parameter:

```
inctype = restore
```

> **c)** What do you think this parameter provides information about?

_____

_____

> **d)** What command should you write to run the IMP utility against your new parameter file? Write down this command, run the utility, then check your new log file for errors.

_____

_____

> **e)** What result do you receive after running your import? Are there any differences between the student_data_imp.log file you receive now and the one you receive in your answer to Question b)? If so, what are they?

Edit your student_data_imp.par parameter file. Take out the "inctype" parameter and add the following additional parameter:

```
tables = grade_type
```

    f) What do you suppose this parameter provides information about?

    g) Re-run the command you executed in Question d), then check your log file for errors. What happened this time? Why do you think you received this result?

LAB 14.1 EXERCISE ANSWERS

14.1.1 ANSWERS

    a) What do you think these particular parameters provide information for?

    Answer: The first parameter, "userid", provides information about which user ID/password the EXP utility should use when logging in to the database to perform the export. The second parameter, "file", provides information about the export file (logical backup) to be created with the EXP command. The third parameter, "direct", reads the data blocks directly, providing a faster export. The final parameter, "log", specifies the name of the file that the output of the export action should be logged to. This is the file that will contain a log of any errors that occur during the export.

    b) What result do you receive after running your export? What do you think this result means?

    Answer: After running your export, you should have received a result similar to the following:

Connected to: Oracle8i Enterprise Edition Release 8.1.5.0.0 - Production

With the Partitioning and Java options

PL/SQL Release 8.1.5.0.0 - Production

Export done in WE8ISO8859P1 character set and WE8ISO8859P1 NCHAR character set

. exporting pre-schema procedural objects and actions

. exporting foreign function library names for user STUDENT

. exporting object type definitions for user STUDENT

About to export STUDENT's objects ...

. exporting database links

. exporting sequence numbers

. exporting cluster definitions

. about to export STUDENT's tables via Direct Path ...

. . exporting table	COURSE	30 rows exported
. . exporting table	ENROLLMENT	226 rows exported
. . exporting table	GRADE	2004 rows exported
. . exporting table	GRADE_CONVERSION	15 rows exported
. . exporting table	GRADE_TYPE	6 rows exported
. . exporting table	GRADE_TYPE_WEIGHT	300 rows exported
. . exporting table	INSTRUCTOR	10 rows exported
. . exporting table	MYTAB2	6 rows exported
. . exporting table	MYTAB3	4 rows exported
. . exporting table	SECTION	78 rows exported
. . exporting table	STUDENT	268 rows exported
. . exporting table	ZIPCODE	227 rows exported

. exporting synonyms

. exporting views

. exporting stored procedures

. exporting operators

. exporting referential integrity constraints

. exporting triggers

. exporting indextypes

. exporting bitmap, functional and extensible indexes

. exporting posttables actions

. exporting snapshots

. exporting snapshot logs

. exporting job queues

. exporting refresh groups and children

. exporting dimensions

. exporting post-schema procedural objects and actions

Export terminated successfully without warnings.

> *This result means that all of the logical structures of the STUDENT schema were successfully exported.*

14.1.2 ANSWERS

a) What do you think these particular parameters provide information for?

Answer: The first parameter, "userid", provides information about which user ID/password the IMP utility should use when logging in to the database to perform the import. When you are moving data from one schema to another, you should use the SYSTEM/MANAGER userid and password (or that of any user with DBA privileges), the "fromuser" parameter to specify the owner of the schema objects that you wish to import, and the "touser" parameter to specify to which user (schema) the logical backup should be imported. The fourth parameter, "file", provides information about the export file (logical backup) to be used in the import. And the final parameter, "log", specifies the name of the file that the output of the import action should be logged to. This is the file that will contain a log of any errors that occur during the import.

Specifying the FROMUSER parameter indicates the source schemas in the export file. Unless this parameter is complemented with the TOUSER parameter, the IMP command will import the objects in the export file into identically named schemas (in the case above, the STUDENT schema). If any schema named in the FROMUSER parameter does not exist (and no TOUSER parameter is included), objects are imported into the USERID schema (in the case above, the SYSTEM schema).

b) What result do you receive after running your import? What do you think this result means?

Answer: After running your import, you should have received a result similar to the following:

Connected to: Oracle8i Enterprise Edition Release 8.1.5.0.0 - Production

With the Partitioning and Java options

PL/SQL Release 8.1.5.0.0 - Production

Export file created by EXPORT:V08.01.05 via direct path

Warning: the objects were exported by STUDENT, not by you

import done in WE8ISO8859P1 character set and WE8ISO8859P1 NCHAR character set

. . importing table	"COURSE"	30 rows imported
. . importing table	"ENROLLMENT"	226 rows imported
. . importing table	"GRADE"	2004 rows imported
. . importing table	"GRADE_CONVERSION"	15 rows imported
. . importing table	"GRADE_TYPE"	6 rows imported
. . importing table	"GRADE_TYPE_WEIGHT"	300 rows imported
. . importing table	"INSTRUCTOR"	10 rows imported
. . importing table	"MYTAB2"	6 rows imported

. . importing table	"MYTAB3"	4 rows imported
. . importing table	"SECTION"	78 rows imported
. . importing table	"STUDENT"	268 rows imported
. . importing table	"ZIPCODE"	227 rows imported

About to enable constraints...

Import terminated successfully without warnings.

> *This result means that all of the logical structures of the STUDENT schema were successfully imported into the PTH01 schema.*

c) What do you think this parameter provides information about?

> *Answer: This parameter provides information about the type of recovery that you would like to perform. It accepts one of two input keywords: RESTORE or SYSTEM. Specifying SYSTEM means that only the SYSTEM schema objects from the last incremental export should be imported. Specifying RESTORE means that user objects that have changed since the last time an incremental export was created should be imported.*

d) What command should you write to run the IMP utility against your new parameter file? Write down this command, run the utility, then check your new log file for errors.

> *Answer: An example of the command you should use to run your IMP utility is:*

```
imp parfile=student_data_imp.par
```

e) What result do you receive after running your import? Are there any differences between the student_data_imp.log file you receive now and the one you receive in your answer to Question b)? If so, what are they?

> *Answer: If you are using a version of Oracle later than 7.3.x, after running your new import, you should receive a result similar to the following:*

Connected to: Oracle8i Enterprise Edition Release 8.1.5.0.0 - Production

With the Partitioning and Java options

PL/SQL Release 8.1.5.0.0 - Production

Export file created by EXPORT:V08.01.05 via direct path

Warning: the objects were exported by STUDENT, not by you

import done in WE8ISO8859P1 character set and WE8ISO8859P1 NCHAR character set

IMP-00083: dump file does not contain an incremental export

IMP-00000: Import terminated unsuccessfully

Though you've added a table and in so doing changed the STUDENT schema, specifying an incremental parameter value of RESTORE in the IMP utility command simply isn't enough to import just those user objects that have changed since the last time you ran the EXP utility on the STUDENT schema. It is necessary to first perform an incremental export before any type of incremental import can be performed.

If you are using Oracle7.3.x or earlier, your import will try to run as it did in Question b); however, you will receive error messages to the effect that your CREATE statements have failed because the objects they are trying to create already exist in the target schema.

f) What do you suppose this parameter provides information about?

Answer: This parameter provides information about which tables should be imported. If this parameter is specified, the value supplied to it is usually a list of one or more tables. If it is not specified, then all tables are imported.

g) Re-run the command you executed in Question d), then check your log file for errors. What happened this time? Why do you think you received this result?

Answer: After re-executing the import, you should have received a result similar to the following:

Connected to: Oracle8i Enterprise Edition Release 8.1.5.0.0 - Production

With the Partitioning and Java options

PL/SQL Release 8.1.5.0.0 - Production

Export file created by EXPORT:V08.01.05 via direct path

Warning: the objects were exported by STUDENT, not by you

import done in WE8ISO8859P1 character set and WE8ISO8859P1 NCHAR character set

IMP-00015: following statement failed because the object already exists:

"CREATE TABLE "GRADE_TYPE" ("GRADE_TYPE_CODE" CHAR(2), "DESCRIPTION" VARCHAR"

"2(50), "CREATED_BY" VARCHAR2(30), "CREATED_DATE" DATE,
"MODIFIED_BY" VARCHA"

"R2(30), "MODIFIED_DATE" DATE)   PCTFREE 10 PCTUSED 40 INITRANS 1
MAXTRANS 25"

"5 LOGGING STORAGE(INITIAL 10240 NEXT 10240 MINEXTENTS 1
MAXEXTENTS 121 PCTI"

"NCREASE 50 FREELISTS 1 FREELIST GROUPS 1 BUFFER_POOL DEFAULT)
TABLESPACE "U"

"SERS""

Import terminated successfully with warnings.

> *This time, the import statement failed because the GRADE_TYPE table already exists in the target PTH01 schema. The import statement will not overwrite the structure of existing database objects in the target schema. For the above import statement to run successfully, you would need to either first drop the GRADE_TYPE table in the PTH01 schema, or include the parameter IGNORE=Y in your import statement. This parameter is used to indicate whether the import statement should ignore any errors that occur during import if the object already exists. With the value of this parameter specified as "Y", you are able to import the table; however, all the same actions that the Server would usually perform against newly inserted rows would be performed against the rows inserted during the import. For example, if you include the parameter IGNORE=Y in your student_data_imp.par parameter file, you can import the GRADE_TYPE table, but rows that have primary key values that match rows already in the table will violate the primary key constraint and be rejected.*

LAB 14.1 SELF-REVIEW QUESTIONS

To test your progress, you should be able to answer the following questions.

1) Which of the following database components do the Oracle-provided import (IMP) and export (EXP) utilities help to back up and recover? Check all that apply.

   a) _____ Control files
   b) _____ Tables
   c) _____ Indexes
   d) _____ Datafiles

2) Which of the following circumstances can lead to logical data loss? Check all that apply.

   a) _____ An ill-formed WHERE clause in a DELETE statement
   b) _____ A disk crash
   c) _____ An accidental table drop
   d) _____ An accidental datafile deletion
   e) _____ A critical database file being overwritten

3) The three different types of EXPORT data collection are:

   a) _____ Full, Partial, and Cumulative
   b) _____ Complete, Partial, and Incremental
   c) _____ Incremental, Cumulative, and Full
   d) _____ System, Full, and Restore

4) In addition to performing full database exports, you can export data in which other modes? Check all that apply.

   a) _____ Schema
   b) _____ Table
   c) _____ Cumulative
   d) _____ User

Quiz answers appear in Appendix A, Lab 14.1.

CHAPTER 14

TEST YOUR THINKING

1) Perform an incremental backup and an incremental recovery of the STUDENT schema data using the tools and terminology you've learned in this chapter. Discuss the various error messages you encounter (if any) and how you resolve them.

2) Why do you think Oracle provides three different levels of data accumulation: Incremental, Cumulative, and Full? Can you think of any business situations and/or justifications for each level? Describe them.

3) At the UNIX or MS-DOS command line, type the command:

```
exp HELP=y
```

What other parameters for the EXP utility do you see listed and what do you think those parameters provide information for? Choose three or four of them and comment on them. Then, type the command:

```
imp HELP=y
```

and repeat the exercise for the IMP utility.

CHAPTER 15

PHYSICAL BACKUP AND RECOVERY

CHAPTER OBJECTIVES

In this chapter, you will learn about:

✔ Backup and Recovery Using ARCHIVELOG Mode   Page 328

As Chapter 7, "Redo Logs" mentions, in the course of day-to-day activity, your database may be subject to different types of failure. Some of the most common types of failure are user process (such as when a user suddenly quits an application without explicitly committing or rolling back changes), Instance (such as when the operating system crashes), and media (whereby a datafile is corrupted or a physical disk is lost). Each type of failure causes data inaccuracy and inconsistency.

A DBA should put in place a schedule for backing up the database (making physical copies of the datafiles, control files, redo log files, and all configuration files) that allows for recovery in the event of a database failure. Understanding the different types of failure that can occur helps the DBA to determine what he or she must do to recover the database from failure. Neither user process or Instance failure requires DBA intervention. However, performing regular backups of the Database is the only way to recover from a media failure. It is, therefore, important to learn how DBAs safeguard data in the event of these types of failure.

LAB 15.1

BACKUP AND RECOVERY
USING ARCHIVELOG MODE

LAB OBJECTIVES

After this lab, you will be able to :

✔ Perform a Physical Backup and Perform Different
   Types of Archiving
✔ Simulate a Media Failure
✔ Perform a Complete Offline Recovery
✔ Perform a Complete Online Recovery

LAB 15.1 EXERCISES

15.1.1 PERFORM A PHYSICAL BACKUP AND PERFORM DIFFERENT TYPES OF ARCHIVING

As mentioned in the chapter overview, user process failures and Instance failures do not require DBA intervention. User process failures affect only a single user process; therefore, only one incomplete transaction requires resolution. The Server remains unaffected. Automatically and at regular intervals, the PMON (Process Monitor) background process checks for user processes that ended unexpectedly. When it comes across one, it rolls back that process's uncommitted transactions, thereby restoring the database to a consistent state.

Instance failures are more serious than user process failures because they involve multiple users and transactions. Recall from Chapter 7, "Redo Logs," that when a user issues a COMMIT statement, changed data is not automatically written to the datafiles. Instead, the Oracle Server performs a "deferred write" by having LGWR write redo information to the online redo log files, while the changed data remains in the Database Buffer Cache until some event, like a checkpoint, causes DBWR to write the changed data to the datafiles. Therefore, when an Instance dies as the result of say, someone killing a background process or the underlying operating system crashing, the SGA, along with the Database Buffer Cache, is gone. And since the SGA is gone, modified data can no longer be written to the datafiles.

This lost data must be recovered from the redo log files. When you restart the failed Instance, the Oracle Server uses the SMON (System Monitor) background process to recover any transactions not already contained in the datafiles. The first action performed by SMON is that of taking all the changes recorded in the redo log files and applying them to the datafiles. This action is called *rolling forward*. In rolling forward, all transactions, committed and uncommitted, are applied to the datafiles. It is then necessary for SMON to roll back any of those transactions applied to the datafiles that were not committed. Thus, this action is called *rolling back*.

Media failure takes place when a storage device becomes lost or corrupted. Naturally, a media failure is more difficult to recover from since physical files are no longer available. Therefore, the DBA must take precautions to try to prevent losses of data due to possible media failure. Making regular backups of the Database helps the DBA in achieving this goal.

Backing up the data in your Database is much like the actions you take to copy a document you are working on to a floppy disk. If the hard disk containing your original document crashes (a situation known as a media failure), you have a copy of your work and will be able to restore the document up to the point where you last saved your work on the floppy disk. Of course, if you made any changes to the document on the hard disk since your last copy onto the floppy disk, you will not be able to recover those changes.

The Oracle Server, however, allows you to recover a Database even if your backup copy of the Database is not current as of the moment of your database failure. The first part of your database recovery involves restoring the copy of the Database from your backup. The second part involves recovering all transactions that took place between the time of your most recent backup and the database failure.

PERFORMING A PHYSICAL BACKUP

If your database is not used on a 24x7 basis (a database that is available 24 hours a day, seven days a week), then it can be backed up with a *cold backup* (also known as an *offline* backup). If your database must always be available (24×7), then you must perform a *hot backup* (also known as an *online* backup). In this chapter, you practice performing a *cold backup*.

To perform a cold backup, you must first shut down all Instances connected to the Database, and then close the Database.

Perform a physical backup of your Database by completing the following exercise.

Connect to Server Manager in line mode as INTERNAL (if you are working in Windows NT, you may accomplish this in an MS-DOS session) and close your database by issuing the following command:

```
SHUTDOWN IMMEDIATE
```

Now that you've closed your database, you need to create backup copies of all of your physical files (datafiles, redo log files, and control files) and configuration files (init.ora).

In your oracle/admin/<SID> directory, create a new directory called "backup". If you are using Windows NT, you can create this directory using Windows Explorer functionality. If you are using UNIX, you can create this directory by navigating to the oracle/admin/<SID> directory and issuing the following command:

```
mkdir backup
```

Once you have created this directory, open it and create two additional directories underneath it. These directories should be named oradata and pfile (this name is short for "parameter file").

Copy the contents of your oracle/oradata/<SID> directory to your new oracle/admin/<SID>/backup/oradata directory. If you are using Windows NT, you can perform this action by using Windows Explorer's copy and paste functionality. If you are using UNIX, you can perform this action by navigating to the oracle/admin/<SID>/backup directory and issuing a command similar to the following at the command line:

```
cp -p -R oracle/oradata/db00/*.* oradata
```

This action will copy (cp), keeping all sets of existing permissions on the files (-p), all the contents of the oracle/oradata/<SID> directory (*.*) to the oradata directory that it will create dynamically (-R) and place in the current directory path to where you've just navigated. The contents of this file include all the datafiles, redo log files, and control files.

Now copy the most recent version of your init.ora file to your newly created pfile directory.

In this exercise, you are only backing up one location's worth of physical files (datafiles, redo log files, and control files). In a real-world situation, your datafiles, redo log files, and control files could be located on separate disks and filesystems. You would then back up multiple files located in several locations. Additionally, you would back up archived redo logs. At this point, you have not yet created any. Finally, if you have more than one configuration file, you must be sure to create backup copies of them as well.

Backing Up the Control Files

In this exercise, you back up the control files simply by copying them to a designated backup directory. Alternatively, you may back up the control files one at a time by using an ALTER DATABASE command. An example of this kind of statement is:

```
ALTER DATABASE BACKUP CONTROLFILE TO
'e:\oracle\admin\db00\backup\oradata\control01.ctl';
```

You are now ready to create a starting point for recovery. Connect to Server Manager in line mode as INTERNAL and restart your database by issuing the following command:

```
STARTUP OPEN
```

This action creates the Instance, starts all of the necessary background processes, allocates the memory resources, mounts the database to the Instance, and opens the datafiles.

Before you begin backing up, you must make sure you have the most current names and sizes of your datafiles, control files, redo log files, and configuration files.

a) Perform four queries. Select the name of your database and the log mode from the V$DATABASE view. Select the names of your redo log files and control files from the V$LOGFILE and V$CONTROLFILE views. Also select the names of the datafiles from the DBA_DATA_FILES data dictionary view. Write down these queries, execute them, and record their results. Remember which user you must log into SQL*Plus as to be able to perform these queries. Why do you think this set of steps is necessary?

Display the current archiving information for your database by issuing the following command as INTERNAL (if you are prompted for a password, it is ORACLE):

```
ARCHIVE LOG LIST
```

b) Write down the results of this action. According to the results you receive, are you currently archiving your redo logs? How do you know?

Shut down your database using the SHUTDOWN IMMEDIATE command.

Make a backup copy of your init.ora file in your pfile directory. The name of your backup file should be init.ora.07, or whatever the next highest version number is. Open your init.ora file for editing and add the following parameters:

```
log_archive_dest = <the destination directory for your archive
logs>
```

An example of this path is:

```
log_archive_dest = e:\oracle\admin\db00\arch
```

Oracle7.x versions require you to append an additional suffix to your log_archive_dest parameter value before the Oracle Server is able to successfully create archived redo log files. For example, the above listing for the log_archive_dest parameter value would have to be changed to a value similar to the following:

```
log_archive_dest = e:\oracle\admin\db00\arch\arch
```

Now add the following parameter to denote a naming convention for your archived redo log files:

```
log_archive_format = "%S.arc"
```

The following table displays the different types of format masks available for archived redo logs.

Format Mask	Description
%T	Thread number; left-zero-padded
%t	Thread number; not padded
%S	Log sequence number; left-zero-padded
%s	Log sequence number; not padded

Save and exit the file.

Issue the following command while logged onto Server Manager in line mode as INTERNAL:

```
STARTUP MOUNT EXCLUSIVE
```

This type of startup mode is necessary, because to put the database in ARCHIVELOG mode, you must mount the database to the Instance without opening the datafiles. The "exclusive" option ensures that you are the only session connected to the database so that your action of enabling archiving is unimpeded.

Put the database in ARCHIVELOG mode by issuing the following command:

```
ALTER DATABASE ARCHIVELOG;
```

c) Issue the ARCHIVE LOG LIST command again and write down your new results. Compare the results you receive now with the results you received in Question b).

Open the datafiles of the database by issuing the following command:

```
ALTER DATABASE OPEN;
```

Since you have not, at this point, configured the Instance for automatic archiving, the type of archiving you are performing is *manual*. Manual archiving simply means that you must issue a command manually after each log switch for the Oracle Server to create an archived copy of the redo log. The opposite of *manual* archiving is *automatic* archiving, which uses the ARCH (or in Oracle8i, ARCn) background process to perform the archiving automatically. You explore automatic archiving later in this chapter.

ARCHIVELOG mode is particularly important during hot backups. If you want to recover a consistent database after restoring with an online backup, the backup must have been created while archiving was enabled. If your database is not in ARCHIVELOG mode, the only way you can create a consistent backup is to create a cold backup.

Force a manual log switch now by issuing the following command:

```
ALTER SYSTEM SWITCH LOGFILE;
```

d) Issue the ARCHIVE LOG LIST command again and write down your new results. Compare the results you receive now with the results you received in Question c). Do you notice any difference in the log sequence numbers? Why or why not?

Open a new SQL*Plus session and issue the following two consecutive commands while logged on as user SYSTEM:

```
ALTER SYSTEM SWITCH LOGFILE;
ALTER SYSTEM SWITCH LOGFILE;
```

e) What happened when you twice more attempted to switch your log files? Do not try to correct the situation yet. Write down your theory about why this problem occurred.

You should see a noticeable effect after performing the actions just before Question e). If you performed the above steps out of order in even the slightest way, you may not receive this effect.

In the Server Manager session (if you are using Windows NT, this is the MS-DOS window session), issue the following command to manually archive the log file:

```
ARCHIVE LOG ALL
```

f) Does this action correct the situation in user SYSTEM's SQL*Plus session? Why or why not?

g) Issue the ARCHIVE LOG LIST command again and write down your new results. Compare the results, particularly the log sequence numbers, you receive now with the results you received in Question d).

Look in your /oracle/admin/db00/arch (ADMIN/db00/arch) directory to see your archived redo log files.

h) What are the names of your archived redo log files?

In user SYSTEM's SQL*Plus session, issue the following command to see which background processes your database is currently running:

```
SELECT vb.name, vb.description
  FROM v$bgprocess vb, v$session vs
 WHERE vb.paddr = vs.paddr;
```

    i) What unique background processes is your database currently running?

_____

_____

Exit from user SYSTEM's SQL*Plus session. DO NOT close your Server Manager session.

Shut down your database by issuing the SHUTDOWN IMMEDIATE command.

Make a backup copy of your init.ora file in your pfile directory. The name of your backup file should be init.ora.08, or whatever the next highest version number is. Open your init.ora file for editing and enable automatic archiving by adding the following parameter:

```
log_archive_start = true
```

Save and exit the file.

Restart your database by issuing the following command in Server Manager as INTERNAL:

```
STARTUP OPEN
```

    j) In your Server Manager session, issue the same query you executed in Question i) to see which background processes your database is currently running. Do you notice any difference between the result set you receive here and the one you received in Question i)? If so, what is it?

_____

_____

These next few steps help you to prove that the redo log files are being automatically archived.

Force a manual log switch by issuing the following command:

```
ALTER SYSTEM SWITCH LOGFILE;
```

k) Issue the ARCHIVE LOG LIST command again and write down your new results. Compare the results, particularly the log sequence numbers, you receive now with the results you received in Question g).

_____

_____

Open an additional SQL*Plus session and issue the following two consecutive commands while logged on as user SYSTEM:

```
ALTER SYSTEM SWITCH LOGFILE;
ALTER SYSTEM SWITCH LOGFILE;
```

l) Did the SQL*Plus session freeze again like last time? Why or why not?

_____

_____

m) Issue the ARCHIVE LOG LIST command again and write down your new results. Compare the results, particularly the log sequence numbers, you receive now with the results you received in Question k).

_____

_____

n) Look in your arch directory to see your archived redo log files. What are their names?

_____

_____

Make the current state of the database the new starting point by exiting from your SQL*Plus session and shutting down the database by issuing the SHUTDOWN IMMEDIATE command.

You MUST NOW BACKUP your datafiles, control files, redo log files, archived redo log files, and configuration files using the methods discussed in the beginning of this lab.

o) Briefly explain what was accomplished in the lab you just completed.

_____

_____

15.1.2 SIMULATE A MEDIA FAILURE

You will now simulate a media failure by setting up a datafile loss problem.

Do not proceed unless you have successfully completed the following tasks:
- *Put your database in ARCHIVELOG mode.*
- *Enabled automatic archiving.*
- *Backed up all of the files in your ORADATA directory (control files, datafiles, redo log files).*

Log onto Server Manager as INTERNAL and restart the database by issuing the STARTUP OPEN command.

a) In your Server Manager session, issue the ARCHIVE LOG LIST command and write down the log sequence numbers.

_____

_____

Open an additional SQL*Plus session and issue the following query while logged on as user STUDENT:

```
SELECT COUNT(*)
  FROM course;
```

b) How many rows are in the COURSE table?

_____

_____

Again in user STUDENT's session, issue the following DML statement:

```
INSERT INTO course (course_no, description, cost,
                    prerequisite, created_by,
                    created_date, modified_by,
                    modified_date)
         VALUES (460, 'DB Admin', 1195, 350,
                'TAMRANEW', SYSDATE, 'LORIECKH',
                SYSDATE);

COMMIT;
```

In your Server Manager session, force a manual log switch by issuing the following command:

```
ALTER SYSTEM SWITCH LOGFILE;
```

c) In your Server Manager session, issue the ARCHIVE LOG LIST command and write down the log sequence numbers. Compare the results you receive here with those you received in Question a). Did the log sequence numbers increase? If not, something is wrong with your configuration.

_____

_____

In user STUDENT's session, issue the following transaction:

```
INSERT INTO course (course_no, description, cost,
                    prerequisite, created_by,
                    created_date, modified_by,
                    modified_date)
         VALUES (470, 'Adv DB', 1195, 460,
                'MICHAELN', SYSDATE, 'MATTHEWN',
                SYSDATE);

COMMIT;
```

In your Server Manager session, force a manual log switch by issuing the following command:

```
ALTER SYSTEM SWITCH LOGFILE;
```

d) In the Server Manager session, issue the ARCHIVE LOG LIST command and write down the log sequence numbers. Compare the results you receive here with those you received in Question c).

_____

_____

e) Obtain the number of rows in the COURSE table again. How many rows are there?

_____

_____

In user STUDENT's session, write the DML statement to insert one last row into the COURSE table. DO NOT issue a COMMIT command and DO NOT exit from this SQL*Plus session until instructed to do so.

f) Write down the DML statement you created and execute it.

_____

_____

In your Server Manager session, issue the following query to determine which datafile(s) supports the USERS tablespace:

```
SELECT file_name
  FROM dba_data_files
 WHERE tablespace_name = 'USERS';
```

g) What is the name(s) of the datafile(s) that supports the USERS tablespace?

_____

_____

In your Server Manager session, close the database by issuing the following command:

```
SHUTDOWN IMMEDIATE
```

The shutdowns performed in this chapter may take longer than usual.

Exit from Server Manager and from the SQL*Plus session.

In the operating system, delete the datafile(s) that supports the USERS tablespace. If you are using Windows NT, this file may be removed using Windows Explorer functionality. If you are using UNIX, navigate to your '/oracle/ora-data/<SID>' (ORADATA) directory and issue a command with the following syntax:

```
rm <name of datafile>
```

The "rm" in the above UNIX command stands for "remove."

You have just simulated a serious crash in the database.

15.1.3 PERFORM A COMPLETE OFFLINE RECOVERY

Attempt to start up the database while logged onto Server Manager as INTERNAL by issuing the STARTUP OPEN command.

a) What is the response from the system?

_____

_____

Issue the SHUTDOWN IMMEDIATE command and exit Server Manager.

Copy the existing copy of the missing datafile, located in your /oracle/admin/ <SID>/backup/oradata directory (the backup for the ORADATA directory), to the /oracle/oradata/<SID> (ORADATA) directory.

Attempt to start up the database again while logged onto Server Manager as INTERNAL by issuing the STARTUP OPEN command.

> **b)** What is the response from the system this time?

_____

_____

> **c)** To what level did your database start up: nomount, mount, or open (i.e., what level is it at currently)?

_____

_____

Recover the datafile by issuing the following command in your Server Manager session:

```
RECOVER DATABASE
```

> **d)** Follow the prompts to restore your database. Write down exactly what options are supplied to you, which ones you choose, and the response you receive from the system after making your selection(s).

_____

_____

In your recovery process, you may receive a message similar to the following:

```
ORA-00278:  Logfile
'e:\oracle\admin\db00\arch\
arch0000000131.arc' no longer needed for this recovery
```

    e) What does this message tell you about the current stage of your recovery process? Is any action required involving the listed archived redo log file? Why?

Open a new SQL*Plus session and attempt to connect as user STUDENT.

    f) What message do you receive? Do not attempt to correct the situation yet. Leave the SQL*Plus session in this state.

    g) Write down your theory about what needs to be done to correct this situation (i.e., what startup level must the database be brought to in order to allow users to connect to the database?).

Bring the database to its proper startup level by issuing the following command in your Server Manager session:

```
ALTER DATABASE OPEN;
```

h) In your SQL*Plus session, re-attempt to connect to the database as user STUDENT. What is the response from the system this time? Why do you think you received this response?

_____

_____

i) Write a query to determine the number of rows in the COURSE table. Execute it and compare the result you receive with the result you received in Question e) of Lab 15.1.2.

_____

_____

If the two result sets match, then you have successfully recovered your database.

15.1.4 PERFORM A COMPLETE ONLINE RECOVERY

In this lab you recover the database by recovering only the part that is problematic, while those parts that are not remain online.

Exit your SQL*Plus session.

In your Server Manager session, issue the SHUTDOWN IMMEDIATE command and log out.

In the operating system, delete the datafiles that supports the USERS tablespace.

a) Attempt to start up the database while logged onto Server
Manager as INTERNAL by issuing the STARTUP OPEN
command. What is the response from the system?

_____

_____

Shut down the database using the SHUTDOWN IMMEDIATE command and
exit your Server Manager session.

Copy the existing copy of the missing datafile, located in your /oracle/
admin/<SID>/backup/oradata directory (the backup for the ORADATA directory), to the /oracle/oradata/<SID> (ORADATA) directory.

b) Re-attempt to start up the database while logged onto Server
Manager as INTERNAL by issuing the STARTUP OPEN
command. What is the response from the system this time?

_____

_____

Set the datafile offline by issuing a command similar to the following, substituting the location of your datafile:

```
ALTER DATABASE DATAFILE
'e:\oracle\oradata\db00\users01.dbf' OFFLINE;
```

For the third time, attempt to start up the database by issuing the following
command:

```
ALTER DATABASE OPEN;
```

c) Open a new SQL*Plus session and attempt to connect to the
database as user STUDENT. What is the response from the
system? Is your attempt successful?

_____

_____

d) Write a query to obtain the number of rows in the COURSE table and execute it. What response do you receive from the system?

e) What are the advantages and disadvantages of allowing user STUDENT to log on when this user does not have access to the datafile just taken offline?

Recover the datafile by issuing a command similar to the following in your Server Manager session:

```
RECOVER DATAFILE 'e:\oracle\oradata\db00\users01.dbf'
```

f) In user STUDENT's session, re-execute the query you wrote in Question d) to obtain the number of rows in the COURSE table. What response do you receive from the system this time? Are there any other necessary tasks still left to perform? If so, what are they?

Set the newly recovered datafile online by issuing a command similar to the following in your Server Manager session:

```
ALTER DATABASE DATAFILE
'e:\oracle\oradata\db00\users01.dbf' ONLINE;
```

g) In user STUDENT's session, re-execute the query you wrote in Question d) to obtain the number of rows in the COURSE table. What response do you receive from the system this time? Compare the result you receive now with the results you

received in both Question e) of Lab 15.1.2 and Question i) of
Lab 15.1.3. Do all three result sets match?

LAB 15.1 EXERCISE ANSWERS

15.1.1 ANSWERS

a) Perform four queries. Select the name of your database and the log mode from the V$DATABASE view. Select the names of your redo log files and control files from the V$LOGFILE and V$CONTROLFILE views. Also select the names of the datafiles from the DBA_DATA_FILES view. Write down these queries, execute them, and record their results. Remember which user you must log into SQL*Plus as in order to be able to perform these queries. Why do you think this set of steps is necessary?

Answer: Some examples of the queries you may use to obtain the most current names of your datafiles, control files, and redo log files are:

```
SELECT name, log_mode
  FROM v$database;

SELECT group#, member
  FROM v$logfile;

SELECT name
  FROM v$controlfile;

SELECT file_name
  FROM dba_data_files
 WHERE tablespace_name = 'USERS';
```

*Upon issuing these queries while logged onto SQL*Plus as user SYSTEM, you should have received results similar to the following:*

```
SQL> SELECT name, log_mode
  2    FROM v$database;
```

```
NAME        LOG_MODE
--------    -----------
DB00        NOARCHIVELOG

SQL> SELECT group#, member
  2     FROM v$logfile;

GROUP#      MEMBER
------      ------------------------------------
1           E:\ORACLE\ORADATA\DB00\REDO_01A.LOG
1           E:\ORACLE\ORADATA\DB00\REDO_01B.LOG
2           E:\ORACLE\ORADATA\DB00\REDO_02A.LOG
2           E:\ORACLE\ORADATA\DB00\REDO_02B.LOG
3           E:\ORACLE\ORADATA\DB00\REDO_03A.LOG
3           E:\ORACLE\ORADATA\DB00\REDO_03B.LOG
6 rows selected.

SQL> SELECT name
  2     FROM v$controlfile;

NAME
--------------------------------------
E:\ORACLE\ORADATA\DB00\CONTROL01.CTL
E:\ORACLE\ORADATA\DB00\CONTROL02.CTL

SQL> SELECT file_name
  2     FROM dba_data_files
  3    WHERE tablespace_name = 'USERS';

FILE_NAME
--------------------------------------
E:\ORACLE\ORADATA\DB00\USERS01.DBF
```

This set of steps is necessary because you want to make sure that you have a record of all the names and locations of all the files of your Database before you begin your Database backup. After you perform your backup and recovery, you should re-execute these same queries. The goal is to compare the results of those queries you receive before your backup with the results you receive after your recovery. If your backup and recovery are successful, the two sets of results should match. Knowing which log mode your database is currently running in helps you to determine whether to perform a cold or hot backup. If you place your database in ARCHIVELOG mode and enable automatic archiving, you can perform a hot backup. If not, you have no choice but to perform a cold backup if you expect to be able to recover your Database to a consistent state.

b) Write down the results of this action. According to the results you receive, are you currently archiving your redo logs? How do you know?

Answer: Upon issuing this command, you should have received a result similar to the following:

```
SVRMGR> ARCHIVE LOG LIST
Database log mode               No Archive Mode
Automatic archival              Disabled
Archive destination             E:\Oracle\admin\DB00\arch
Oldest online log sequence      40
Current log sequence            42
```

According to the results, you are not currently archiving your redo logs since the "Database log mode" field shows that you are currently running in "No Archive Mode."

c) Issue the ARCHIVE LOG LIST command again and write down your new results. Compare the results you receive now with the results you received in Question b).

Answer: Upon issuing this command again, you should have received a result similar to the following:

```
SVRMGR> ARCHIVE LOG LIST
Database log mode               Archive Mode
Automatic archival              Disabled
Archive destination             E:\Oracle\admin\DB00\arch
Oldest online log sequence      40
Next log sequence to archive    42
Current log sequence            42
```

Notice that you are now running in "Archive Mode". However, you are still not automatically archiving. At this point, you are manually archiving. Since you are now in ARCHIVELOG mode, your "Next log sequence to archive" is displayed. When LGWR finishes writing to the "Current log sequence," then you can archive it. In this example, the values for the "Current log sequence" and "Next log sequence to archive" are the same. These values become different from each other as log switches occur and log files are not yet archived.

d) Issue the ARCHIVE LOG LIST command again and write down your new results. Compare the results you receive now with the results you received in Question c). Do you notice any difference in the log sequence numbers? Why or why not?

Answer: Upon issuing this command again, you should have received a result similar to the following:

```
SVRMGR> ARCHIVE LOG LIST
Database log mode              Archive Mode
Automatic archival             Disabled
Archive destination            E:\Oracle\admin\DB00\arch
Oldest online log sequence     41
Next log sequence to archive   42
Current log sequence           43
```

You should notice a difference in the log sequence numbers in that, due to the manual log file switch, the values for both the "Current log sequence" and the "Oldest online log sequence" have increased by one. The "Next log sequence to archive" value has not changed since log sequence 42 is still waiting to be archived. Meanwhile, the "Current log sequence" value has increased due to the log switch. You are now running out of log groups to switch to that are not in need of archiving. This leads you into the upcoming problem in the following question.

e) What happened when you twice more attempted to switch your log files? Do not try to correct the situation yet. Write down your theory about why this problem occurred.

Answer: When you twice more attempted to switch your log files, you should have noticed that your SQL*Plus session was hanging. This problem occurred because you are still manually archiving. You have not enabled automatic archiving yet.

f) Does this action correct the situation in user SYSTEM's SQL*Plus session? Why or why not?

Answer: Yes, this action corrects the situation in user SYSTEM's SQL*Plus session in that the Oracle Server is not waiting for archiving to occur and the session is no longer hanging. The message "System altered", returned by the Oracle Server in the Server Manager session, indicates that this session's last action is now complete.

g) Issue the ARCHIVE LOG LIST command again and write down your new results. Compare the results, particularly the log sequence numbers, you receive now with the results you received in Question d).

Answer: Upon issuing this command again, you should have received a result similar to the following:

```
SVRMGR> ARCHIVE LOG LIST
Database log mode              Archive Mode
Automatic archival             Disabled
Archive destination            E:\Oracle\admin\DB00\arch
Oldest online log sequence     43
Next log sequence to archive   44
Current log sequence           45
```

After forcing two manual log switches, the values for each of the three fields, "Oldest online log sequence", "Next log sequence to archive", and "Current log sequence", has increased by two.

h) What are the names of your archived redo log files?

Answer: The names of your archived redo log files should be similar to "arch0000000042.arc" and "arch0000000043.arc."

i) What unique background processes is your database currently running?

Answer: The background processes your database is currently running should look similar to the following:

```
SQL> SELECT vb.name, vb.description
  2    FROM v$bgprocess vb, v$session vs
  3   WHERE vb.paddr = vs.paddr;

NAME   DESCRIPTION
-----  --------------------------
PMON   process cleanup
DBWR   db writer process
LGWR   Redo etc.
CKPT   checkpoint
SMON   System Monitor Process

5 rows selected.
```

In the answer to this question, you are shown the most common background processes that your database is likely to be currently running.

j) In your Server Manager session, issue the same query you executed in Question i) to see which background processes your database is currently running. Do you notice any difference between the result set you receive here and the one you received in Question i)? If so, what is it?

Answer: Upon issuing this query, you should have received a result set similar to the following:

```
SQL> SELECT vb.name, vb.description
  2    FROM v$bgprocess vb, v$session vs
  3   WHERE vb.paddr = vs.paddr;
```

```
NAME   DESCRIPTION
-----  --------------------------
PMON   process cleanup
DBWR   db writer process
ARCH   Archival Process
LGWR   Redo etc.
CKPT   checkpoint
SMON   System Monitor Process

6 rows selected.
```

The difference between the result set you receive here and the one you received in Question i) is that a new background process, ARCH (ARCn for Oracle8i), is now running as a result of your having enabled automatic archiving by setting the "log_archive_start" parameter in your init.ora file equal to "true", and then restarting the database.

k) Issue the ARCHIVE LOG LIST command again and write down your new results. Compare the results, particularly the log sequence numbers, you receive now with the results you received in Question g).

Answer: Upon issuing this command again, you should have received a result similar to the following:

```
SVRMGR> ARCHIVE LOG LIST
Database log mode              Archive Mode
Automatic archival             Enabled
Archive destination            E:\Oracle\admin\DB00\arch
Oldest online log sequence     44
Next log sequence to archive   46
Current log sequence           46
```

Notice that "Automatic archival" is now "Enabled", and the values for the "Oldest online log sequence" and "Current log sequence" fields have both been incremented by one due to the log switch. Since we restarted the database, the value for the "Next log sequence to archive" field is the same as that of "Current log sequence" field.

l) Did the SQL*Plus session freeze again like last time? Why or why not?

*Answer: The SQL*Plus session did not freeze again like last time because automatic archiving is enabled. It is no longer necessary for the Oracle Server to wait for you to manually archive a redo log file before it can successfully perform a log switch.*

m) Issue the ARCHIVE LOG LIST command again and write down your new results. Compare the results, particularly the log sequence numbers, you receive now with the results you received in Question k).

Answer: Upon issuing this command again, you should have received a result similar to the following:

```
SVRMGR> ARCHIVE LOG LIST
Database log mode              Archive Mode
Automatic archival             Enabled
Archive destination            E:\Oracle\admin\DB00\arch
Oldest online log sequence     46
Next log sequence to archive   48
Current log sequence           48
```

All three fields, "Oldest online log sequence", "Next log sequence to archive", and "Current log sequence", have been automatically incremented by two as a result of the two log switches just performed.

n) Look in your arch directory to see your archived redo log files. What are their names?

Answer: The names of your archived redo log files should now be similar to "arch0000000042.arc," "arch0000000043.arc," "arch0000000044.arc," "arch0000000045.arc," "arch0000000046.arc," and "arch0000000047.arc."

o) Briefly explain what was accomplished in the lab you just completed.

Answer: In the lab you just completed, you increased your chances for a successful recovery by making backup copies of all files necessary to restore the Database, monitoring the ARCHIVE LOG LIST output, performing checkpoints (by issuing log switches), enabling automatic archiving, and ensuring that you have all relevant information about the Database now either archived or backed up.

15.1.2 ANSWERS

a) In your Server Manager session, issue the ARCHIVE LOG LIST command and write down the log sequence numbers.

Answer: Upon issuing this command, you should have received a result similar to the following:

```
SVRMGR> ARCHIVE LOG LIST
Database log mode              Archive Mode
```

```
Automatic archival                  Enabled
Archive destination                 E:\Oracle\admin\DB00\arch
Oldest online log sequence          46
Next log sequence to archive        48
Current log sequence                48
```

b) How many rows are in the COURSE table?

Answer: Upon issuing this query, you should have received a result similar to the following:

```
SQL> SELECT COUNT(*)
  2     FROM course;

  COUNT(*)
---------
       30
```

There are 30 rows in the COURSE table.

c) In your Server Manager session, issue the ARCHIVE LOG LIST command and write down the log sequence numbers. Compare the results you receive here with those you received in Question a). Did the log sequence numbers increase? If not, something is wrong with your configuration.

Answer: Upon issuing this command again, you should have received a result similar to the following:

```
SVRMGR> ARCHIVE LOG LIST
Database log mode                   Archive Mode
Automatic archival                  Enabled
Archive destination                 E:\Oracle\admin\DB00\arch
Oldest online log sequence          47
Next log sequence to archive        49
Current log sequence                49
```

As you can see, due to the log switch, all of the log sequence numbers increased by one.

d) In the Server Manager session, issue the ARCHIVE LOG LIST command and write down the log sequence numbers. Compare the results you receive here with those you received in Question c).

Answer: Upon issuing this command again, you should have received a result similar to the following:

```
SVRMGR> ARCHIVE LOG LIST
Database log mode              Archive Mode
Automatic archival             Enabled
Archive destination            E:\Oracle\admin\DB00\arch
Oldest online log sequence     48
Next log sequence to archive   50
Current log sequence           50
```

Once again, due to the log switch, all log sequence numbers have been incremented by one.

e) Obtain the number of rows in the COURSE table again. How many rows are there?

Answer: Upon issuing this query again, you should have received a result similar to the following:

```
SQL> SELECT COUNT(*)
  2    FROM course;

  COUNT(*)
---------
       32
```

There are currently 32 committed rows in the COURSE table.

f) Write down the DML statement you created and execute it.

Answer: One example of a DML statement you can use to insert one last row into the COURSE table is:

```
INSERT INTO course (course_no, description, cost,
                prerequisite, created_by,
                created_date, modified_by,
                modified_date)
     VALUES (475, 'DBA Tips/Tricks', 1195, 470,
            'DONALDNE', SYSDATE, 'FRANCESN',
            SYSDATE);
```

Upon issuing this DML statement, you should have received a result similar to the following:

```
SQL> INSERT INTO course (course_no, description, cost,
  2                      prerequisite, created_by,
  3                      created_date, modified_by,
```

```
  4                              modified_date)
  5               VALUES (475, 'DBA Tips/Tricks', 1195,
  6                       470, 'DONALDNE', SYSDATE,
  7                       'FRANCESN', SYSDATE);
```

1 row created.

g) What is the name(s) of the datafile(s) that supports the USERS tablespace?

Answer: Upon issuing this query, you should have received a result similar to the following:

```
SQL> SELECT file_name
  2    FROM dba_data_files
  3    WHERE tablespace_name = 'USERS';
```

FILE_NAME

E:\ORACLE\ORADATA\DB00\USERS01.DBF

The name of the datafile that supports the USERS tablespace is USERS01.DBF.

15.1.3 ANSWERS

a) What is the response from the system?

Answer: Upon attempting to issue the STARTUP OPEN command, the response from the system should be similar to:

```
SVRMGR> STARTUP OPEN
```
ORACLE instance started.
Total System Global Area   36437964 bytes
Fixed Size   65484 bytes
Variable Size   19521536 bytes
Database Buffers   16777216 bytes
Redo Buffers   73728 bytes
Database mounted.
ORA-01157: cannot identify data file 2 - file not found
ORA-01110: data file 2:
'E:\ORACLE\ORADATA\DB00\USERS01.DBF'

b) What is the response from the system this time?

Answer: Upon attempting to re-issue the STARTUP OPEN command after copying the backup datafile to the oracle/oradata/db00 (ORADATA) directory, the response from the system should be similar to:

```
SVRMGR> STARTUP OPEN
ORACLE instance started.
Total System Global Area     36437964 bytes
Fixed Size                      65484 bytes
Variable Size                19521536 bytes
Database Buffers             16777216 bytes
Redo Buffers                    73728 bytes
Database mounted.
ORA-01113: file 2 needs media recovery
ORA-01110: data file 2:
'E:\ORACLE\ORADATA\DB00\USERS01.DBF'
```

c) To what level did your database start up: nomount, mount, or open (i.e., what level is it at currently)?

Answer: The database is currently at the "mount" level. It is still unable to open the datafiles since the USERS01.DBF datafile has not yet been fully recovered.

d) Follow the prompts to restore your database. Write down exactly what options are supplied to you, which ones you choose, and the response you receive from the system after making your selection(s).

Answer: If you are using Oracle 8.1.x, chances are that when you issued the following command:

```
SVRMGR> RECOVER DATABASE
```

the response you received from the system was simply:

Media recovery complete.

You received this message because Oracle8i will automatically apply the archived redo logs if they are in the location and format specified in the initialization parameters LOG_ARCHIVE_DEST and LOG_ARCHIVE_FORMAT. However, if you are using versions of Oracle prior to 8.1.x, it is more likely that you would receive a list of messages and prompts similar to the following:

```
ORA-00279: Change 10390 generated at 04/29/00 16:47:11
needed for Thread 1
ORA-00289: Suggestion:
e:\oracle\admin\db00\arch\arch0000000049.arc
ORA-00280: Change 10390 for Thread 1 is in sequence #49
Specify log: {<RET>=suggested | filename | AUTO | CANCEL}
```

After pressing the RETURN key as suggested by this list of messages and prompts, you would probably receive a response from the system similar to the following:

```
Log applied.
Media recovery complete.
```

e) What does this message tell you about the current stage of your recovery process? Is any action required involving the listed archived redo log file? Why?

Answer: The following message:

```
ORA-00278:  Logfile
'e:\oracle\admin\db00\arch\arch0000000131.arc' no longer
needed for this recovery
```

tells you that the datafile has been successfully recovered. Since it has been recovered, the originally recommended archived redo log file is no longer needed for media recovery.

f) What message do you receive? Do not attempt to correct the situation yet. Leave the SQL*Plus session in this state.

Answer: Upon attempting to connect to the database as user STUDENT directly after performing your media recovery, you should have received a response from the system similar to the following:

```
ERROR: ORA-01033: ORACLE initialization or shutdown in
progress
```

g) Write down your theory about what needs to be done to correct this situation (i.e., what startup level must the database be brought to in order to allow users to connect to the database?).

Answer: Although you have performed media recovery successfully, the Database is still only at the mount level. It has not yet been opened. The Database must be opened for users to be able to connect to it.

h) In your SQL*Plus session, re-attempt to connect to the database as user STUDENT. What is the response from the system this time? Why do you think you received this response?

Answer: After re-attempting to connect to the database as user STUDENT, the response from the system this time should be similar to the following:

```
Connected to:
Oracle8i Enterprise Edition Release 8.1.5.0.0 - Production
With the Partitioning and Java options
PL/SQL Release 8.1.5.0.0 - Production
```

You received this response because you opened your Database, an action that enables users to connect to (access) the database.

i) Write a query to determine the number of rows in the COURSE table. Execute it and compare the result you receive with the result you received in Question e) of Lab 15.1.2.

Answer: One example of a query you can use to determine the number of rows in the COURSE table is:

```
SELECT COUNT(*)
  FROM course;
```

This example should already be familiar to you. Upon executing this query, you should have received a result similar to the following:

```
SQL> SELECT COUNT(*)
  2     FROM course;

COUNT(*)
---------
       32
```

There are 32 committed rows currently in the COURSE table. The result received here matches the result received in Question e) of Lab 15.1.2 because, although you inserted one last row in the COURSE table, you shut down the database and simulated a media failure before you issued a COMMIT command. The last INSERT transaction was rolled back during the action of SHUTDOWN IMMEDIATE.

15.1.4 ANSWERS

a) Attempt to start up the database while logged onto Server Manager as INTERNAL by issuing the STARTUP OPEN command. What is the response from the system?

Answer: Upon attempting to issue the STARTUP OPEN command, the response from the system should be similar to:

```
SQL> STARTUP OPEN
ORACLE instance started.
Total System Global Area     36437964 bytes
Fixed Size                      65484 bytes
Variable Size                19521536 bytes
Database Buffers             16777216 bytes
Redo Buffers                    73728 bytes
Database mounted.
ORA-01157: cannot identify data file 2 - file not found
ORA-01110: data file 2:
'E:\ORACLE\ORADATA\DB00\USERS01.DBF'
```

b) Re-attempt to start up the database while logged onto Server Manager as INTERNAL by issuing the STARTUP OPEN command. What is the response from the system this time?

Answer: This time, the response from the system should be similar to:

```
SQL> STARTUP OPEN
ORACLE instance started.
Total System Global Area     36437964 bytes
Fixed Size                      65484 bytes
Variable Size                19521536 bytes
Database Buffers             16777216 bytes
Redo Buffers                    73728 bytes
Database mounted.
ORA-01113: file 2 needs media recovery
ORA-01110: data file 2:
'E:\ORACLE\ORADATA\DB00\USERS01.DBF'
```

c) Open a new SQL*Plus session and attempt to connect to the database as user STUDENT. What is the response from the system? Is your attempt successful?

Answer: Upon attempting to connect to the database as user STUDENT after opening the Database, the response from the system should be similar to:

```
Connected to:
Oracle8i Enterprise Edition Release 8.1.5.0.0 - Production
With the Partitioning and Java options
PL/SQL Release 8.1.5.0.0 - Production
```

If you receive this result, your attempt is successful.

d) Write a query to obtain the number of rows in the COURSE table and execute it. What response do you receive from the system?

Answer: With the example used throughout this chapter, you can determine the number of rows in the COURSE table by issuing the following:

```
SELECT COUNT(*)
  FROM course;
```

Upon executing this query, you should have received a result similar to the following:

```
SQL> SELECT COUNT(*)
  2   FROM course;
 FROM course
      *
ERROR at line 2:
ORA-00376: file 2 cannot be read at this time
ORA-01110: data file 2:
'E:\ORACLE\ORADATA\DB00\USERS01.DBF'
```

e) What are the advantages and disadvantages of allowing user STUDENT to log on when this user does not have access to the datafile just taken offline?

Answer: One advantage of allowing user STUDENT to log on when this user does not have access to the datafile just taken offline (USERS01.DBF) is that the user can still access the rest of the Database. If the user needs to access objects contained in other online datafiles, he or she is not kept from doing so. A disadvantage, however, is that if the data needed by the user is contained in the datafile just taken offline, then the user's success in accessing the Database is not ultimately helpful.

f) In user STUDENT's session, re-execute the query you wrote in Question d) to obtain the number of rows in the COURSE table. What response do you receive from the system this time? Are there any other necessary tasks still left to perform? If so, what are they?

Answer: Upon re-executing the query issued in Question d), you should have received a result similar to the following:

```
SQL> SELECT COUNT(*)
  2     FROM course;
   FROM course
        *
ERROR at line 2:
ORA-00376: file 2 cannot be read at this time
ORA-01110: data file 2:
'E:\ORACLE\ORADATA\DB00\USERS01.DBF'
```

The result received here is exactly the same as the one received in Question d). There are still necessary tasks left to perform. Remember that you explicitly placed the USERS01.DBF datafile offline so that users would still be able to access the Database while you were performing media recovery. Even though the media recovery is now complete, the datafile must now explicitly be placed back online for any of its data to become available to users.

g) In user STUDENT's session, re-execute the query you wrote in Question d) to obtain the number of rows in the COURSE table. What response do you receive from the system this time? Compare the result you receive now with the results you received in both Question e) of Lab 15.1.2 and Question i) of Lab 15.1.3. Do all three result sets match?

Answer: Upon re-executing the query issued in Question d), you should have received a result similar to the following:

```
SQL> SELECT COUNT(*)
  2     FROM course;

COUNT(*)
---------
       32
```

The result received here matches both the result received in Question e) of Lab 15.1.2 and the result received in Question i) of Lab 15.1.3. Therefore, you have successfully recovered your database.

LAB 15.1 SELF-REVIEW QUESTIONS

To test your progress, you should be able to answer the following questions.

1) Which of the following is TRUE about manual archiving?

    a) _____ Log switches take place automatically

    b) _____ The ARCH background process is not running

c) _____ You do not have to be in ARCHIVELOG mode
d) _____ The ARCH background process has been invoked
e) _____ None of the above

2) Which of the following types of failure requires DBA intervention?

a) _____ Instance
b) _____ Media
c) _____ User process
d) _____ All of the above

3) The Oracle Server does not allow you to recover a Database if your backup copy of the Database is not current as of the moment of media failure.

a) _____ True
b) _____ False

4) The different types of backup you can perform are: (Check all that apply.)

a) _____ Fast (online)
b) _____ Cold (offline)
c) _____ Slow (offline)
d) _____ Hot (online)
e) _____ Slow (online)

5) To put the database in ARCHIVELOG mode, you must first do the following:

a) _____ Start the database to mount level
b) _____ Force a manual log switch
c) _____ Start the Instance, then mount and open the Database
d) _____ Alter all of the datafiles to be offline
e) _____ Issue a DML statement followed by a COMMIT

6) If you are in ARCHIVELOG mode, you have invoked automatic archiving.

a) _____ True
b) _____ False

7) To safeguard against possible data loss due to media failure, what SQL command should you include at the end of every transaction?

a) _____ RECOVER DATABASE
b) _____ ALTER SYSTEM SWITCH LOGFILE
c) _____ COMMIT
d) _____ SELECT * FROM dual;

Quiz answers appear in Appendix A, Lab 15.1.

CHAPTER 15

TEST YOUR THINKING

1) Based on the knowledge of backup and recovery you have acquired so far, which method of recovery, online or offline, do you think would be most efficient for a stock brokerage firm on Wall Street? Why? And which do you think would be most efficient for a public library? Why?

2) Oracle makes it impossible to perform an online backup without the database being in ARCHIVELOG mode. Although you do not practice creating an online backup in this set of exercises, why do you think an online backup must be performed with this restriction?

C H A P T E R   1 6

APPLICATION AND SQL OPTIMIZATION

CHAPTER OBJECTIVES

In this chapter, you will learn about:

✔ Using the AUTOTRACE Command
and the TKPROF Utility   Page 366

One or a combination of problems typically causes poor database performance. These problems can be placed into the following categories: database design that does not take performance issues into consideration, incorrect tuning of the Oracle database server, and inefficient SQL statements.

A well-thought-out database design has the greatest positive impact on database performance, followed by efficient SQL statements, and lastly tuning the Oracle Server itself. The next chapter, "Database Tuning and Optimization," discusses the tuning of the Oracle database. This chapter shows you how to determine the efficiency of SQL statements.

The Oracle Server provides you with a number of tools to help you tune SQL statements, specifically the TKPROF utility and the SQL*Plus AUTOTRACE command. These utilities illustrate the execution steps of the Oracle optimizer. Examining the output of these tools allows you to focus on tuning problem areas with alternate SQL statements.

365

LAB 16.1

USING THE AUTOTRACE COMMAND AND TKPROF UTILITY

LAB OBJECTIVES

After this Lab, you will be able to:

✔ Set up SQL*Plus's AUTOTRACE Utility
✔ Determine the Optimizer Mode
✔ Analyze Tables and Indexes
✔ Interpret the Output of the Execution Plan
✔ Use the TKPROF Utility

Before executing a SQL statement, the Oracle optimizer examines it and chooses the best *execution plan*. An *execution plan* is a sequence of steps that needs to be carried out to perform a specific action in the database, such as the return of a result set. The Oracle Server employs two optimizers: the *rule-based* optimizer and the *cost-based* optimizer.

 Oracle continually enhances the optimizer with each subsequent version. Carefully read the release notes to determine the impact on your database.

THE RULE-BASED OPTIMIZER

The rule-based optimizer considers a number of rules when evaluating a SQL statement. Each rule has a ranking, and the rule with a higher ranking is executed first because the optimizer considers it to be more efficient.

Following is the 15-step ranking used by the rule-based optimizer. According to Table 16.1, the access by ROWID is considered the most efficient way to execute a SQL statement. The least desirable way to retrieve data is to access it via a full table scan.

For example, if a WHERE clause condition contains a column with a unique index as well as a non-indexed column, the optimizer creates a plan to process the condition with the unique index first because it is considered to be more efficient. The rule-based approach always assumes that the full table scan is the worst access method.

Table 16.1 ■ Rule-based Optimizer ranking

Rank	Access Path
1	Single row by ROWID
2	Single row by cluster join
3	Single row by hash cluster key with unique or primary key
4	Single row by unique or primary key
5	Cluster join
6	Hash cluster key
7	Indexed cluster key
8	Composite index (consists of more than one column)
9	Single column index
10	Bounded range search on an indexed column, i.e., >= AND <=
11	Unbounded range search on indexed columns
12	Sort-merge join
13	MIN or MAX function on an indexed column
14	ORDER BY clause on indexed column
15	Full table scan

THE COST-BASED OPTIMIZER

The cost-based optimizer takes statistics into consideration rather than rigid rules. To determine the best execution plan, the optimizer takes into account the number of rows in the table and the selectivity of columns, among other factors. These column and table statistics are collected with the ANALYZE command and stored in the data dictionary.

When you compare the two optimizers, you will note that the cost-based optimizer does not assume that the full table scan is the worst access method. In fact, the cost-based optimizer may choose the full table scan, if column(s) in the WHERE clause of a SQL statement exhibit low selectivity, or if a large number of returned rows is expected.

The statistics used by the cost-based optimizer are gathered with the ANALYZE command. You can either compute statistics exactly or estimate them by sampling a subset of the table's rows. The syntax to obtain exact statistics of a table together with the associated indexes is as follows:

```
ANALYZE TABLE course COMPUTE STATISTICS;
Table analyzed.
```

If your database or application employs the cost-based optimizer, you will want to analyze periodically, especially if the number of records in the table and/or the distribution of the values in the columns changes significantly. A DBMS_ JOB (PL/SQL background job), cron job (UNIX background job), or any other job that is set up to run on a regular basis can easily perform this.

CHOOSING AN OPTIMIZER

The choice of optimizer can be determined either at the instance level with the OPTIMIZER_MODE initialization parameter, at the session level with the ALTER SESSION command, or for an individual SQL statement using a *hint*.

If the optimizer is in CHOOSE mode, then the Oracle Server chooses the cost-based optimizer when statistics are present for any of the tables involved in the SQL statement. If none of the tables involved have been analyzed, then the rule-based optimizer is employed.

THE EXECUTION PLAN

The optimizer creates the execution plan showing the individual steps necessary to execute a statement. The most indented step is the first step performed by the statement. If two steps are listed at the same level of indentation, then the steps are executed in the order in which they are listed. Note there is one exception to this rule, the nested loop join, which is discussed shortly.

The following text shows a SQL statement and its execution plan. You can obtain the execution plan using either the AUTOTRACE command or the TKPROF utility, which are both discussed later in this chapter.

```
SELECT course_no, description
  FROM course
 WHERE course_no = 122;
Execution Plan
----------------------------------------------------------
0        SELECT STATEMENT Optimizer=CHOOSE
         (Cost=1 Card=1 Bytes=53)
1    0     TABLE ACCESS (BY INDEX ROWID) OF 'COURSE'
           (Cost=1 Card=1 Bytes=53)
2    1        INDEX (UNIQUE SCAN) OF 'CRSE_PK' (UNIQUE)
```

The numbers at the far left indicate the line or step number, and the numbers immediately to the right indicate the parent step number. The most indented step is line number two, which will be executed first. This step performs an index lookup of the primary key index, CRSE_PK. The lookup of the value for COURSE_NO 122 retrieves the ROWID from the index. The next step, line number one, retrieves the row from the COURSE table via the ROWID.

In this example, the text in line 0 indicates that the optimizer is set in CHOOSE mode. Since the table was analyzed beforehand, the cost-based optimizer is used. Notice that each line shows the cost in parentheses.

The COST value in each step is an indicator of the amount of work involved with each step. Using this, you can focus on tuning the steps with the highest COST. The COST is a relative number that is determined using several system parameters, including the amount of memory and expected CPU time required to execute the step. The CARD parameter indicates the cardinality of the step—that is, the number of rows that the optimizer expects to process. The last parameter, BYTES, indicates the size in bytes expected for the step.

OBTAINING AN EXECUTION PLAN

An execution plan can be obtained using one of several methods. The simplest way is to use the AUTOTRACE command in SQL*Plus. The Oracle TKPROF utility is an alternate method which allows you to collect information about multiple SQL statements and sort them by specified criteria, such as by execution time or by CPU usage. The exercises in this lab illustrate the basics of the AUTOTRACE command and the TKPROF utility.

HINTS

If you are not satisfied with the plan produced by the optimizer, you can change it by re-writing the statement using an alternative syntax, or by using hints. *Hints* are simply directives to the optimizer. Using hints, you can force the optimizer to use a particular index, or to choose a specific join order. In certain instances, this may result in a better plan. For example, if you know that a particular index is more selective for certain queries, you can tell the optimizer to use this index instead. The following example contains a hint (which looks like a comment with a plus sign) that specifies that the rule-based optimizer should be used.

```
SELECT /*+ RULE */ *
  FROM student
 WHERE student_id = 123;
```

JOIN TYPES

Before examining the execution plan in more detail, you need to understand the different join types the Oracle Server performs. Choosing the correct type of join, and joining tables in the proper order, has a significant impact on how efficiently your SQL statement executes. Four types of join operations are available to the Oracle Server: *nested loop join, sort-merge join, hash join,* and *cluster join*. This lab discusses only the first three, which are the most popular.

THE NESTED LOOP JOIN

For the nested loop join, the optimizer picks a *driving table*, which is the first table in the join chain. Suppose that, in the following SQL statement, the driving table is the STUDENT table.

```
SELECT /*+ RULE */ *
  FROM enrollment e, student s
 WHERE s.student_id = e.student_id;
```

A full table scan is always executed on the driving table. Therefore, in this example, a full table scan of the STUDENT table is performed. For each row of the STUDENT table, the primary key index of the ENROLLMENT table is then probed to determine if the WHERE clause condition is satisfied. If so, the row is included in the result set. This probing is repeated until all the rows of the STUDENT table have been tested.

The following execution plan describes a nested loop join:

```
Execution Plan
------------------------------------------------------------
0        SELECT STATEMENT Optimizer=RULE
1    0     NESTED LOOPS
2    1       TABLE ACCESS (FULL) OF 'STUDENT'
3    1       TABLE ACCESS (BY INDEX ROWID) OF 'ENROLLMENT'
4    3         INDEX (RANGE SCAN) OF 'ENR_PK' (UNIQUE)
```

The execution plan for a nested loop is read differently from other execution plans because it contains a loop. The most indented row is NOT the first to be executed, but is rather probed for every row of the driving table.

The nested loop join is typically the fastest join when the goal is to retrieve the first row as quickly as possible. It is also the most efficient join type when you access less than approximately 10% of the total rows from the tables involved. (This percentage will vary depending on the total number of rows returned, the values of parameters in your init.ora file, and the version of Oracle you are running. Still, this metric provides a general indication of the situations in which this type of join would be useful.)

The selection of the driving table is crucial to good performance of the nested loop join. You should choose the table that returns the least number of records for the driving table, since this will require fewer records to be probed in each subsequent join.

SORT-MERGE JOIN

The sort-merge join performs sorts on the tables involved, then merges the sorted result set. In the following example, a full table scan is performed on the ENROLLMENT table. Then, the result is sorted by the joining column, and the STUDENT table is scanned and sorted. The two result sets are merged, and the matching rows are returned for output. Note that the first result row is returned only after all the records from both tables have been processed.

```
SELECT /*+ USE_MERGE (e, s)*/ *
  FROM enrollment e, student s
 WHERE s.student_id = e.student_id;
```

The sort-merge join is typically used when a large number of rows in a table are retrieved. Sort-merge joins are also performed when no indexes exist on the table to support the join condition or when the indexes are disabled through the use of a function. You can force the use of a sort-merge join by using the USE_MERGE hint as shown in the statement above.

```
Execution Plan
------------------------------------------------------------
0   SELECT STATEMENT Optimizer=HINT: CHOOSE
    (Cost=37 Card=226 Bytes=38420)
1     0   MERGE JOIN (Cost=37 Card=226 Bytes=38420)
2     1     SORT (JOIN) (Cost=10 Card=226 Bytes=10622)
3     2       TABLE ACCESS (FULL) OF 'ENROLLMENT'
                (Cost=2 Card=226 Bytes=10622)
4     1     SORT (JOIN) (Cost=27 Card=268 Bytes=32964)
5     4       TABLE ACCESS (FULL) OF 'STUDENT'
                (Cost=4 Card=268 Bytes=32964)
```

HASH JOIN

The hash join is only available if you use the cost-based optimizer and if the init.ora parameter HASH_JOIN_ENABLED is set to TRUE. During a hash join, the Oracle Server performs a full table scan on each of the tables being joined and splits each into many partitions in memory. The Oracle Server then builds a *hash table* from one of these partitions and probes it against the partition of the other table as shown in the statement below. The hash join typically outperforms the sort-merge join when the tables involved are relatively small.

```
SELECT /*+ USE_HASH (e, s)*/ *
  FROM enrollment e, student s
 WHERE s.student_id = e.student_id;
Execution Plan
```

```
0   SELECT STATEMENT Optimizer=CHOOSE:
    (Cost=10 Card=226 Bytes=38420)
1     0   HASH JOIN (Cost=10 Card=226 Bytes=38420)
2     1     TABLE ACCESS (FULL) OF 'ENROLLMENT'
              (Cost=2 Card=226 Bytes=10622)
3     1     TABLE ACCESS (FULL) OF 'STUDENT'
              (Cost=4 Card=268 Bytes=32964)
```

LAB 16.1 EXERCISES

16.1.1 SET UP SQL*PLUS'S AUTOTRACE UTILITY

a) Log into SQL*Plus as user STUDENT. Issue the following command. What is the response?

```
SET AUTOTRACE ON
```

_____

_____

b) Find the script plustrce.sql in the **ORACLE_HOME**/sqlplus/ admin directory. View the file and read the instructions. Explain the purpose of this script.

_____

_____

c) Connect as user SYS (the password, if you have not already changed it, is CHANGE_ON_INSTALL) and run the script. Then grant the role to user STUDENT. Write down the results of these actions.

_____

_____

If you change the password for user SYS, MAKE SURE YOU DO NOT FORGET THE NEW PASSWORD! Write it down and keep it in a secure place.

d) Find and view the script utlxplan.sql in the **ORACLE_HOME**/ rdbms/admin/utlxplan.sql directory. Explain the purpose of this script and then execute it. Next connect as user STUDENT in SQL*Plus and execute it once more.

_____

_____

e) Issue the following command as user STUDENT and describe the result:

```
SET AUTOTRACE ON
```

_____

_____

f) Issue the following SELECT statement with the AUTOTRACE command still set to ON. What do you observe?

```
SELECT zip, city
  FROM zipcode
 WHERE state = 'FL';
```

_____

_____

g) The following text describes syntax options for the AUTOTRACE command. Explain the meanings for different variations of these options (e.g., what kind of output you will include and/or what kind of output you will exclude), including the difference between the ON option and the TRACEONLY option.

```
SET AUTOT[RACE] {OFF|ON|TRACE[ONLY]} [EXP[LAIN]] [STAT[ISTICS]]
```

_____

_____

**16.1.2 DETERMINE THE
OPTIMIZER MODE**

a) While logged on as user SYSTEM, issue the following query in Server Manager. Describe the result, particularly as it refers to the optimizer mode.

```
SELECT name, value
  FROM v$parameter
 WHERE name = 'optimizer_mode';
```

Alternatively, you can also issue the following command in SQL*Plus on Oracle versions above 7.3:

```
SHOW PARAMETER optimizer
```

---

b) Only perform this exercise if the value for the optimizer_mode parameter in your init.ora file is not set to CHOOSE.

Add or change the optimizer_mode parameter in your init.ora file so that it is equal to CHOOSE, then restart the database. Re-execute the command from Question a). What is the result?

16.1.3 ANALYZE TABLES AND INDEXES

Log into SQL*Plus as user STUDENT.

a) For each of the tables in the STUDENT schema, issue the following command. Create a master/slave script to simplify the task.

```
ANALYZE TABLE <tablename> ESTIMATE STATISTICS;
```

---

b) While logged into SQL*Plus as user STUDENT, execute the following commands. What do you observe about the values in the columns of the USER_TABLES data dictionary view after each step?

```
SELECT num_rows, avg_row_len, sample_size, last_analyzed
  FROM user_tables
 WHERE table_name = 'ZIPCODE';
```

```
ANALYZE TABLE zipcode DELETE STATISTICS;

SELECT num_rows, avg_row_len, sample_size, last_analyzed
  FROM user_tables
WHERE table_name = 'ZIPCODE';

ANALYZE TABLE zipcode ESTIMATE STATISTICS;
```

16.1.4 INTERPRET THE OUTPUT OF THE EXECUTION PLAN

The following is the basic test query you will be using for this exercise. Save it in a file called studenttest01.sql in your adhoc directory.

```
SELECT /*+ RULE */ *
  FROM    student st, enrollment e,
          zipcode z
  WHERE   st.student_id = e.student_id
    AND   st.zip = z.zip
ORDER BY st.registration_date DESC, st.last_name ASC,
          st.first_name ASC;
```

a) Log in as user STUDENT and set AUTOTRACE ON together with the TRACEONLY EXPLAIN option. Then, execute the script studenttest01.sql and spool the output to a file named studenttest01.log. According to the execution plan, which step is executed first?

b) Copy studenttest01.sql to a new file named studenttest02.sql. Modify studenttest02.sql to change the order of the tables in the FROM clause. The final version of the FROM clause should list the tables in this order: ZIPCODE, STUDENT,

ENROLLMENT. Save the file and execute the statement. How does the execution plan change, if at all?

_____

_____

c) Copy studenttest01.sql to a new file named studenttest03.sql. Modify studenttest03.sql by changing the SELECT list line to include a hint that tells the optimizer to use the STU_ZIP_FK_I index on the STUDENT table. Record the effect this change has on the execution plan.

_____

_____

16.1.5 USE THE TKPROF UTILITY

a) Open your init.ora file and record the values for the parameters USER_DUMP_DEST and MAX_DUMP_FILE_SIZE. Also make sure the parameter for TIMED_STATISTICS is set to TRUE. If this value is not set to TRUE, shut down your database, then add or uncomment the line for the parameter and restart your database. Explain the purposes of these three parameters.

_____

_____

b) Log in as user STUDENT and issue the following SQL statements. Record the result you receive after executing each statement.

```
CREATE INDEX stu_i_last_name ON student(last_name);

ANALYZE INDEX stu_i_last_name COMPUTE STATISTICS;

ALTER SESSION SET SQL_TRACE = TRUE;
```

_____

_____

c) Execute the following SQL statements. What feedback do you receive when you issue the last SQL statement?

```
SELECT 'DONALD '||
       TO_CHAR(SYSDATE, 'MM/DD HH24:MI')
  FROM DUAL;

SELECT student_id
  FROM student
 WHERE last_name LIKE 'Rodri%';

SELECT student_id
  FROM student
 WHERE last_name LIKE '%odri%';

ALTER SESSION SET SQL_TRACE = FALSE;
```

d) Identify your trace file in the USER_DUMP_DEST directory. You can either do this by listing the files by date and time or by searching through the files where the file contains the string 'DONALD'. This illustrates the usefulness of tagging a file with an identifier and the date and time. You can search for the file with this identifier using the Find utility if you are using the Windows NT operating system or by using the grep command on the UNIX operating system. Write down your filename.

e) Run the TKPROF utility at your operating system prompt. The simplified syntax is as follows:

```
C:\>tkprof <trace_file> <formatted_output_file>
explain=schema/password sys=no
```

In an NT environment, the command you execute may look similar to the following:

```
C:\>tkprof c:\oracle\admin\db00\udump\ora00125.trc
c:\guest\ora00125.txt explain=student/learn sys=no
```

Note that the name of the TKPROF executable program can vary depending on the Oracle version and operating system. If the TKPROF executable program is not in your path, then prefix the program with the path and drive name. You also may not have permission to write to the USER_DUMP_DEST directory, and therefore you need to store the formatted output file elsewhere; in the previous example, it is stored in the c:\guest directory. Add the optional parameter SYS=NO to avoid showing Oracle Server-generated SQL statements. Record the command you execute to run TKPROF.

When you execute your command, TKPROF returns only the following message if it did not encounter any errors:

```
TKPROF: Release 8.1.5.00 - Production on Thu May 4
21:30:10 2000
(c) Copyright 1999 Oracle Corporation.  All rights
reserved.
```

If TKPROF returns with syntax errors, fix the necessary errors. Typically the errors relate to file permissions problems or incorrectly spelled file or directory names.

---

f) Use your text editor to view the formatted trace file. Determine if the statements issued against the STUDENT table used the index on the LAST_NAME column.

---

g) Drop the index created in Question b) to restore the schema back to its original state.

LAB 16.1 EXERCISE ANSWERS

16.1.1 ANSWERS

a) Log into SQL*Plus as user STUDENT. Issue the following command. What is the response?

```
SET AUTOTRACE ON

SP2-0613: Unable to verify PLAN_TABLE format or existence
SP2-0611: Error enabling EXPLAIN report
SP2-0618: Cannot find the Session Identifier.  Check
PLUSTRACE role is enabled
SP2-0611: Error enabling STATISTICS report
```

*Answer: SQL*Plus returns several errors that indicate that the STUDENT user is missing some objects and roles that it needs to perform an AUTOTRACE.*

b) Find the script plustrce.sql in the **ORACLE_HOME**/sqlplus/admin directory. View the file and read the instructions. Explain the purpose of this script.

Answer: The script creates the PLUSTRACE role.

The script must be run as the SYS user and it grants access to dynamic performance views. Because the PLUSTRACE role is granted to the DBA role with the ADMIN option, any user with the DBA role can grant the PLUSTRACE role to other users.

c) Connect as user SYS (the password, if you have not already changed it, is CHANGE_ON_INSTALL) and run the script. Then grant the role to user STUDENT. Write down the results of these actions.

Answer: By granting the role to user STUDENT, you have granted this user SELECT privileges on these views.

```
GRANT plustrace TO student;
Grant succeeded.
```

d) Find and view the script utlxplan.sql in the **ORACLE_HOME**/rdbms/admin directory. Explain the purpose of this script and then execute it. Next, connect as user STUDENT in SQL*Plus and execute it once more.

Answer: This script creates a table called PLAN_TABLE. This table is used to store the execution plan for AUTOTRACE and TKPROF.

e) Issue the following command as user STUDENT and describe the result:

```
SET AUTOTRACE ON
```

Answer: The SQL*Plus prompt is returned to you, indicating that the AUTOTRACE command is now ready to show the execution plan.

f) Issue the following SELECT statement with the AUTOTRACE command still set to ON. What do you observe?

```
SELECT zip, city
  FROM zipcode
 WHERE state = 'FL';
```

Answer: First, the result of the SELECT statement is returned, followed by the execution plan. Lastly, you see a set of statistics indicating the resources required to process the SQL statement.

The result may look similar to the following output.

```
ZIP    CITY
-----  -------------------------
33431  Boca Raton


Execution Plan
----------------------------------------------------------
0        SELECT STATEMENT Optimizer=CHOOSE
1    0     TABLE ACCESS (FULL) OF 'ZIPCODE'


Statistics
----------------------------------------------------------
         0    recursive calls
         4    db block gets
        10    consistent gets
         0    physical reads
         0    redo size
      1149    bytes sent via SQL*Net to client
       687    bytes received via SQL*Net from client
         4    SQL*Net roundtrips to/from client
         1    sorts (memory)
         0    sorts (disk)
         1    rows processed
```

The statistics displayed last are relevant to database tuning. Of the statistics listed, those statistics necessary for obtaining information about the database's current *cache hit ratio*, along with the definition of this term, are discussed in Chapter 17, "Database Tuning and Optimization."

g) The following text describes syntax options for the AUTOTRACE command. Explain the meanings for different variations of these options (e.g., what kind of output you will include and/or what kind of output you will exclude), including the difference between the ON option and the TRACEONLY option.

```
SET AUTOT[RACE] {OFF|ON|TRACE[ONLY]} [EXP[LAIN]] [STAT[ISTICS]]
```

Answer: The AUTOTRACE command includes several options which allow you to display the execution plan, the statistics, or both.

The SET AUTOTRACE TRACEONLY option only shows the execution plan and the statistics, but excludes the resulting query output. The command SET AUTOTRACE TRACEONLY EXPLAIN shows the execution plan only and suppresses the statistics and result set. To disable the AUTOTRACE command, issue the SET AUTOTRACE OFF command.

16.1.2 ANSWERS

a) While logged on as user SYSTEM, issue the following query in Server Manager. Describe the result, particularly as it refers to the optimizer mode.

Answer: After executing this query, you should have received a result similar to the following:

```
SQL> SELECT name, value
  2     FROM v$parameter
  3     WHERE name = 'optimizer_mode';
```

NAME	VALUE
optimizer_mode	CHOOSE

Here, the optimizer mode is set to CHOOSE.

b) Only perform this exercise if the value for the optimizer_mode parameter in your init.ora file is not set to CHOOSE.

Add or change the optimizer_mode parameter in your init.ora file to be equal to CHOOSE, then restart the database. Re-execute the command from Question a). What is the result?

Answer: After executing this query, you should have received a result similar to the following:

```
SQL> SELECT name, value
  2    FROM v$parameter
  3   WHERE name = 'optimizer_mode';

NAME            VALUE
-------------   ------
optimizer_mode  CHOOSE
```

Here, as in the answer to Question a), the optimizer mode is set to CHOOSE.

16.1.3 ANSWERS

a) For each of the tables in the STUDENT schema, issue the following command. Create a master/slave script to simplify the task.

```
ANALYZE TABLE <tablename> ESTIMATE STATISTICS;
```

Answer: *The following master/slave, also known as "the SQL to generate SQL" or "dynamic SQL," script executes the ANALYZE TABLE statements for all the tables in the current user's schema.*

```
- File Name: analyze.sql
- Purpose: Analyze all the tables in a user's schema
- Created Date: May 1, 2000
- Author: Alice Rischert
SET PAGESIZE 0
SET LINESIZE 80
SET FEEDBACK OFF
SET TERM OFF
SPOOL analyze.out
SELECT 'ANALYZE TABLE '|| table_name ||
       ' ESTIMATE STATISTICS;'
  FROM user_tables;
SPOOL OFF
SET PAGESIZE 20
SET LINESIZE 100
SET FEEDBACK ON
SET TERM ON
```

Execute the analyze.sql script. If the sample size is omitted, as in this example, the Oracle Server estimates the statistics based on 1064 rows. If the table contains less than 1064 rows, the statistics are computed, rather than estimated. The following is an example of an ANALYZE command with a sample size:

```
SQL> ANALYZE TABLE course ESTIMATE STATISTICS SAMPLE 40
PERCENT;
Table analyzed.
```

The SAMPLE integer specifies 40 percent of the rows to be examined to determine the statistics. If more than 50 percent is specified as a sample size, the Oracle Server reads all the data and computes the statistics. Instead of using a percentage, you can also choose the exact number of rows to be analyzed.

```
ANALYZE TABLE course ESTIMATE STATISTICS SAMPLE 5000 ROWS;
```

ANALYZING THE ENTIRE SCHEMA

Rather than writing a dynamic SQL script to analyze all of the tables and indexes in the schema, you can execute the PL/SQL procedure GATHER_SCHEMA_STATS from the DBMS_STATS package and pass the schema name as a parameter.

```
SQL> EXECUTE DBMS_STATS.GATHER_SCHEMA_STATS('STUDENT');
PL/SQL procedure successfully completed.
```

Be sure to analyze your schema periodically, especially after the distribution of the data changes significantly, since these changes may affect the optimizer's execution plan.

If you add an index to a table after you've analyzed the table, no statistics about the index are available. You subsequently need to analyze the index as well! The syntax to analyze the index only is as follows:

ANALYZE INDEX <INDEX_NAME> COMPUTE STATISTICS;

b) While logged into SQL*Plus as user STUDENT, execute the following commands. What do you observe about the values in the columns of the USER_TABLES data dictionary view after each step?

Answer: The columns in the data dictionary view USER_TABLES are filled in with statistics values when a table is analyzed, and are set to NULL when the statistics are deleted.

```
SQL> ANALYZE TABLE zipcode ESTIMATE STATISTICS;
Table analyzed.
```

```
SQL> SELECT num_rows, avg_row_len, sample_size,
  2            last_analyzed
  3     FROM user_tables
  4     WHERE table_name = 'ZIPCODE';
NUM_ROWS   AVG_ROW_LEN SAMPLE_SIZE LAST_ANAL
---------  ----------- ----------- ---------
     227            56        1064 30-APR-00

1 row selected.

SQL> ANALYZE TABLE zipcode DELETE STATISTICS;
Table analyzed.

SQL> SELECT num_rows, avg_row_len, sample_size,
  2            last_analyzed
  3     FROM user_tables
  4     WHERE table_name = 'ZIPCODE';
NUM_ROWS   AVG_ROW_LEN SAMPLE_SIZE LAST_ANAL
---------  ----------- ----------- ---------


1 row selected.

SQL> ANALYZE TABLE zipcode ESTIMATE STATISTICS;
Table analyzed.
```

The data dictionary is updated as a result of executing the ANALYZE command. The new values can be seen in a number of data dictionary views, including USER_TABLES, USER_TAB_COLUMNS, USER_INDEXES, and USER_IND_COLUMNS.

16.1.4 ANSWERS

a) Log in as user STUDENT and set AUTOTRACE ON together with the TRACEONLY EXPLAIN option. Then, execute the script studenttest01.sql and spool the output to a file named studenttest01.log. According to the execution plan, which step is executed first?

Answer: In this statement, the first step executed is the access to the ZIPCODE table via a full table scan (Line 4).

In a nested loop join, the most indented row is not the first to be executed. The first step is the full table access of the ZIPCODE table. For every row that is read from the ZIPCODE table, the index of the STUDENT table, called STU_ZIP_FK_I, is probed to see if the zip code exists in the STUDENT table. Once all the records have been probed for the condition in the WHERE clause, another nested loop is performed. This time, the result from the prior join is probed against the ENR_PK index to determine if the student ID exists in the ENROLLMENT table.

Your execution plan may look similar to the following.

```
SET AUTOTRACE TRACEONLY EXPLAIN

SQL> SELECT /*+ RULE */ *
  2     FROM    student st, enrollment e,
  3             zipcode z
  4     WHERE   st.student_id = e.student_id
  5     AND     st.zip = z.zip
  6   ORDER BY  st.registration_date DESC, st.last_name
  7             ASC, st.first_name ASC;


Execution Plan
----------------------------------------------------------
   0        SELECT STATEMENT Optimizer=HINT: RULE
   1    0     SORT (ORDER BY)
   2    1       NESTED LOOPS
   3    2         NESTED LOOPS
   4    3           TABLE ACCESS (FULL) OF 'ZIPCODE'
   5    3           TABLE ACCESS (BY INDEX ROWID) OF
                      'STUDENT'
   6    5             INDEX (RANGE SCAN) OF 'STU_ZIP_FK_I'
                        (NON-UNIQUE)
   7    2         TABLE ACCESS (BY INDEX ROWID) OF
                    'ENROLLMENT'
   8    7           INDEX (RANGE SCAN) OF 'ENR_PK' (UNIQUE)
```

Note that the Oracle Server may choose a different access path and your resulting execution plan may look different depending on the version of Oracle you are using and the configuration of your database, among other things.

A hint is always enclosed by either a multi-line comment with a plus sign (/*+ */) or a single line comment with a plus sign (--+).

Table 16.2 displays examples of some commonly used hints.

Note that all hints, except for the RULE hint, use the cost-based optimizer.

Table 16.2 ■ Commonly-used hints

Hint	Purpose
FIRST_ROWS	This hint uses the cost-based optimizer to return the *first* row as quickly as possible.
ALL_ROWS	This hint uses the cost-based optimizer to return *all* rows as quickly as possible.
CHOOSE	This hint chooses between the cost-based optimizer and the rule-based optimizer, depending on the presence of statistics. If statistics are available, the cost-based optimizer then defaults to the ALL_ROWS costing model.
RULE	This hint chooses the rule-based optimizer.
ORDERED	This hint joins the tables in the order listed in the FROM clause using the cost-based optimizer.
INDEX(tablename indexname)	The index hint tells the cost-based optimizer to perform an index scan on a specified index. Specify the name of the table on which the index is built. **Note: If you use an alias on the table, use the alias name instead of the table name.**

JOINS AND THE ALL_ROWS AND FIRST_ROWS HINTS

If you choose the FIRST_ROWS hint in a SQL statement involving a join, the Oracle Server most often uses the nested loop join, since it most quickly retrieves the first row. In the case of an ALL_ROWS hint, the Oracle Server typically uses the sort-merge join or the hash join.

b) Copy studenttest01.sql to a new file named studenttest02.sql. Modify studenttest02.sql to change the order of the tables in the FROM clause. The final version of the FROM clause should list the tables in this order: ZIPCODE, STUDENT, ENROLLMENT. Save the file and execute the statement. How does the execution plan change, if at all?

Answer: Upon executing this query, you should have received a result set similar to the following:

```
SQL> SELECT /*+ RULE */ *
  2     FROM   zipcode z, student st,
```

```
3              enrollment e
4    WHERE     st.student_id = e.student_id
5       AND    st.zip = z.zip
6   ORDER BY   st.registration_date DESC, st.last_name
7              ASC, st.first_name ASC;
```

Execution Plan
```
------------------------------------------------------------
0       SELECT STATEMENT Optimizer=HINT: RULE
1    0    SORT (ORDER BY)
2    1      NESTED LOOPS
3    2        NESTED LOOPS
4    3          TABLE ACCESS (FULL) OF 'ENROLLMENT'
5    3          TABLE ACCESS (BY INDEX ROWID) OF
                'STUDENT'
6    5            INDEX (UNIQUE SCAN) OF 'STU_PK'
                  (UNIQUE)
7    2        TABLE ACCESS (BY INDEX ROWID) OF 'ZIPCODE'
8    7          INDEX (UNIQUE SCAN) OF 'ZIP_PK' (UNIQUE)
```

The execution plan changes. The first step to be executed is now the full table scan of the ENROLLMENT table.

The optimizer chooses the join order based on the order of the tables listed in the FROM clause, provided the WHERE clause conditions of the tables are equivalent. For example, a WHERE clause listing the STUDENT_ID column of the STUDENT table and the STUDENT_ID column of the ENROLLMENT table are equivalent WHERE clause conditions. Both are primary key columns of their respective tables, and therefore, both have a unique index and their ranking is the same.

```
SELECT *
  FROM student s, enrollment e
 WHERE s.student_id = e.student_id;
```

Comparing the execution plans of the same SQL statement issued under the rule-based and cost-based optimizer, you notice that the join order is different.

```
SQL> SELECT /*+ RULE */ *
  2    FROM student s, enrollment e
  3   WHERE s.student_id = e.student_id;
```
Execution Plan
```
------------------------------------------------------------
0       SELECT STATEMENT Optimizer=HINT: RULE
1    0    NESTED LOOPS
```

```
2     1         TABLE ACCESS (FULL) OF 'ENROLLMENT'
3     1         TABLE ACCESS (BY INDEX ROWID) OF 'STUDENT'
4     3             INDEX (UNIQUE SCAN) OF 'STU_PK' (UNIQUE)
```

For the rule-based optimizer, the last table listed in the FROM clause is the driving table.

```
SQL> SELECT /*+ FIRST_ROWS */ *
  2  FROM enrollment e, student s
  3 WHERE s.student_id = e.student_id;
Execution Plan
------------------------------------------------------------
0         SELECT STATEMENT Optimizer=HINT: FIRST_ROWS
          (Cost=228 Card=226 Bytes=35482)
1    0      NESTED LOOPS (Cost=228 Card=226 Bytes=35482)
2    1        TABLE ACCESS (FULL) OF 'ENROLLMENT'
               (Cost=2 Card=226 Bytes=10622)
3    1        TABLE ACCESS (BY INDEX ROWID) OF 'STUDENT'
               (Cost=1 Card=268 Bytes=29480)
4    3          INDEX (UNIQUE SCAN) OF 'STU_PK' (UNIQUE)
```

The cost-based optimizer chooses the first table listed in the FROM clause unless you use the ORDERED hint to override the table order.

The driving table should be the table that retrieves the smallest result set. Try to eliminate as many rows as possible for the driving table by choosing selective indexes or restrictive criteria. Having a small driving table is more efficient, because subsequent joins do not need to examine as many records.

The following query result shows information about the student with the ID of 123 who lives in the state of New York. In this example, it is best to first start the join with the STUDENT table as the driving table because the WHERE condition s.STUDENT_ID = 123 returns, at most, one row. The condition z.STATE = 'NY' can yield multiple rows, and the STATE column is not indexed, therefore causing a full table scan. This also means that you only need to retrieve one row from the STUDENT table and one row from the ZIPCODE table. If you start the join with the ZIPCODE table, you need to probe many more records to retrieve the final result.

```
SQL> SELECT last_name, state, city
  2     FROM student s, zipcode z
  3    WHERE s.zip = z.zip
  4      AND s.student_id = 123
  5      AND z.state = 'NY';
```

Execution Plan

```
-----------------------------------------------------------
0         SELECT STATEMENT Optimizer=CHOOSE
          (Cost=3 Card=1 Bytes=55)
1     0     NESTED LOOPS (Cost=3 Card=1 Bytes=55)
2     1       TABLE ACCESS (BY INDEX ROWID) OF 'STUDENT'
              (Cost=2 Card=1 Bytes=31)
3     2         INDEX (UNIQUE SCAN) OF 'STU_PK' (UNIQUE)
                (Cost=1 Card=2)
4     1       TABLE ACCESS (BY INDEX ROWID) OF 'ZIPCODE'
              (Cost=1 Card=23 Bytes=552)
5     4         INDEX (UNIQUE SCAN) OF 'ZIP_PK' (UNIQUE)
```

c) Copy studenttest01.sql to a new file named studenttest03.sql. Modify studenttest03.sql by changing the SELECT list line to include a hint that tells the optimizer to use the STU_ZIP_FK_I index on the STUDENT table. Record the effect this change has on the execution plan.

Answer: The execution plan uses the cost-based optimizer. It also uses the index hint, forcing the use of the STU_ZIP_FK_I index.

The hint forces the scan of the STU_ZIP_FK_I index on the STUDENT table. This index is actually a very poor choice, but the example demonstrates how you can override the optimizer's index choice.

```
SQL> SELECT - -+ INDEX(st stu_zip_fk_i)
  2             *
  3     FROM    zipcode z, student st,
  4             enrollment e
  5     WHERE   st.student_id = e.student_id
  6       AND   st.zip = z.zip
  7  ORDER BY st.registration_date DESC, st.last_name
  8             ASC, st.first_name ASC;
Execution Plan
-----------------------------------------------------------
0         SELECT STATEMENT Optimizer=CHOOSE
          (Cost=296 Card=226 Bytes=46330)
1     0     SORT (ORDER BY) (Cost=296 Card=226 Bytes=46330)
2     1       HASH JOIN (Cost=265 Card=226 Bytes=46330)
3     2         TABLE ACCESS (FULL) OF 'ZIPCODE'
                (Cost=2 Card=227 Bytes=10896)
4     2         HASH JOIN (Cost=259 Card=226 Bytes=35482)
5     4           TABLE ACCESS (FULL) OF 'ENROLLMENT'
```

```
                    (Cost=2 Card=226 Bytes=10622)
   6      4          TABLE ACCESS (BY INDEX ROWID) OF
                     'STUDENT' (Cost=253 Card=268 Bytes=29480)
   7      6             INDEX (FULL SCAN) OF 'STU_ZIP_FK_I'
                       (NON-UNIQUE) (Cost=5 Card=268)
```

INCORRECTLY SPECIFYING HINTS

If you incorrectly specify a hint, the optimizer ignores the hint and you are left to wonder why the hint does not work.

Here is an example of an index hint that is specified incorrectly.

```
SELECT --+ INDEX(student stu_zip_fk_i)
       *
```

Instead of the table name, STUDENT, the table alias, st, should be used because an alias is used in the FROM clause of the statement. This incorrectly specified hint causes the optimizer to ignore the hint.

ALTERNATIVE SQL STATEMENTS

Poorly performing SQL statements can sometimes be rewritten for faster execution. For example, the following SQL statement determines which students are not enrolled in any classes:

```
SELECT student_id
  FROM student
 WHERE student_id NOT IN
       (SELECT student_id
          FROM enrollment
       );
```

The statement could also be written as a set operation or as a statement that uses a NOT EXISTS operator.

```
SELECT student_id
  FROM student
MINUS
SELECT student_id
  FROM enrollment;

SELECT student_id
  FROM student s
 WHERE NOT EXISTS
       (SELECT NULL
```

```
    FROM enrollment
   WHERE s.student_id = student_id
);
```

INDEXES AND THE OPTIMIZER

When you look at the execution plan of a statement, you may notice that an index is not used if a function modifies a database column.

Assume the STUDENT table's EMPLOYER column is indexed. Then, the following statement does not use the index on the column because the column is modified by a function in the WHERE clause:

```
SELECT *
  FROM student
 WHERE UPPER(employer) = 'SMITH';
```

Sometimes the Oracle Server will also determine not to use an index on a column because the Oracle Server considers it faster to retrieve the rows than searching through the index, if the column is not very *selective*—that is, if the column does not have many distinct values. Another reason why the Oracle Server may not use an index is if the Oracle Server performs an implicit data type conversion, as in the following example:

```
SELECT *
  FROM zipcode
 WHERE zip = 10025;
```

Here the optimizer will rewrite the query as

```
SELECT *
  FROM zipcode
 WHERE TO_NUMBER(zip) = 10025;
```

This kind of statement causes the index on the ZIP column of VARCHAR2 data type to be disabled. Note that numeric columns compared with character literals are not affected in the same way because the implicit data conversion is done on the character literal. You can supplement your learning of SQL optimization with one of the other books in this series, *The Oracle SQL Interactive Workbook,* by Alex Morrison and Alice Rischert.

16.1.5 ANSWERS

a) Open your init.ora file and record the values for the parameters USER_DUMP_DEST and MAX_DUMP_FILE_SIZE. Also, make sure the parameter for TIMED_STATISTICS is set to TRUE. If this value is not set to TRUE, shut down your database, then add or uncomment the line for the parameter and restart your database. Explain the purposes of these three parameters.

Answer: The value for the USER_DUMP_DEST parameter specifies the directory where trace files are stored. The MAX_DUMP_FILE_SIZE parameter specifies the maximum file size for each individual trace file. The parameter TIMED_STATISTICS is set to TRUE to enable the collecting of timed execution statistics in your TKPROF results.

b) Log in as user STUDENT and issue the following SQL statements. Record the result you receive after each statement.

```
CREATE INDEX stu_i_last_name ON student(last_name);

ANALYZE INDEX stu_i_last_name COMPUTE STATISTICS;

ALTER SESSION SET SQL_TRACE=TRUE;
```

Answer: The CREATE INDEX statement returns the INDEX CREATED message, and the ANALYZE command reports the message INDEX ANALYZED, indicating the newly created index is analyzed. Lastly, the ALTER SESSION command displays the message SESSION ALTERED.

The ALTER SESSION command with the SET SQL_TRACE=TRUE option sets up a trace file you will be using for the TKPROF utility. The SQL trace facility will record all the SQL statements issued and provide statistics such as the CPU and elapsed time, the number of rows processed, and the number of physical and logical reads, until you set SQL_TRACE equal to FALSE. The trace file will be written to the USER_DUMP_DEST directory.

c) Execute the following SQL statements. What feedback do you receive when you issue the last SQL statement?

```
SELECT 'DONALD '||
       TO_CHAR(SYSDATE, 'MM/DD HH24:MI')
   FROM DUAL;
```

```
SELECT student_id
  FROM student
 WHERE last_name LIKE 'Rodri%';

SELECT student_id
  FROM student
 WHERE last_name LIKE '%odri%';


ALTER SESSION SET SQL_TRACE=FALSE;
```

Answer: The ALTER SESSION command responds with the feedback message SESSION ALTERED.

The tracing of SQL statements is now stopped. The ALTER SESSION command with the SET SQL_TRACE option enables or disables tracing for your session only. You can enable the tracing of all sessions in the Instance by setting the SQL_TRACE initialization parameter in the init.ora file equal to TRUE. To trace a session other than your own, you can use one of Oracle's built-in packages called DBMS_SYSTEM.SET_SQL_TRACE_IN_SESSION. This is useful if you need to trace the statements generated by an application, without enabling the tracing of the entire Instance or modifying the application to issue the ALTER SESSION command.

d) Identify your trace file in the USER_DUMP_DEST directory. You can either do this by listing the files by date and time or by searching through the files where the file contains the string 'DONALD.' This illustrates the usefulness of tagging a file with an identifier and the date and time. You can search for the file with this identifier using the Find utility if you are using the Windows NT operating system or by using the grep command on the UNIX operating system. Write down your filename.

Answer: The filename will vary for each session.

Typically the filename begins with the letters ora and ends with a .trc extension, e.g., ora00125.trc.

e) Run the TKPROF utility at your operating system prompt. The simplified syntax is as follows:

```
C:\>tkprof <trace_file> <formatted_output_file>
explain=schema/password sys=no
```

In an NT environment, the command you execute may look similar to the following:

```
C:\>tkprof c:\oracle\admin\db00\udump\ora00125.trc
c:\guest\ora00125.txt explain=student/learn sys=no
```

Note that the name of the TKPROF executable program can vary depending on the Oracle version and operating system. If the TKPROF executable program is not in your path, then prefix the program with the path and drive name. You also may not have permission to write to the USER_DUMP_DEST directory, and therefore you need to store the formatted output file elsewhere. In the previous example, it is stored in the c:\guest directory. Add the optional parameter SYS=NO to avoid showing Oracle Server-generated SQL statements. Record the command you execute to run TKPROF.

Answer: The answer varies depending on your operating system, the destination of your udump directory, the trace file name, and the name you give to your formatted trace file.

The TKPROF program is executed at the operating system prompt. If the executable is not in your path, prefix TKPROF with the name of the drive and directory where it is found. Next, specify the location and name of the trace file. Finally, specify the directory and filename for the formatted file TKPROF creates.

TKPROF also has several optional parameters, some of which are discussed in this exercise. For example, you can instruct TKPROF to sort the SQL statements in the formatted output file by many different criteria. This is particularly useful if you are collecting many SQL statements. If you want to sort the statement by the statement that had the longest elapsed time, you can use the parameters PRSELA (elapsed time spent parsing), EXEELA (elapsed time spent executing), and FCHELA (elapsed time spent fetching).

```
C:\>tkprof c:\oracle\admin\db00\udump\ora00125.trc
c:\guest\ora00125.txt explain=student/learn sort=(prsela,
exeela, fchela) sys=no
```

When you issue the TKPROF statement with the EXPLAIN parameter, an execution plan is generated. The SYS = NO parameter eliminates from the resulting trace file any internal SQL statements issued by the Oracle Server to execute your statement.

f) Use your text editor to view the formatted trace file. Determine if the statements issued against the STUDENT table used the index on the LAST_NAME column.

Answer: The SELECT statement with the % wildcard at the beginning of the text literal did not use the index. This result is in contrast to the result received from the statement that uses a text literal as the leading string.

The TKPROF program transforms the trace binary file into a readable text file. You can use your editor to view the file. Your TKPROF file may vary from the result shown here.

The formatted trace file can be divided into a header, body, and summary. The body lists the individual statements executed, along with the execution plan. In addition, it shows statistics in tabular format. These statistics show you how long it takes to parse, execute, and fetch each individual SQL statement and how many rows are processed during each step.

The parsing of an SQL statement is the process the Oracle Server performs to validate the syntax of your statement and to check if you are authorized to perform this action. The execute step identifies the rows in a SELECT statement. In case of a DML statement, it modifies the rows. The fetch step retrieves the rows; this step is only applicable in SELECT statements.

Furthermore, you see that the SQL statement with the LIKE operator and text literal 'Rodri%' used an index, while the statement with the text literal '%odri%' did not. The execution plan also shows how many rows are processed during each step. You can use this information to determine which steps require tuning of your statement.

The following output is a partial listing of the formatted TKPROF result; it does not show the ALTER SESSION statement, the SELECT statement that creates the name tag (in the example, it's the name, DONALD), and the date and time.

```
*******************************************************************
SELECT student_id
  FROM student
 WHERE last_name LIKE 'Rodri%'
```

call	count	cpu	elapsed	disk	query	current	rows
Parse	1	0.01	0.03	0	0	0	0
Execute	1	0.00	0.00	0	0	0	0
Fetch	1	0.00	0.01	1	2	0	0
total	3	0.01	0.04	1	2	0	0

```
Misses in library cache during parse: 1
Optimizer goal: CHOOSE
Parsing user id: 54   (STUDENT)


Rows     Row Source Operation
-------- -------------------------------------------------
      0  TABLE ACCESS BY INDEX ROWID STUDENT
      1    INDEX RANGE SCAN (object id 12961)
```

```
Rows        Execution Plan
--------    ----------------------------------------------------------------
      0     SELECT STATEMENT    GOAL: CHOOSE
      0      TABLE ACCESS    GOAL: ANALYZED (BY INDEX ROWID) OF 'STUDENT'
      1        INDEX    GOAL: ANALYZED (RANGE SCAN) OF 'STU_I_LAST_NAME
                  (NON-UNIQUE)


**********************************************************************


SELECT student_id
  FROM student
 WHERE last_name LIKE '%odri%'
```

call	count	cpu	elapsed	disk	query	current	rows
Parse	1	0.00	0.03	0	0	0	0
Execute	1	0.00	0.00	0	0	0	0
Fetch	1	0.00	0.03	0	24	4	0
total	3	0.00	0.06	0	24	4	0

```
Misses in library cache during parse: 1
Optimizer goal: CHOOSE
Parsing user id: 54   (STUDENT)

Rows        Row Source Operation
--------    -----------------------------------------------
      0     TABLE ACCESS FULL STUDENT


Rows        Execution Plan
--------    -----------------------------------------------
      0     SELECT STATEMENT    GOAL: CHOOSE
      0      TABLE ACCESS    GOAL: ANALYZED (FULL) OF 'STUDENT'
*********************************************************************
```

The header of your TKPROF output may look similar to the following listing. It lists the TKPROF version, the day the file was formatted, and the name of the trace file and sort options used. It also describes the individual columns shown in the tabular statistics.

```
TKPROF: Release 8.1.5.0.0 - Production on Sun May 7 12:24:16 2000

(c) Copyright 1999 Oracle Corporation.  All rights reserved.

Trace file: ora00125.trc
Sort options: default


******************************************************************
```

```
count      = number of times OCI procedure was executed
cpu        = cpu time in seconds executing
elapsed    = elapsed time in seconds executing
disk       = number of physical reads of buffers from disk
query      = number of buffers gotten for consistent read
current    = number of buffers gotten in current mode (usually for
             update)
rows       = number of rows processed by the fetch or execute call
*************************************************************************
```

The following is the end of the TKPROF output file. It shows all the statistics in summary. It separates recursive and non-recursive SQL statements. The recursive statements are those suppressed with the SYS=NO parameter.

```
*************************************************************************

OVERALL TOTALS FOR ALL NON-RECURSIVE STATEMENTS
```

call	count	cpu	elapsed	disk	query	current	rows
Parse	4	0.01	0.10	0	0	0	0
Execute	5	0.02	0.13	0	0	0	0
Fetch	4	0.00	0.06	1	27	8	1
total	13	0.03	0.29	1	27	8	1

```
Misses in library cache during parse: 2
Misses in library cache during execute: 1


OVERALL TOTALS FOR ALL RECURSIVE STATEMENTS
```

call	count	cpu	elapsed	disk	query	current	rows
Parse	0	0.00	0.00	0	0	0	0
Execute	0	0.00	0.00	0	0	0	0
Fetch	0	0.00	0.00	0	0	0	0
total	0	0.00	0.00	0	0	0	0

```
Misses in library cache during parse: 0

    5  user SQL statements in session.
    0  internal SQL statements in session.
    5  SQL statements in session.
    3  statements EXPLAINed in this session.
*************************************************************************
```

```
Trace file: ora00125.trc
Trace file compatibility: 7.03.02
Sort options: default

    1   session in trace file.
    5   user SQL statements in trace file.
    0   internal SQL statements in trace file.
    5   SQL statements in trace file.
    5   unique SQL statements in trace file.
    3   SQL statements EXPLAINed using schema:
        STUDENT.prof$plan_table
          Default table was used.
          Table was created.
          Table was dropped.
   63   lines in trace file.
```

g) Drop the index created in Question b) to restore the schema back to its original state.

Answer: The SQL statement issued is as follows:

```
SQL> DROP INDEX stu_i_last_name;
Index dropped.
```

LAB 16.1 SELF-REVIEW QUESTIONS

To test your progress, you should be able to answer the following questions.

1) You cannot use the rule-based optimizer if the tables have been analyzed.

a) _____ True
b) _____ False

2) Indexes should never be analyzed when using the cost-based optimizer.

a) _____ True
b) _____ False

3) The order in which tables are joined can be changed using an ORDERED hint in the cost-based optimizer.

a) _____ True
b) _____ False

4) Typically, the nested loop join is most efficient when returning all the records from a table.

a) _____ True
b) _____ False

5) Statistics collected by the ANALYZE command are stored in the data dictionary.

a) _____ True
b) _____ False

Quiz answers appear in Appendix A, Lab 16.1.

CHAPTER 16

TEST YOUR THINKING

1) As user STUDENT, execute the following SQL statement using the rule-based optimizer:

```
SELECT s.student_id, s.last_name, g.grade_type_code
  FROM student s, enrollment e, grade g
 WHERE s.student_id = e.student_id
   AND e.student_id = g.student_id
   AND e.section_id = g.section_id
   AND e.section_id = 87
   AND numeric_grade = 99;
```

2) Obtain the execution plan for the statement using the AUTOTRACE command.
3) Describe the steps performed in the execution plan.
4) Obtain an execution plan using the TKPROF utility.
5) Create an index on the EMPLOYER column of the STUDENT table. Observe the statistics for the index in the USER_IND_COLUMN data dictionary view. What needs to be done for these statistics to be filled in?

CHAPTER 17

DATABASE TUNING AND OPTIMIZATION

CHAPTER OBJECTIVES

In this chapter, you will learn about:

✔ Optimizing the Use of Memory
  and Disk Resources   Page 404

Chapter 16, "Application and SQL Optimization," discusses database performance in terms of the efficiency of SQL statements. This chapter discusses performance in terms of how the Oracle Server uses memory and what can be done to reduce the number of reads from disk. This discussion provides a survey of different database tuning techniques. For a more in-depth discussion on database tuning, you may wish to refer to one of the reference manuals listed in Appendix B. An increase in performance means a decrease in the time it takes for users to be able to access data in an Oracle database.

Since the Oracle Server relies heavily on memory, one of the steps a DBA can take to optimize performance is to increase the size of the SGA. Other steps to be taken include analyzing performance statistics (e.g., finding out the ratio of successful reads from memory to those attempts which result in necessary reads from disk) and distributing disk I/O (input/output) evenly across disk drives (i.e., keeping datafiles on devices separate from redo log files, and storing tables and indexes separate from each other). Additionally, a DBA can reduce some kinds of contention for database resources by creating additional rollback segments, if necessary. Ideally, a well-tuned database keeps as much information in memory as possible. Keep in mind, however, that database tuning is only necessary if your database performance is not acceptable to your users. This means that you have to work with your users to agree upon performance guidelines.

403

LAB 17.1

OPTIMIZING THE USE OF MEMORY AND DISK RESOURCES

LAB OBJECTIVES

After this lab, you will be able to :

✔ Gather Performance Statistics
✔ Monitor and Enhance Memory Usage
✔ Determine I/O Distribution and Level of Contention
✔ Analyze Performance Statistics

LAB 17.1 EXERCISES

17.1.1 GATHER PERFORMANCE STATISTICS

As mentioned in the chapter overview, in general, one of the most effective ways to improve the performance of your database is to increase the size of your SGA. Additionally, it is just as crucial to appropriately allocate the amount of memory you have available within the SGA to the various parts of the SGA. Chapter 2, "Creating Your Database," discusses the main parts of the SGA: the Database Buffer Cache, the Redo Log Buffer, and the Shared Pool (which consists of, among other things, the Library Cache and the Data Dictionary Cache). The Database Buffer Cache contains a specific number of data block buffers. A *buffer* is simply a temporary storage area in memory for data.

To control how the memory in the SGA is used, you must manage values for the following initialization parameters: DB_BLOCK_SIZE, DB_BLOCK_BUFFERS, LOG_BUFFER, SHARED_POOL_SIZE, and (if you are using Oracle8.1.x) JAVA_POOL_SIZE. In a dedicated server configuration, for example, the size of the SGA results from the following formula:

SGA = (DB_BLOCK_SIZE   x   DB_BLOCK_BUFFERS) + LOG_BUFFER + SHARED_POOL_SIZE + JAVA_POOL_SIZE (Again, this last parameter is included as of Oracle8.1.x)

Note that although it plays a role in tuning, the value for the DB_BLOCK_SIZE parameter CANNOT be changed after database creation. If you feel that you must change the value for this parameter, then you must re-create the entire database.

To determine how much space to allocate to each part of the SGA, you can gather statistics regarding cache hits and cache misses to the SGA memory. A *cache* is a particular type of buffer. Besides providing temporary storage for data, it retains information regarding that data to avoid unnecessary extra reads from disk. A *cache hit* takes place when a user requests information that is already in the cache. For instance, a user issues a query and the result set for that query, is already residing in the Database Buffer Cache. This circumstance indicates that the query has already been issued before the current user issued his or her query, and therefore, it is not necessary for the information to be read again from the datafiles. A *cache miss* takes place when the information requested is not in the cache. In this case, the Oracle Server (dedicated server or shared-server processes as described in Chapter 3, "Oracle Networking: Configuring Basic Net8/SQL*Net Components") must read the relevant information from disk into the Database Buffer Cache. The *cache hit ratio* is the percentage of information requests that result in a cache hit. The following formula can be used to determine the cache hit ratio:

Cache Hit Ratio = (1 − (physical reads / logical reads)) * 100

In this formula, "physical reads" denotes cache misses, and "logical reads" denotes total data requests.

To begin gathering performance statistics, navigate to the directory where the Oracle-provided UTLBSTAT.SQL script resides. If you are working in a UNIX environment, you can navigate to this directory using the following path:

```
cd $ORACLE_HOME/rdbms/admin
```

If you are working in a Windows NT environment, you can navigate to this directory through Windows Explorer. For example, your directory path should look similar to the following:

```
E:\Oracle\Ora81\RDBMS\ADMIN
```

Remember from Chapter 2, "Creating your Database," that the location of this directory is Oracle Server version-dependent. In Oracle7.3.x, the location is ORACLE_HOME\Rdbms73\admin. In Oracle8.0.x, the location is ORACLE_HOME\Rdbms80\admin.

a) Open the UTLBSTAT.SQL script and view it. What do you think this script is used for?

_____

_____

If you have not already set the init.ora parameter TIMED_STATISTICS = TRUE, then you should set it now as described in Chapter 16, Lab 16.1.5.

Now, gather the beginning statistics with the following steps:

If you are working in a UNIX environment, issue the command from within SQL*Plus:

```
@$ORACLE_HOME/rdbms/admin/utlbstat
```

Alternatively, if you are working in a Windows NT environment, issue a command similar to the following:

```
@e:\oracle\ora81\rdbms\admin\utlbstat
```

b) What result do you receive after running this script?

_____

_____

This script, along with a companion script called UTLESTAT.SQL, allows you to capture the database's performance monitoring information at a particular moment in time. UTLBSTAT.SQL is run to *begin* gathering diagnostic database performance statistics, and UTLESTAT.SQL is run to *end* the gathering of these statistics.

Optimally, these two scripts should be run during peak daily processing. In other words, you will gather more useful statistics by running these scripts during peak production load and consistent transaction processing. Two typical periods in which to run the two scripts in a system in which users are normally logged on for an eight-hour workday might be from 10:00 a.m. to 12:00 p.m. and again from 2:00 p.m. to 4:30 p.m.. Running these two scripts when there are no users on the system, or running these scripts for a full 24-hour period, may give you distorted and misleading results. Usually, these two scripts cause very little overhead.

Exit Server Manager.

Statistics gathering restarts with each shutdown and startup of the database, so do not shut down your database again until you are instructed to do so.

Running the UTLBSTAT.SQL script creates beginning collection tables and views in the SYS schema. These objects will have names with the word *BEGIN* in them. The beginning statistics are selected from several dynamic performance views and stored in these objects. Remember that *dynamic performance views* primarily provide information about the current state of the database. The Oracle Server constantly updates and maintains these views with information of the changing status and/or activity of the database.

A DBA often supplements the diagnostics gathered from these two scripts by executing queries or creating scripts that access the V$ dynamic performance views, such as V$ROWCACHE, V$LIBRARYCACHE, and V$SYSSTAT. Keep in mind, though, that it is from these exact views (along with the X$ tables) that the two scripts collect their statistics to begin with.

17.1.2 MONITOR AND ENHANCE MEMORY USAGE

Monitor the Shared Pool by completing the following exercise:

Logon to SQL*Plus as user STUDENT and issue the following query:

```
SELECT *
  FROM student st, enrollment e, section se, course c,
       zipcode z, instructor i
 WHERE   st.student_id = e.student_id
   AND   e.section_id = se.section_id
   AND   se.course_no = c.course_no
   AND   se.instructor_id = i.instructor_id
```

```
        AND   st.zip = z.zip
        AND   ROWNUM = 1
   ORDER BY st.registration_date DESC, st.last_name ASC,
            st.first_name ASC;
```

Issue the statement again without the ORDER BY clause.

Now, connect as user SYSTEM and obtain the Oracle Server's numeric ID for user STUDENT by issuing the following query:

```
SELECT user_id
  FROM dba_users
 WHERE username = 'STUDENT';
```

a) What is the USER_ID for user STUDENT? Write down this value because you will need it for the next step.

_____

_____

Issue the following query to find out which statements user STUDENT has parsed in the Library Cache of the Shared Pool. **HINT:** You may want to first issue the SQL*Plus command SET PAUSE ON.

```
SELECT sql_text
  FROM v$sqlarea
 WHERE parsing_user_id = <Use the value obtained in
                          Question a)>
```

b) Write down the SQL_TEXT value that is specific to the queries you just ran.

_____

_____

Your cache hit ratio can be monitored by looking at how the various caches of the SGA are currently being used. To wisely adjust the SGA parameters, it is important to know which ratio values are acceptable per cache. Table 17.1 illustrates acceptable values for good cache hit ratios for the different caches.

Table 17.1 ■ Cache Hit ratios for the various caches

Type of Cache	Cache Hit Ratio Should Be >=
Library	90%
Data Dictionary	80%
Database Buffer	80%

Issue the following statement to find out the current cache hit ratio to the Library Cache:

```
SELECT SUM(pins) "Pins", SUM(reloads) "Reloads",
       SUM(pins) / (SUM(pins) + SUM(reloads)) * 100
       "Cache Hit Ratio"
  FROM v$librarycache;
```

c) Write down the result of this query. What is your current cache hit ratio to the Library Cache?

_____

_____

d) What do you think the V$LIBRARYCACHE columns PINS and RELOADS provide information about?

_____

_____

Compare the cache hit ratio value you receive in Question c) to the acceptable value for the Library Cache listed in Table 17.1. If the value you receive in Question c) is below the minimum value listed in Table 17.1, you will need to increase the value of the SHARED_POOL_SIZE parameter in your init.ora file.

You are merely gathering information at this point. Do not change any initialization file parameters until instructed to do so since any changes to the init.ora file require a restart of the database. You cannot restart the database until you are finished gathering statistics.

e) Based on your comparison between the answer you receive in Question c) and the corresponding value for the Library Cache in Table 17.1, will you need to do anything to increase your cache hit ratio after you have finished gathering your statistics? If so, what will you need to do?

Now, issue the following statement to find out the current cache hit ratio to the Data Dictionary Cache:

```
SELECT SUM(gets) "Gets", SUM(getmisses) "Misses",
       1 - (SUM(getmisses) / SUM(gets))
       "Cache Hit Ratio"
  FROM v$rowcache;
```

f) Write down the result of this query. What is your current cache hit ratio to the Data Dictionary Cache?

g) What do you think the V$ROWCACHE columns GETS and GETMISSES provide information about?

Compare the cache hit ratio value you receive in Question f) to the acceptable value for the Data Dictionary Cache listed in Table 17.1. If the value you receive in Question f) is below the minimum value listed in Table 17.1, you will need to increase the value of the SHARED_POOL_SIZE parameter in your init.ora file.

h) Based on your comparison between the answer you receive in Question f) and the corresponding Data Dictionary Cache value in Table 17.1, will you need to do anything to increase your cache hit ratio after you have finished gathering your statistics? If so, what will you need to do?

_____

_____

Now, issue the following statement to find out the current cache hit ratio to the Database Buffer Cache:

```
SELECT (1 - (a.value / (b.value + c.value))) * 100
       "Cache Hit Ratio"
  FROM v$sysstat a, v$sysstat b, v$sysstat c
 WHERE a.name = 'physical reads'
   AND b.name = 'db block gets'
   AND c.name = 'consistent gets';
```

i) Write down the result of this query. What is the current cache hit ratio to the Database Buffer Cache?

_____

_____

j) What do you think the various values supplied for the NAME column in the WHERE clause for the query in Question i) provide information about?

_____

_____

Compare the cache hit ratio value you receive in Question i) to the acceptable value for the Database Buffer Cache listed in Table 17.1. If the value you receive in Question i) is below the value listed in Table 17.1, you will need to increase the value of the DB_BLOCK_BUFFERS parameter in your init.ora file.

The size for the DB_BLOCK_BUFFERS parameter is specified in number of Oracle data blocks (since each buffer contains one data block), not bytes.

k) Based on your comparison between the answer you receive in Question i) and the corresponding value in Table 17.1, will you need to do anything to increase your cache hit ratio after you have finished gathering your statistics? If so, what will you need to do?

To find out both the number of sorts currently occurring and within which part(s) of the database they can be found, issue the following query:

```
SELECT name, value
  FROM v$sysstat
 WHERE name = 'sorts (memory)'
    OR name = 'sorts (disk)';
```

l) Write down the result of this query. How many sorts are currently occurring and within which areas of the database can they be found?

These values will be used to help determine the correctness of the SORT_AREA_SIZE parameter in your init.ora file.

Based on the values you receive in Question l), calculate the following value: disk sorts/memory sorts.

m) Write down the result of this calculation. Ideally, this calculation should yield a result that is less than 25% (or less than .25). Does your result meet this criterion?

If the result of this calculation is more than 25%, you will need to increase the size of the SORT_AREA_SIZE parameter in your init.ora file.

17.1.3 DETERMINE I/O DISTRIBUTION AND LEVEL OF CONTENTION

Create the following SQL*Plus script to find out how evenly (or unevenly, as the case may be) your disk I/O is spread out, and save it in your adhoc directory with the name i_o_test.sql.

```
COLUMN Name FORMAT A40 WRAP
SET PAGES 100
SELECT    name "Name", phyrds "Phys. Reads",
          phywrts "Phys. Writes",
          phyrds + phywrts "Sum"
  FROM    v$datafile df, v$filestat fs
 WHERE    df.file# = fs.file#
ORDER BY name;
```

a) After you've created the above script in your adhoc directory, execute it. What result do you receive? What do you think this result means?

_____

_____

You identify "hot" datafiles by how frequently they're accessed (relative to other datafiles), as shown by the physical read and write values in the previous query. You may find that some disks or filesystems stand out as being frequently accessed. You may then wish to spread disk I/O more evenly, by changing the location of your datafiles, changing the tablespaces in which those objects reside, and/or making use of an operating system or machine solution such as RAID (Redundant Array of Inexpensive Disks). RAID is a topic that merits its own book. Therefore, it is given only a brief mention here so that you may be aware of the possible options (and complexities) of managing your I/O distribution.

b) Using the result you receive in Question a), if you had to accomplish each of the three tasks mentioned in the above paragraph to more effectively manage your I/O distribution, how would you go about it? Your answer need only be based on the knowledge you've gained thus far.

_____

_____

Find out what your level of contention for rollback segments is (i.e., whether you are waiting too long for rollback segments) by issuing the following query:

```
SELECT a.class "Class", a.count "Count",
       SUM(b.value) "Total Requests",
       ROUND(((a.count / SUM(b.value)) * 100), 3)
       "Percent Waits"
  FROM v$waitstat a, v$sysstat b
 WHERE a.class IN ('system undo header',
                   'system undo block', 'undo header',
                   'undo block'
                   )
   AND b.name IN   ('db block gets', 'consistent gets')
 GROUP BY a.class, a.count;
```

If the result for "Percent Waits" is greater than 1% for any of the rows returned, you will need to create additional rollback segments.

> **c)** Write down the results of this query. What kind of information do you think this query provides you? Is the result for "Percent Waits" greater than 1%? If so, what will you need to do to reduce the level of contention?

_____

_____

17.1.4 ANALYZE PERFORMANCE STATISTICS

This lab section could also be titled "Stop Gathering Performance Statistics," for you will now stop gathering performance statistics and begin analyzing them. You can use the resultant statistics, along with the answers obtained for the questions in Lab Sections 17.1.2 – 17.1.3, to help you tune your database.

To stop gathering performance statistics, navigate to the directory where the Oracle-provided UTLESTAT.SQL script resides. It will be located in the same directory in which the UTLBSTAT.SQL script resides.

a) Open the UTLESTAT.SQL script and view it. Comment on what you think this script does.

_____

_____

Navigate to your adhoc directory. Log on to Server Manager in line mode as INTERNAL and run the script UTLESTAT.SQL. If you are working in a UNIX environment, issue the command:

```
@$ORACLE_HOME/rdbms/admin/utlestat
```

Alternatively, if you are working in a Windows NT environment, issue a command similar to the following:

```
@e:\oracle\ora81\rdbms\admin\utlestat
```

b) What result do you receive after running this script?

_____

_____

This script creates your *ending* and *differences* collection tables and views. The *ending* objects will have names with the word *END* in them. The ending statistics are stored in these objects. The *differences* objects store the differences between the beginning and ending statistics. Then, UTLESTAT.SQL selects information from the differences objects, formats it, and stores the output in a file the script creates called REPORT.TXT.

c) View the REPORT.TXT file. You will see that it contains database statistics – many of them similar to the ones you observed in the answers for the questions in Lab Sections 17.1.2 – 17.1.3. What other kind of information does it contain?

_____

_____

Now you can shut down your database and, using the information you gathered in the above steps, make appropriate changes, if any are required. Remember that tuning is an iterative process, so increase or decrease values for your init.ora parameters **in small increments** and track exactly what you change.

Remember also that each time you make a change to your initialization parameter file, you must restart your database to see the effect of the change. Also, be aware that the first time you issue a query after a database has been started, the caches are "cold" (empty). Therefore, if you make a change to one of your init.ora parameters and subsequently restart your database, issue a few random queries to "warm up" the caches before you issue any statistics-gathering queries (such as the types of queries you issue in Lab Sections 17.1.2 – 17.1.3). This practice should be used particularly when you have just changed an initialization parameter and would like to see if the change impacts the cache hit ratio.

LAB 17.1 EXERCISE ANSWERS

17.1.1 ANSWERS

a) Open the UTLBSTAT.SQL script and view it. What do you think this script is used for?

Answer: This script is used for gathering the beginning statistics regarding database performance (most notably, how memory and disk I/O are being used) and creating the objects and views that store those statistics.

b) What result do you receive after running this script?

Answer: After running this script, you should see that all beginning statistics tables and views are created and the beginning statistics are selected from the relevant V$ and X$ views and stored in the newly-created objects.

17.1.2 ANSWERS

a) What is the USER_ID for user STUDENT? Write down this value because you will need it for the next step.

Answer: Upon issuing this query, you should have received a result similar to the following:

```
SQL> SELECT user_id
  2    FROM dba_users
  3    WHERE username = 'STUDENT';

  USER_ID
---------
       41
```

The USER_ID for user STUDENT is 41.

b) Write down the sql_text value that is specific to the queries you just ran.

Answer: Upon issuing the query from V$SQLAREA, you should have received a result similar to the following:

```
SQL> SELECT sql_text
  2    FROM v$sqlarea
  3   WHERE parsing_user_id = 41;
```

SQL_TEXT

```
SELECT *    FROM student st, enrollment e, section se,
course c,         zipcode z, instructor i   WHER
E    st.student_id = e.student_id     AND    e.section_id =
se.section_id    AND    se.course_no = c.cou
rse_no    AND    se.instructor_id = i.instructor_id    AND
st.zip = z.zip    AND    ROWNUM = 1

SELECT *    FROM student st, enrollment e, section se, course
c,         zipcode z, instructor i   WHER
E    st.student_id = e.student_id     AND    e.section_id =
se.section_id    AND    se.course_no = c.cou
rse_no    AND    se.instructor_id = i.instructor_id    AND
st.zip = z.zip    AND    ROWNUM = 1 ORDER
 BY st.registration_date DESC, st.last_name ASC,
st.first_name ASC
```

c) Write down the result of this query. What is your current cache hit ratio to the Library Cache?

Answer: Upon issuing this query, you should have received a result similar to the following:

```
SQL> SELECT SUM(pins) "Pins", SUM(reloads) "Reloads",
  2          SUM(reloads)/(SUM(pins) + SUM(reloads))* 100
  3          "Cache Hit Ratio"
  4    FROM v$librarycache;
```

Pins	Reloads	Cache Hit Ratio
129497	10	.99922822

This example shows that the current cache hit ratio to the Library Cache is approximately 1 (100%).

d) What do you think the V$LIBRARYCACHE columns PINS and RELOADS provide information about?

Answer: The V$LIBRARYCACHE columns PINS and RELOADS provide information about reads from memory and reads from disk, respectively.

e) Based on your comparison between the answer you receive in Question c) and the corresponding value for the Library Cache in Table 17.1, will you need to do anything to increase your cache hit ratio after you have finished gathering your statistics? If so, what will you need to do?

Answer: Based on the comparison between the example answer received in Question c) and the corresponding value in Table 17.1, no further action is required to increase the cache hit ratio. If this had not been the case, then it would be necessary to increase the value for the SHARED_POOL_SIZE parameter in the init.ora file.

f) Write down the result of this query. What is your current cache hit ratio to the Data Dictionary Cache?

Answer: Upon issuing this query, you should have received a result similar to the following:

```
SQL> SELECT SUM(gets) "Gets", SUM(getmisses) "Misses",
  2           1 - (SUM(getmisses) / SUM(gets))
  3           "Cache Hit Ratio"
  4      FROM v$rowcache;

    Gets     Misses Cache Hit Ratio
--------- ---------- ---------------
   18732        505       .97304079
```

This example shows that the current cache hit ratio to the Data Dictionary Cache is 97.30%.

g) What do you think the V$ROWCACHE columns GETS and GETMISSES provide information about?

Answer: The V$ROWCACHE columns GETS and GETMISSES provide information about reads from memory and reads from disk, respectively.

h) Based on your comparison between the answer you receive in Question f) and the corresponding Data Dictionary Cache value in Table 17.1, will you need to do anything to increase your cache hit ratio after you have finished gathering your statistics? If so, what will you need to do?

Answer: Based on the comparison between the example answer received in Question f) and the corresponding value in Table 17.1, no further action is required to increase the cache hit ratio. If this had not been the case, then it would be necessary to increase the value for the SHARED_POOL_SIZE parameter in the init.ora file. Note that if the cache hit ratio is extraordinarily poor, it could show as a negative number (prompting you to increase the value of the SHARED_POOL_SIZE parameter).

i) Write down the result of this query. What is your current cache hit ratio to the Database Buffer Cache?

Answer: Upon issuing this query, you should have received a result similar to the following:

```
SQL> SELECT (1 - (a.value / (b.value + c.value))) * 100
  2          "Cache Hit Ratio"
  3     FROM v$sysstat a, v$sysstat b, v$sysstat c
  4    WHERE a.name = 'physical reads'
  5      AND b.name = 'db block gets'
  6      AND c.name = 'consistent gets';

Cache Hit Ratio
---------------
      99.154833
```

This example shows that the current cache hit ratio to the Database Buffer Cache is 99.154833%.

j) What do you think the various values supplied for the NAME column in the WHERE clause for the query in Question i) provide information about?

Answer: The various values supplied for the NAME column in the WHERE clause for the query in Question i) provide information about the following:

Physical Reads—The Oracle data blocks retrieved from the datafiles (when interpreting the statistics portion of TKPROF output, this value is known as "disk").

DB Block Gets—The Oracle data block buffers read from the Database Buffer Cache (when interpreting the statistics portion of TKPROF output, this value is known as "current"). These buffers are read in "current mode," which means that the data contained in these buffers is consistent with the data in the datafiles.

Consistent Gets—The Oracle data block buffers read for consistency from the Rollback Buffer Cache, stored in the Database Buffer Cache (when interpreting the statistics portion of TKPROF output, this value is known as "query"). These buffers contain modified data, and therefore, the data is not yet consistent with the data in the datafiles. If you have forgotten what kind of information the TKPROF utility provides, please read Chapter 16, "Application and SQL Optimization," once more.

k) Based on your comparison between the answer you receive in Question i) and the corresponding value in Table 17.1, will you need to do anything to increase your cache hit ratio after you have finished gathering your statistics? If so, what will you need to do?

Answer: Based on the comparison between the example answer received in Question i) and the corresponding value in Table 17.1, no further action is required to increase the cache hit ratio. If this had not been the case, then it would be necessary to increase the value for the DB_BLOCK_BUFFERS parameter in the init.ora file.

l) Write down the result of this query. How many sorts are currently occurring and within which areas of the database can they be found?

Answer: Upon issuing this query, you should have received a result similar to the following:

```
SQL> SELECT name, value
  2      FROM v$sysstat
  3     WHERE name = 'sorts (memory)'
  4        OR name = 'sorts (disk)';
```

NAME	VALUE
sorts (memory)	901
sorts (disk)	3

There are currently 901 sorts occurring in memory and 3 sorts occurring on disk.

m) Write down the result of this calculation. Ideally, this calculation should yield a result that is less than 25% (or less than .25). Does your result meet this criterion?

Answer: Upon performing this calculation, you should have received a result similar to the following:

disk sorts (3) / memory sorts (901) = 0.00333 (or, .33%)

This result definitely meets the specified criterion by falling well below the ideal goal of less than 25%. Ideally, it is much faster and more efficient for the Oracle Server to perform sorts in memory than on disk.

17.1.3 ANSWERS

a) After you've created the above script in your adhoc directory, execute it. What result do you receive? What do you think this result means?

Answer: Upon issuing the i_o_test.sql script, you should have received a result similar to the following:

```
SQL> @i_o_test
SQL> COLUMN name FORMAT a40 WRAP
SQL> SET PAGES 100
SQL> SELECT    name "Name", phyrds "Phys. Reads",
  2            phywrts "Phys. Writes",
  3            phyrds + phywrts "Sum"
  4    FROM    v$datafile df, v$filestat fs
  5    WHERE   df.file# = fs.file#
  6    ORDER BY name;
```

Name	Phys. Reads	Phys. Writes	Sum
E:\ORACLE\ORADATA\DB00\INDX01.DBF	4	2	6
E:\ORACLE\ORADATA\DB00\RBS01.DBF	39	181	220
E:\ORACLE\ORADATA\DB00\SYSTEM01.DBF	1797	204	2001
E:\ORACLE\ORADATA\DB00\TEMP01.DBF	50	188	238
E:\ORACLE\ORADATA\DB00\TOOLS01.DBF	4	2	6
E:\ORACLE\ORADATA\DB00\USERS01.DBF	22	2	24

```
6 rows selected.
```

If you look at the values supplied for Phys. Reads, Phys. Writes, and the sum of both of these values together, you should notice that currently, most of the database's I/O activity is taking place on the SYSTEM01.DBF datafile.

b) Using the result you receive in Question a), if you had to accomplish each of the three tasks mentioned in the above paragraph to more effectively manage your I/O distribution, how would you go about it? Your answer need only be based on the knowledge you've gained thus far.

Answer: Using the result received in Question a), if you had to accomplish each of the three tasks mentioned in the above paragraph to more effectively manage your I/O distribution, you could move datafiles to new disk locations (for instance, you could move the SYSTEM01.DBF datafile to a new disk, perhaps F: or G:). If the frequently accessed datafile could be taken offline, you could move some of its objects to a different tablespace. Oracle's IMPORT/EXPORT utilities could be used to export the objects from one tablespace and import them into another. Additionally, you could work with your systems administrator to design a strategy for evening out disk access, possibly using a RAID configuration.

c) Write down the results of this query. What kind of information do you think this query provides you? Is the result for "Percent Waits" greater than 1%? If so, what will you need to do to reduce the level of contention?

Answer: Upon issuing this query, you should have received a result similar to the following:

```
SQL> SELECT a.class "Class", a.count "Count",
  2          SUM(b.value) "Total Requests",
  3          ROUND(((a.count / SUM(b.value)) * 100), 3)
  4          "Percent Waits"
  5     FROM v$waitstat a, v$sysstat b
  6    WHERE a.class IN ('system undo header',
  7                      'system undo block',
  8                      'undo header',
  9                      'undo block'
 10                     )
 11      AND b.name IN ('db block gets',
 12                     'consistent gets')
 13    GROUP BY a.class, a.count;
```

Class	Count	Total Requests	Percent Waits
system undo block	0	132397	0
system undo header	0	132397	0
undo block	0	132397	0
undo header	0	132397	0

This query uses the relevant values related to rollback segment activity (essentially, any value from the V$WAITSTAT.CLASS column with the word "undo" in it) to find out the number of requests from the Database Buffer Cache and the Rollback Buffer Cache that result in any amount of time spent waiting to gain access to a rollback segment. The result for "Percent Waits" is not greater than 1%. It is 0%. If it had been greater than 1%, you would have had to create additional rollback segments to reduce the level of contention.

17.1.4 ANSWERS

a) Open the UTLESTAT.SQL script and view it. Comment on what you think this script does.

Answer: This script is used for gathering the ending and differences (the differences between the beginning and ending statistics) statistics, creating the objects and views that store those statistics, and selecting information from the differences objects, formatting that information, and storing it in a file called REPORT.TXT. Once it has created the REPORT.TXT file, it drops all of the beginning, ending, and differences objects and views it originally created.

b) What result do you receive after running this script?

Answer: After running this script, you should see that the REPORT.TXT file has been created and stored in your adhoc directory and all tables and views used for gathering the statistics and providing information for the creation of the REPORT.TXT file no longer exist.

c) View the REPORT.TXT file. You will see that it contains database statistics – many of them similar to the ones you observed in the answers for the questions in Lab Sections 17.1.2 – 17.1.3. What other kind of information does it contain?

Answer: Notice that the REPORT.TXT file also contains information about which initialization parameters have been changed since database creation, system-wide wait events for background processes (PMON, SMON, etc.), and the average write queue length for the dirty buffer queue, among other things.

LAB 17.1 SELF-REVIEW QUESTIONS

To test your progress, you should be able to answer the following questions.

1) Which of the following parts of the SGA should you gather statistics about to determine whether you need to increase the Shared Pool size? Check all that apply.

    a) _____ Redo Log Buffer
    b) _____ Data Dictionary Cache
    c) _____ Library Cache
    d) _____ Rollback Buffer Cache
    e) _____ Database Buffer Cache

2) Which of the following steps can be performed to tune your database? Check all that apply.

a) _____ Run the UTLBSTAT.SQL script
b) _____ Monitor your cache hit ratios
c) _____ Run the UTLESTAT.SQL script
d) _____ Adjust associated parameter settings in your init.ora file
e) _____ Try to more evenly distribute your I/O

3) The purpose of the REPORT.TXT file is to help you more effectively tune your:

a) _____ Application
b) _____ Database

4) Ideal times to gather database statistics for cache hit ratio analysis are:

a) _____ Over a holiday weekend
b) _____ From midnight to 5:00 a.m on a workday
c) _____ From 8:00 a.m. to 10:00 a.m. on a workday
d) _____ From 10:00 a.m. to 2:00 p.m. on a workday
e) _____ From 5:00 p.m. to 10:00 p.m. on a workday

Ideal times to gather database statistics for cache hit ratio analysis are ac-tually simply during peak business hours (whenever those hours may be).

5) You can more evenly distribute your physical disk I/O by performing which of the following? Check all that apply.

a) _____ Change the location of one or more datafiles
b) _____ Change the tablespace of one or more particular datafiles' objects
c) _____ Increase the value for the DB_BLOCK_BUFFERS parameter in your init.ora file
d) _____ Stripe your objects across multiple disks using RAID
e) _____ Increase the size of the SGA

6) Ideally, you should try to minimize the amount of information held in memory.

a) _____ True
b) _____ False

Quiz answers appear in Appendix A, Lab 17.1.

C H A P T E R   1 7

TEST YOUR THINKING

1) How do you suppose that application tuning and database tuning tie together? Answer in terms of what you can deduce from the database statistics (and/or application statistics, specifically the information available in TKPROF output) you gather.

2) Create a test plan for conducting database tuning. Make each step contingent on the step before it. For instance, begin with gathering statistics, then supplementing those statistics with a few ad-hoc queries of your own. Based on the analysis of the statistics and query results, state what you should do next, and so forth, explaining the necessity for each step.

A P P E N D I X   A

ANSWERS TO SELF-REVIEW QUESTIONS

CHAPTER 1

Lab 1.1 ■ Self–Review Answers

Question	Answer	Comments
1)	b	DBAs come from a varied set of technical backgrounds and paths. To start as a junior DBA, you should have already developed good SQL and PL/SQL skills. You're in an even better position if you understand the database architecture and the workings of at least one operating system.

Lab 1.2 ■ Self–Review Answers

Question	Answer	Comments
1)	b	Remember to specify the Message Type as the first parameter to the oerr command.
2)	a	To create a TAR with Oracle Support, you need to have purchased an Oracle Support package. Some products come with limited support in their trial license period.

CHAPTER 2

Lab 2.1 ■ Self–Review Answers

Question	Answer	Comments
1)	b	
2)	b	Even though you are not required to install Oracle software in an OFA-compliant manner, it is recommended that you do so. The Oracle Installer will create the directories it needs below the ORACLE_HOME location.
3)	a-2, b-4, c-3, d-1	
4)	b, d	

Lab 2.2 ■ Self–Review Answers

Question	Answer	Comments
1)	b, d	
2)	b, e, f	
3)	c	
4)	b	In Oracle8.x, there are some additional components: the Large Pool (which holds some information when the MTS—described in Chapter 3—is employed), the Keep Buffer Pool, the Recycle Buffer Pool, and the Default Buffer Pool. The last three take over space in the area that in Oracle7.3 is simply referred to as the Database Buffer Cache. The sizes of those areas are controlled by init.ora parameters. In Oracle8i, another area is added called the Java Pool.
5)	e	These processes all must run with Oracle7.x—Oracle8.x. In Oracle 7.x, the CKPT process is an optional background process. Starting with Oracle8.x, CKPT starts automatically with the Instance.
6)	c	

7)	c	TRANSACTIONAL is only available as of Oracle8i.
8)	d	
9)	a	
10)	c	The Dictionary Cache is also known as the Data Dictionary Cache.

CHAPTER 3

Lab 3.1 ■ Self–Review Answers

Question	Answer	Comments
1)	b	
2)	c	
3)	b	
4)	b	
5)	a, c	
6)	a	

Lab 3.2 ■ Self–Review Answers

Question	Answer	Comments
1)	d	
2)	b	
3)	b	
4)	b	
5)	a, b, e	You can find all of these with the command `lsnrctl help`. Issue this command and you will see that dbsnmp_status is one of the parameters.
6)	c, d	

Lab 3.3 ■ Self–Review Answers

Question	Answer	Comments
1)	c	
2)	b	
3)	b	

CHAPTER 4

Lab 4.1 ■ Self–Review Answers

Question	Answer	Comments
1)	b	
2)	a	However, if these tablespaces are shared, the data in them cannot be updated. They are read-only.
3)	c	
4)	b	
5)	a, b, c, d	
6)	a, c	

Lab 4.2 ■ Self–Review Answers

Question	Answer	Comments
1)	b	A datafile corresponds to one, and only one, tablespace.
2)	b	A user must be assigned a default tablespace and be granted permission to create objects in the database.
3)	c	
4)	d	
5)	b	
6)	b	Often this keyword is never specified, and therefore the default value, PERMANENT, is used.

CHAPTER 5

Lab 5.1 ■ Self–Review Answers

Question	Answer	Comments
1)	b	A segment is automatically created each time an object is created to support data storage for that object.
2)	b	Segments have a one-to-one relationship with a database object.
3)	b	A segment corresponds to one, and only one, table-space.
4)	b	Temporary segments store information for sorts that are too large to perform in memory (e.g., those kinds of sorts that are incurred via the ORDER BY clause in an SQL statement).
5)	a–3, b–4, c–2, d–1	

Lab 5.2 ■ Self–Review Answers

Question	Answer	Comments
1)	a	
2)	b	
3)	b	An extent corresponds to one, and only one, segment.
4)	a	
5)	c	
6)	b	

CHAPTER 6

Lab 6.1 ■ Self–Review Answers

Question	Answer	Comments
1)	b	If you want to change your block size, (an action that is rarely recommended), you will be required to re-create your entire database.
2)	b	
3)	b	The actual data contained in rows of a table is stored in the row data portion, not the header, of a data block.
4)	b	Transaction entries are typically stored in the header portion of a data block.
5)	a–2, b–5, c–1, d–3, e–4	

Lab 6.2 ■ Self–Review Answers

Question	Answer	Comments
1)	b	Only the PCTFREE parameter can be specified during a CREATE INDEX statement.
2)	a	
3)	a	Both row migration and row chaining create the necessity for at least two reads in obtaining data for one row. Row chaining can potentially create the necessity for two or more reads.
4)	c, d	
5)	a	
6)	b	If you have a table with a low number of updates, you are probably safe specifying a low PCTFREE value (for example, 5 or 10).

CHAPTER 7

Lab 7.1 ■ Self–Review Answers

Question	Answer	Comments
1)	c	
2)	a	
3)	b	

Lab 7.2 ■ Self–Review Answers

Question	Answer	Comments
1)	c	Though many of the other listed events occur AS A RESULT OF a checkpoint taking place, of the events listed, only a log switch CAUSES a checkpoint to occur.
2)	a	In versions of Oracle prior to version 8, you were required to set the init.ora parameter, CHECKPOINT_PROCESS, equal to TRUE if you wanted the CKPT background process to be invoked upon Instance startup.

CHAPTER 8

Lab 8.1 ■ Self–Review Answers

Question	Answer	Comments
1)	a	
2)	b	
3)	d	
4)	b	A dirty buffer is one that contains modified data.
5)	a	
6)	c	Dirty and Least Recently Used
7)	b	

Lab 8.2 ■ Self–Review Answers

Question	Answer	Comments
1)	b	
2)	d, e	
3)	e	

CHAPTER 9

Lab 9.1 ■ Self–Review Answers

Question	Answer	Comments
1)	b	By default, Oracle assigns SYSTEM as a user's default tablespace.
2)	c	
3)	a	
4)	b	Even though these statements will create the user and give them the system-level privileges to create objects, it does not give them a quota allocation to any of the tablespaces.
5)	f	
6)	d	

CHAPTER 10

Lab 10.1 ■ Self–Review Answers

Question	Answer	Comments
1)	d	
2)	b, c	
3)	c	
4)	a	
5)	b	

6)	b
7)	b
8)	c

Lab 10.2 ■ Self–Review Answers

Question	Answer	Comments
1)	a	
2)	d	
3)	b	
4)	b	

Lab 10.3 ■ Self–Review Answers

Question	Answer	Comments
1)	c	
2)	g	
3)	b	An expired account can only be re-enabled by a user with DBA privileges using the ALTER USER command.
4)	d	
5)	b	
6)	b	
7)	d	

CHAPTER 11

Lab 11.1 ■ Self–Review Answers

Question	Answer	Comments
1)	d	
2)	a, c, d	
3)	b	
4)	d	

CHAPTER 12

Lab 12.1 ■ Self–Review Answers

Question	Answer	Comments
1)	b	
2)	b	
3)	b	Rollback segments require a minimum of two extents.
4)	b, c, d	
5)	d	
6)	b	
7)	e	

CHAPTER 13

Lab 13.1 ■ Self–Review Answers

Question	Answer	Comments
1)	e	
2)	c	
3)	b	
4)	d	
5)	c	
6)	b	Oracle uses row-level locking.
7)	b	

CHAPTER 14

Lab 14.1 ■ Self–Review Answers

Question	Answer	Comments
1)	b, c	
2)	a, c	
3)	c	
4)	b, d	

CHAPTER 15

Lab 15.1 ■ Self–Review Answers

Question	Answer	Comments
1)	b	
2)	b	
3)	b	In this situation, you recover your Database using your most recent logical and physical backup(s), your archived redo log files, and your online redo log files.
4)	b, d	
5)	a	
6)	b	
7)	c	

CHAPTER 16

Lab 16.1 ■ Self–Review Answers

Question	Answer	Comments
1)	b	The rule-based optimizer can still be employed at the statement level if the RULE hint is issued, at the Instance level if the optimizer is set to RULE with the init.ora parameter, or at the session level if the ALTER SESSION SET OPTIMIZER_MODE=RULE; command is issued.
2)	b	The indexes need to be analyzed so that the data dictionary has the necessary statistics and the cost-based optimizer can make intelligent decisions about the SQL statements.
3)	a	
4)	b	Typically, the nested loop join is only the most efficient when a small number of returned rows is expected.
5)	a	

CHAPTER 17

Lab 17.1 ■ Self–Review Answers

Question	Answer	Comments
1)	b, c, e	
2)	a, b, c, d, e	
3)	b	
4)	d	
5)	a, b, d	
6)	b	

APPENDIX B

RECOMMENDED READING LIST

The material in this book is based on pointed discussions and strategic exercises. Since the emphasis is on acquiring the basics of Oracle database administration through a hands-on method of learning, you may wish to read additional material to deepen your understanding of the Oracle Server. Here is a list of books recommended to supplement the material in the *Oracle DBA Interactive Workbook*.

Adams, Steve. *Oracle8i Internal Services for Waits, Latches, Locks, and Memory.* Sebastopol, CA: O'Reilly & Associates, Inc., 1999.

Alomari, Ahmed. *Oracle8 & UNIX Performance Tuning.* Upper Saddle River, NJ: Prentice Hall, 1998.

Bobrowski, Steve. *Oracle8 Architecture.* Berkely, CA: Osborne/McGraw-Hill, 1998.

Devraj S., Venkat. *Oracle 24x7 Tips and Techniques.* Berkeley, CA: Osborne/McGraw-Hill, 1999.

Gennick, Jonathan, McCullough-Dieter, Carol, and Linker, Gerrit-Jan. *Oracle8i DBA Bible.* Foster City, CA: IDG Books Worldwide, 2000.

Gilly, Daniel, and the staff of O'Reilly & Associates, Inc. *UNIX in a Nutshell.* Sebastopol, CA: O'Reilly & Associates, Inc., 1999.

Koletzke, Peter, and Dorsey, Dr. Paul. *Oracle Designer Handbook—2nd Edition.* Berkeley, CA: Osborne/McGraw-Hill, 1998.

Krakovsky, Marina. *Understanding the Oracle Server.* Upper Saddle River, NJ: Prentice Hall, 1996.

Langer, Dr. Arthur M. *Analysis and Design of Information Systems* (2nd Edition of *The Art of Analysis*). New York: Springer-Verlag, 1997.

Loney, Kevin, and Theriault, Marlene. *Oracle8i DBA Handbook.* Berkely, CA: Osborne/ McGraw-Hill, 1999.

McMullen, John. *UNIX User's Interactive Workbook.* Upper Saddle River, NJ: Prentice Hall, 1999.

Morrison, Alex, and Rischert, Alice. *Oracle SQL Interactive Workbook.* Upper Saddle River, NJ: Prentice Hall, 2000.

Page, William G., Austin, David, Baird, Willard, Burke, Mathew, and Duer, Joe. *Special Edition Using Oracle8/8i.* Indianapolis, IN: Que, 1999.

Scherer, Douglas, Gaynor, William Jr., Valentinsen, Arlene, and Cursetjee, Xerxes. *Oracle8i Tips & Techniques.* Berkely, CA: Osborne/McGraw-Hill, 2000.

Stürner, Günther. *Oracle7 A User's and Developer's Guide.* London: International Thomson Publishing, 1994.

Theriault, Marlene, Carmichael, Rachel, and Viscusi, James. *Oracle DBA 101.* Berkeley, CA: Osborne/McGraw-Hill, 1999.

Also review these manuals from the online documentation provided by Oracle Corporation with the Oracle Server (the names may vary slightly from version to version):

- *Oracle Application Developer's Guide*
- *Oracle Concepts Manual*
- *Oracle Server Administrator's Guide*
- *Oracle Network Administrator's Guide*
- *Oracle SQL Language Reference*
- *Oracle Designing and Tuning for Performance*

A P P E N D I X   C

RAID SYNOPSIS

RAID (Redundant Array of Inexpensive Disks) is a technology implemented in either hardware or software that addresses the shortcomings of inexpensive random-access mass storage (i.e., the disk drive). RAID is available on many architectures and platforms and offers its benefits by building logical "volumes" from physical disk blocks. It eliminates the limitations of contiguous storage capacity beyond that of individual drives via concatenation or striping (RAID 0). For example, three 18GB disk drives can be concatenated to create a single 54GB "volume." Unlike concatenation, which allocates data in a linear fashion, striping uses interleaved allocation of disk blocks to improve performance by evenly spreading disk I/O across spindles.

RAID can also improve redundancy. Disks can be "mirrored" (RAID 1) so that data is concurrently written to the disks in the "volume," preventing system outage so long as at least one complete copy of the data remains.

RAID 0 and RAID 1 can be deployed on the same set of disks (RAID 0+1), allowing for very large, redundant volumes. RAID 5 is a technology that simultaneously offers improved performance and redundancy while requiring less raw storage space than RAID 0 and 1. It does this by maintaining parity information on the volume rather than an entire copy. In the event of a failure, the original data is recovered by using this parity data. The tradeoff for requiring fewer disks for the same amount of available storage is slower performance [than a RAID 0/1 volume, for example]. Also, unlike RAID 1, system I/O throughput is significantly impacted during data recovery.

There are many RAID variations involving the concepts of parity, striping, and mirroring (RAID 2, 3, 4, 6, 7, 10, 53, etc.), all having cost/efficiency/performance tradeoffs. RAID 0, 1, and 5, however, are by far the most commonly implemented.

Of particular note to the DBA is that most RAID scenarios introduce another layer of data caching (in addition to that performed by the operating system on a filesystem where applicable), which can have performance implications, depending on the characteristics of the database. While mirroring objects is a feature of many databases, the use of RAID allows for a single system-wide solution for redundancy, since the operating system and any other critical software must be available for the system to run. This frees the DBA from being responsible for responding to hardware failures.

Features of note that are included or integrated with RAID implementations are hot relocation, where data in a failed volume is automatically copied to a delegated "standby" disk, (disk) hot-swap capability (this is really a hardware capability although it is not useful without RAID), runtime filesystem resizing, and even more exotic items like clustering, journaled file-systems, and snapshot functionality. The importance of careful research and the judicious selection and deployment of these technologies cannot be understated.

A P P E N D I X   D

ENVIRONMENT SETTINGS TO REMEMBER

In Chapter 2, "Creating Your Database" there were some environment settings that you were instructed to set for your environment. There are some choices about how to get this done. You can set them at your command line each time you start, you can put them in a script—including the UNIX .profile file, or in NT you can set them as User Environment variables. Forgetting to set these environment variables via one of these methods will lead to some frustration, including the inability to either connect to your database or start Server Manager. Here are some of the most commonly forgotten settings and ways to more easily deal with them. Setting the environment variables to be populated automatically as discussed in this appendix should be done only after successful completion of Chapter 2. Before that time, the environment variables should be set manually at the command line.

ENVIRONMENT VARIABLES

The three environment variables specified in Chapter 2 are:

- ORACLE_HOME: the location of the Oracle program, configuration and script files
- ORACLE_SID: The name of the Oracle Instance
- PFILE: The full path to the init.ora file

Note that in some environments it may be useful to set the ORACLE_BASE environment variable as well as the above three. The Oracle installation documentation for your operating system will contain this information.

Server Manager and SQL*Plus will need to see these environment variables to operate properly. They can be set manually at the OS command line each time you logon to your Server, or they can be populated automatically.

Note that PFILE is not standard in Oracle environments. It was devised for use in a learning environment where the students each create their own databases, but keep all of their configuration files in their own directories. This eliminates the possibility of them accidentally destroying other students' work or the Oracle program files that are kept under ORACLE_HOME. In that setting, the students are not given access to ORACLE_HOME/dbs, and therefore cannot use the default directory and pfile naming convention - ORACLE_HOME/dbs/init<SID>.ora. So, remember that every time you start your database, the location of the init.ora file will need to be specified - as instructed in Chapter 2. If you use the PFILE environment variable, you can specify it at database startup time instead of typing the full path to the init.ora file. The difference can be seen in the following two NT samples:

- Startup without the PFILE environment variable

  ```
  startup pfile=e:\oracle\admin\db00\pfile\init.ora
  ```
- Startup with the PFILE environment variable

  ```
  startup pfile=%PFILE%
  ```

IN UNIX

The ORACLE_HOME, ORACLE_SID and PFILE parameters can be set at the command line each time you connect to your machine. Alternatively, you can include them in your .profile file. Setting these environment variables in your .profile file will automatically make them available to Server Manager and SQL*Plus. An example of the lines you add to your .profile file in kornshell is:

```
export ORACLE_HOME=/u01/app/oracle/product/8.1.6
export ORACLE_SID=db00
export PFILE=/u02/home/cocomo/admin/db00/pfile/init.ora
```

Once you have added these lines to your .profile file, you should either run the .profile file as a script, or log out and then back in to your UNIX session so that you pick up the changes.

FOR INSTRUCTORS

An alternate way to deal with the PFILE issue is to prepare your environment by creating init<SID>.ora files for each database that the students will create on your system, and include an ifile parameter in each initialization parameter file that points to the students' individual pfiles. The students could then edit their local init.ora files, and the Instance would find the initialization parameter file via the ifile parameter. For example, if there are fifty students that each create their own database on your machine (db00-db49), you could include the three export commands shown above in their .profile file, or you could include just ORACLE_HOME and ORACLE_SID. In association with setting only those two variables, you would pre-create fifty init<SID>.ora files in ORACLE_HOME/dbs. The file ORACLE_HOME/dbs/initdb00.ora would include one line similar to:

```
ifile=/u02/home/cocomo/admin/db00/pfile/init.ora
```

The file ORACLE_HOME/dbs/initdb01.ora would include a line similar to:

```
ifile=/u02/home/harry/admin/db01/pfile/init.ora
```

There is a similar issue with the configuration files for Net8. If you want each of those students to create their own listeners, you will not only need to make sure that each student gives their listener a unique name, but also that they set a TNS_ADMIN environment variable to point to their local tnsnames.ora and listener.ora files. Giving the students their own local directories in which to keep their copies of these files negates the need to give them access to the ORACLE_HOME/network directory. At the CTA program, each student names their listener LSNR_<SID>. So, the student managing Instance db00 creates a listener named LSNR_DB00 while the student managing Instance db01 creates a listener named LSNR_DB01.

With slight alteration, we have used this method to run three sections (all meeting on different evenings) of the Introduction to DBA class on the same machine with fifty students. The machine is a Pentium with 512Mb of RAM and runs the Intel Solaris operating system. The one main change to the convention shown above is that the home directories are more generically named. As an instructor, you will need to devise a method that works for your environment.

WINDOWS NT

In NT, you have the choice to set these environment variables manually or automatically. To populate them manually, you set them at the command line each time you open an MS-DOS session. As instructed in Chapter 2, you would issue commands similar to:

```
set ORACLE_HOME=e:\oracle\ora81
set ORACLE_SID=db00
set PFILE=e:\oracle\admin\db00\pfile\init.ora
```

Instead of setting the environment variables every time you open an MS-DOS session you can set them in your NT User Environment. The instructions for this are shown below. Note that setting the environment variables this way is only appropriate for a machine that is used to support only the database for this book's exercises. After you have completed the exercises in this book, you should remove the environment variables and investigate how these variables can be set as key values in the NT Registry. The method for this varies greatly between Oracle versions so you will need to consult your Oracle documentation. At that point, you may wish to create a "Clean Environment" as described in the Oracle8i release notes. This essentially wipes your NT environment clean of all things Oracle, so that you start again with a new installation that is not customized for this book. You will then most likely want to install the Oracle software with a default Oracle database.

In Windows NT, you set the User Environment Variables by navigating to the NT Control Panel and double-clicking on the System icon (Start->Settings->Control Panel->System). In the System Properties dialog select the **Environment** tab. Two windowpanes will be shown; the bottom one is for User Environment Variables. Click once inside that pane. In the **Variable:** field enter the name of the environment variable (ORACLE_HOME, ORACLE_SID, or PFILE). Then enter the value for the variable in the **Value:** field. To keep the entry, click on the **Set** button. When you have done this for each of the environment variables, click the **Apply** button and then click the **OK** button.

In Windows 2000, you set the User Environment Variables by navigating to the Control Panel and double-clicking on the System icon (Start->Settings->Control Panel->System). In the System Properties dialog select the **Advanced** tab and then click on the **Environment Variables** button. Two windowpanes will be shown; the top one is for User Environment Variables. Click once inside that pane and click the **New** button. A New User Variable dialog will appear. In the **Variable** field, enter the name of the environment variable (ORACLE_HOME, ORACLE_SID, or PFILE). Then enter the value for the variable in the **Variable Value:** field. To keep the entry, click the **OK** button. When you have done this for each of the environment variables, click the **OK** button in the New User Variable dialog, then click the **OK** button in the **System Properties** dialog.

To make the changes effective, if you are not in the middle of a chapter's exercises, log out and log back in to NT. Otherwise wait until you've completed the chapter's exercises to re-login.

Note that if you choose to set the environment variables each time you open an MS-DOS window for Oracle database work, you will need to do all of your SQL*Plus and Server Manager work in character mode from within that MS-DOS window. If you make the settings in your User Environment, you can use the SQL*Plus GUI tool to perform exercises that require SQL*Plus.

As stated above, the PFILE environment variable is not standard for Oracle environments. After completing Chapter 2, you can make your environment conform to Oracle's handling of the Optimal Flexible Architecture PFILE location by not adding a PFILE environment variable to your user environment, but instead adding an init<SID>.ora file in the ORACLE_HOME/database directory. That file will have one parameter (ifile) that will point to your init.ora file. Using the db00 Instance as an example you would:

1) Create a text file:

```
e:\oracle\ora81\database\initdb00.ora
```

2) Add one line to the file and save it.

```
ifile=e:\oracle\admin\db00\pfile\init.ora
```

The next time you start your database you will not need to provide a pfile parameter. At the Server Manager prompt, instead of typing:

```
startup pfile=%PFILE%
```

or

```
startup pfile=e:\oracle\admin\db00\pfile\init.ora
```

you can simply enter:

```
startup
```

 If you have trouble with any of these methods of automatically setting your environment variables (UNIX or NT), you can simply undo whatever steps you completed from this appendix and continue to set them manually.

INDEX

A

ACCOUNT UNLOCK clause, ALTER USER
command, 249
Activated rollback segments, 284
Active status, transactions, 273
Active tablespaces, 89
admin directory:
    absolute path of, 22
    identifying/configuring, 19–20
alert*DatabaseName*.log, 31
Alert log, 50
ALL_ROWS hint, 387
ALTER DATABASE command, 191–92, 196
    RESIZE parameter, 192
Alternative SQL statements, 391–92
ALTER ROLLBACK SEGEMENT statement,
    291
ALTER SESSION command, 393–94, 396
ALTER SYSTEM SWITCH LOGFILE, 175–76
ALTERTABLESPACE command, 116–17, 125
    COALESCE clause of, 116
ALTER USER command, ACCOUNT
    UNLOCK clause, 249
ANALYZE command, 368
Application and SQL optimization,
    365–401
ARCH (ARCn for Oracle 8i), 352
ARCHIVELOG LOG LIST command,
    334–35, 337–40, 349–50, 352–53
ARCHIVELOG mode, 328–64
AUDIT_ACTIONS data dictionary view, 259
AUDIT_FILE_DEST, 258–59
Auditing, 251–69
    AUDIT_ACTIONS data dictionary view,
        259
    audit database actions, 252–60
    AUDIT_FILE_DEST, 258–59
    audit objects, 252–60
    audit sessions, 252–60
    AUDIT_TRAIL parameter, 252–53, 258

STMT_AUDIT_OPTION_MAP data
    dictionary view, 259
AUDIT SYSTEM privilege, 254
AUDIT_TRAIL parameter, 252–53, 258
AUTOEXTEND option, ALTER DATABASE
    command, 193
Automatic archiving, 334
AUTOTRACE utility, 366–401
    options to display execution plan, 382
    setting up, 373–74

B

background_dump_dest parameter, 49
Backup:
    ARCHIVELOG LOG LIST command,
        334–35, 337–40, 349–50, 352–53
    ARCHIVELOG mode, 328–64
    automatic archiving, 334
    cold backup, 329
    complete offline recovery, performing,
        341–44
    complete online recovery, performing,
        344–47
    control files, backing up, 331
    Export (EXP) utility, 312–15, 317–19
        complete export, 314
        cumulative export, 314
        full export mode, 314
        incremental export, 314
        parameter options for, 313
        table export mode, 314
        user export mode, 314
    hot backup, 329
    Import (IMP) utility, 315–17, 319–23
    instance failure, 328–29
    logical, 312–26
    manual archiving, 334
    media failure, simulating, 338–41
    offline backup, 329

Backup (*cont.*)
  online backup, 329
  physical, 327–64
    performing, 329–38
  PMON (Process Monitor) background
    process, 328
  SMON (System Monitor) background
    process, 329–30
Before-image information of data, and roll-
    back segments, 271
Block-level locking, 299–300
Block-level storage parameters, 145–56
  defined, 145–46
  free lists, 151–52, 154
  FREELISTS parameter, 152, 155
  INITRANS parameter, 147, 152, 153
  MAXTRANS parameter, 147–48,
    152–53
  PCTFREE parameter, 146, 150, 151, 152,
    154
  PCTUSED parameter, 146, 151, 152
  row chaining, 150, 154
  row migration, 149, 153–54
Blocks:
  defined, 130–34
  See also Data blocks
Buffers, 404

C

Cache hit, 404
Cache hit ratio, 404, 408–9
Cache miss, 404
Caches, 404, 408
CASCADE keyword, DROP USER statement,
    206
catalog.sql script, 53
Chaining, 136
Chaining address, 136, 143
Checkpoints, 172–74
CHOOSE hint, 387
CKPT background process, 172–74
Client database application, 89
Cluster index, 136, 142
Cold backup, 329
Column value with long or raw data type,
    136, 143
COMMIT statement, 273, 297, 305, 329
Commit status, transactions, 273
Complete export, 314
Complete offline recovery, performing,
    341–44

Complete online recovery, performing,
    344–47
Concurrent transactions, 297
CONNECT privilege, 204
CONNECT_TIME, 238
Control files, 25–26, 49
  backing up, 331
core_dump_dest parameter, 49
Cost-based optimizer, 366
CPU_PER_SESSION, 238
CREATE DATABASE statement, 34, 42, 51
createdb00 _01.sql, 34, 42
createdb00 _02.sql, 36–38, 53
CREATE INDEX statement, 393
CREATE PROFILE command, 239
CREATE PROFILE system privilege, 239
CREATE ROLLBACK SEGMENT statement,
    282, 290–91
Create scripts:
  and database, 34–39
  and NT, 40
CREATE SESSION privilege, 204
CREATE TABLESPACE command, 92–93,
    96–98
  DATAFILE keyword, 96
  INITIAL keyword, 98
  MAXEXTENTS/MAXEXTENTS
    UNLIMITED option, 98
  MINEXTENTS option, 98
  PCTINCREASE parameter, 98
  PERMANENT keyword, 93, 99
  TEMPORARY keyword, 93, 99
CREATE TABLE statement, 131–32
  with segment storage parameters
    specified, 121
Cumulative export, 314
Customer Support Identification (CSI)
    number, 6, 9, 10

D

Data backups, *See* Backup; Recovery
Database:
  creating, 15–56
  Optimal Flexible Architecture (OFA), ba-
    sics of, 16–24
Database Buffer Cache, 25, 329, 404–5,
    411, 419
Database file location:
  absolute path to, 23
  identifying, 20–21
Database installation, version of, 49

Database tuning/optimization, 403–25
  I/O distribution, determining, 413–14
  level of contention, determining,
    413–14
  memory usage, monitoring/enhancing,
    407–12
  performance statistics:
    analyzing, 414–16
    gathering, 404–7
Data blocks, 129–56
  block-level storage parameters, 145–56
  chaining, 136
  defined, 130–34
  and extents, 133–34, 141
  free space, 135, 141
  header, 135, 141
  parts of, 134–35, 141
  physical record format, 135–37
  record header, 142
  row data, 135, 136, 141
  row directory, 135, 136, 141
  row header, 136–37, 142
  size of, specifying, 133
  table directory, 135, 141
Data dictionary, 86
  reviewing scripts that create, 48
Data Dictionary Cache, 404, 410, 418
Datafiles, 25, 91, 179–99
  compared to tablespaces, 88
  creating, 189–93
  Database Buffer Cache, 182–84, 186–87
    dirty buffers, 183, 186–87
    free buffers, 182, 186–87
    LRU list, 183, 186
    LRUW/Dirty list, 183, 186
    pinned buffers, 183
  defined, 180–82
  deleting, 189–93
  and instances, 182–85
  manipulating, 189–99
  relationship of tablespaces to, 91–92
  size of, 186
  use of, 185
Data segments, 104, 105–6, 108–9
DBA, and roles, 230–31
DBA_DATA_FILES data dictionary view,
  191–92, 196, 332
DBA privilege, 204
DBA_ROLLBACK_SEGS data dictionary
  view, 281, 287
DBA_TABLES data dictionary view, 281
DBA_TABLESPACES data dictionary view,
  115, 122, 125, 191

DB_BLOCK_BUFFERS parameter, 411, 420
DB_BLOCK_SIZE parameter, 141
DB value, AUDIT_TRAIL parameter, 253
DBWR background process, 171–72
Deactivated rollback segments, 284
Deadlocks, 301
Dedicated server configuration, 59
Default DBA accounts, 28
DELETE operation, auditing, 256
Dictionary Cache, 25
Differences objects, 415
Dirty buffers, 183, 186–87
Dnnn, 77
Driving table, 370

E

Ending objects, 415
Exclusive locks, 299
Execution plan, 366, 368–69
  changing, 370
  hints, 370
  interpreting output of, 376–77
  obtaining, 369
Expired accounts, 241
Export (EXP) utility, 312–15, 317–19
  complete export, 314
  cumulative export, 314
  full export mode, 314
  incremental export, 314
  parameter options for, 313
  table export mode, 314
  user export mode, 314
Extents, 103, 111–27
  additional, 112
  ALTERTABLESPACE command, 116–17,
    125
    COALESCE clause of, 116
  and blocks, 133–34, 141
  data contained in, 119
  DBA_TABLESPACES data dictionary
    view, 115, 122, 125
  defined, 111–13, 119
  free extents, 116, 123
  free space, 115–18
  INITIAL parameter, 113
  MAXEXTENTS parameter, 113, 120
  MINEXTENTS parameter, 113
  NEXT parameter, 113, 120
  parameters, understanding, 113–15
  PCTINCREASE parameter, 113, 116,
    120–21

F

FAILED_LOGIN_ATTEMPTS, 238
Failures, 172
Fallback plan, 7
FALSE value, AUDIT_TRAIL parameter, 253
FIRST_ROWS hint, 387
Free buffers, 182, 186–87
Free extents, 116, 123
Free lists, 14, 151–52
FREELISTS parameter, 152, 155
Free space, data block, 135, 141
Full export mode, 314

G

GRANT statement, 220
    WITH GRANT OPTION clause, 220

H

Hash join, 372
Hash table, 372
Header, data block, 135, 141
Hints, 368, 370, 387
Hot backup, 329

I

IDLE_TIME, 238
ifile parameter, 33
Import (IMP) utility, 315–17, 319–23
Incremental export, 314
Indexes, 392
INDEX hint, 387
Index segments, 104, 105–6, 108–9
INDX tablespace, 88, 89
init.ora file, 28–34, 38
    location of, 33
    in NT, 32–33
    in UNIX, 32
INITRANS parameter, 147, 152, 153
INSERT operation, auditing, 256
Instance, 25
    configuration file, editing, 28–34
instance failures, 172, 328–29
INTERNAL, 28, 50
I/O distribution, determining, 413–14

J

Joins, 370–72
    and FIRST_ROWS and ALL_ROWS hints, 387–91
    hash join, 372
    incorrect specification of, 391
    nested loop join, 370–71
    sort-merge join, 371–72

L

Large Pool, 25
Level of contention, determining, 413–14
LGWR background process, 171–72
Library Cache, 25, 404
listener.ora file, 60
    manually configuring, 62–64
Locked accounts, 241
Locks, 295–310
    automatic locking behavior, 300
    block-level locking, 299–300
    creating, 296–304
    deadlocks, 301
    defined, 298
    elimination of, 296–304
    exclusive, 299
    lost-update problem, 297–98
    purpose of, 295
    review, 296–304
    row, 299
    shared, 299
    statements vs. transactions, 296–97
    table, 300
    use of, 298–99
LOG_ARCHIVE_DEST, 357
LOG_ARCHIVE_FORMAT, 357
Logical backup and recovery, 312–26
    See Backup; Recovery
Log Writer (LGWR) background process, 161–64, 167
Lost-update problem, 297–98
LRU list, 183, 186
LRUW/Dirty list, 183, 186

M

Manual archiving, 334
MAX_DUMP_FILE_SIZE parameter, 377, 392
MAXSIZE clause, ALTER DATABASE command, 193

MAXTRANS parameter, 147–48, 152–53
Media failures, 172, 329
  simulating, 338–41
Memory, 403
Memory usage, monitoring/enhancing, 407–12
Metadata, 86
MetaLink, 6, 10
Millsap, Cary, 16
Morrison, Alex, 392
mts_dispatchers, 77
mts_max_dispatchers, 77
mts_servers, 77
multi-threaded server configuration, 59
Multi-threaded server (MTS):
  configuring, 76–82
    Dnnn, 77
    Snnn, 76–77
  dispatcher, 77
  environment, viewing information about, 76–79
  response and request queues, 77
Multi-version consistency model, 272

N

Nested loop join, 370–71
Net8, 59
Network configuration files:
  listener.ora file, 60
    manually configuring, 62–64
  setting up, 58–66
  TNS_ADMIN directory, 60, 64
    location of, 60–62
  tnsnames.ora file, manually configuring, 58–62
New tablespaces, reasons for creating, 89
NONE value, AUDIT_TRAIL parameter, 253

O

Object privileges, 218
  revoking, 227
oerr command, 7, 11
"OFA Standard, The" (Millsap), 16
Offline backup, 329
Offline tablespaces, 89
Online backup, 329
Online tablespaces, 89
Optimal Flexible Architecture (OFA):
  admin directory, identifying/configuring, 19–20
  basics of, 16–24
  database file location, identifying, 20–21
  Oracle Base (ORACLE_BASE) location, identifying, 17–18
  ORACLE_ HOME directory, identifying, 18–19
OPTIMAL storage clause, 282
OPTIMIZER_MODE initialization parameter, 368
Oracle Base (ORACLE_BASE) location:
  absolute path of, 21
  identifying, 17–18
Oracle Database, 25–26
  control files, 25–26
  creating/configuring, 25–56
    frequently encountered errors, 43
  creating using create scripts, 39–44
  data dictionary, reviewing scripts that create, 48
  datafiles, 25
  and DBWR/LGWR background processes, 179
  ORACLE_HOME environment variable, 40
  ORACLE _SID environment variable, 39–40
  redo log files, 26
  rollback segments, 46–48
  shutdown types, 27
  startup modes, 26
  testing viability of, 44–46
  writing scripts to create, 34–39
Oracle DBA:
  Customer Support Identification (CSI) number, 6, 9, 10
  fallback plan, 7
  MetaLink, 6, 10
  oerr command, 7, 11
  online resources, 10–11
  Oracle Technet, 6, 11
  organizing the task plan, 10
  procedural DBA, tasks of, 4
  resources for, 6–8, 10–11
  role of, 2–13
    paths that lead to, 4
  Technical Assistance Request (TAR), 6–7, 9, 10–11
ORACLE_ HOME directory:
  absolute path of, 21–22
  identifying, 18–19
ORACLE_HOME environment variable, 40, 51
Oracle Installer, 27

Oracle Listener, 67–75
  commands, 67–68, 70–71
  loopback test, performing, 71
  lsnrctl show log_file, 73
  `lsnrctl stop` command, 73
  starting/stopping, 68–69
  `tnsping` command, 72
Oracle networking, 57–82
  dedicated server configuration, 59
  multi-threaded server configuration, 59
  network configuration files, setting up, 58–66
  server process, 59
Oracle Server, 295
  automatic locking behavior, 300
  and concurrent processes, 208
  database recovery, 329
  indexes, analyzing, 375–76
  Instance, 25
    configuration file, 28–34
  joins, 370–72
    and FIRST_ROWS and ALL_ROWS hints, 387–91
    hash join, 372
    nested loop join, 370–71
    sort-merge join, 371–72
  main parts to, 25
  and memory, 403
  optimizers:
    choosing, 368
    cost-based optimizer, 366
    determining optimizer mode, 374–75
    rule-based optimizer, 366, 367
  Oracle Database, 25–26
  tables, analyzing, 375–76
  and tuning of SQL statements, 365
ORACLE_SID environment variable, 39–40, 51
Oracle SQL Interactive Workbook (Morrison/Rishert), 392
Oracle Technet, 6, 11
ORDERED hint, 387
OS value, AUDIT_TRAIL parameter, 253

PASSWORD_REUSE_MAX, 237, 238, 242, 246–47
PASSWORD_REUSE_TIME, 237, 238, 242, 246
PCTFREE parameter, 146, 150, 151, 152, 154
PCTUSED parameter, 146, 151, 152
Performance statistics:
  analyzing, 414–16
  gathering, 404–7
pfile directory, absolute path of, 22
PFILE operating system environment variable:
  in NT, 35
  in UNIX, 34
Physical backup and recovery, 327–64
  performing, 329–38
Physical files, relationship of tablespaces to, 91–92
Pinned buffers, 183
Pinned clean/free buffers, 183
Pinned dirty buffers, 183
PMON (Process Monitor) background process, 328
Primary key constraint, 210
Privileges, 203–4, 217
  ADMIN OPTION, 222, 225, 227
  creating/manipulating, 218–29
  granting, 219–20
  GRANT statement, 220
    GRANT OPTION, 226
    WITH GRANT OPTION clause, 220
  object privileges, 218
    revoking, 227
  revoking, 221–22, 227
  system privileges, 218
    granting, 221
    revoking, 227
Procedural DBA, tasks of, 4
Profiles, 217
  creating/manipulating, 237–49
  defined, 237
  system and database resources, 238
Public synonyms, 233

P

Parallel server configuration, 33
Partitioned segments, 104
PASSWORD_GRACE_TIME, 238
PASSWORD_LIFE_TIME, 238, 241, 244, 246
PASSWORD_LOCK_TIME, 238, 240, 244

R

RAID, 413
RBS tablespace, 88
Record header, 142
Recovering data with redo logs, 170–78
  checkpoints, 172–74, 175

DBWR background process, 171–72
    failures, 172
    instance failures, 172
    LGWR background process, 171–72
    media failures, 172
    process, 170–74
Redo Log Buffer, 25, 404
Redo log files, 26
Redo logs, 157–78
    importance of, 158–59
    Log Writer (LGWR) background process,
        161–64, 167
    Recovering data with, 170–78
    redo entries, 158, 161
    rollback segments vs., 159
Request queues, 77
RESOURCE privilege, 204
Response queues, 77
Revoking privileges, 221–22
Rishert, Alice, 392
Roles, 203–4, 217
    creating/manipulating, 230–49
    defined, 230
    granting, 230–31
Rollback segments, 46–48, 53, 105–6,
        108–9, 271–94
    activated, 284
    ALTER ROLLBACK SEGEMENT
        statement, 291
    and before-image information of data,
        271
    configuring/maintaining, 272–83
    CREATE ROLLBACK SEGMENT
        statement, 282, 290–91
    creating, 276–83
    deactivated, 284
    defined, 271
    extension of, 274–75
    information stored in, 273–74
    management, 272–93
    redo logs vs., 159
    and snapshots, 271
    System Change Number (SCN), 271
    tail, 274
    testing, 276–83
    transaction directory, 273
    transactions, understanding, 272–73
    transaction table, 273
    undo entries, 273
    use of space, 276
ROLLBACK_SEGMENTS parameter, 283
ROLLBACK statement, 272–73, 297, 305
Rolling forward/rolling back, 329

Row chaining, 150, 154
Row data, data block, 135, 136, 141
Row directory, data block, 135, 136, 141
Row header, data block, 136–37, 142
Row locks, 299
Row migration, 149, 153–54
Rule-based optimizer, 366, 367
    ranking, 367
RULE hint, 387

S

Schemas, 87
Security domain, 217
Segments, 103, 104–10
    common types of, identifying, 105–7
    data segments, 104, 105–6, 108
    defined, 104–5, 108
    index segments, 104, 105–6, 108
    managing, 105
    parameters, understanding, 113–15
    partitioned, 104
    rollback segments, 105–6, 108
    table segments, 104, 105–6, 108
    temporary segments, 105–6, 108
SELECT operation, auditing, 256
Self-review questions, answers to, 427–38
Server Manager, 26, 34
    line mode tool, 27
    starting in line mode, 40–42
Server process, 59
SESSIONS_PER_USER, 238
SET AUTOTRACE OFF command, 382
SET AUTOTRACE ON command, 385
SET AUTOTRACE TRACEONLY EXPLAIN,
        382
SET AUTOTRACE TRACEONLY option, 382
SET TRANSACTION READ ONLY
        command, 273
Shared locks, 299
Shared Pool, 25, 404
    size of, 50
SHARED_POOL_SIZE parameter, 418–19
Shutdown types, 27
SMON background process, 170
SMON (System Monitor) background
        process, 329–30
Snapshots, and rollback segments, 271
Snapshot too old error message, 274–75
Snnn, 76–77
SORT_AREA_SIZE parameter, 412
Sort-merge join, 371–72

SQL*Plus, 27
sqlnet.ora file, 60
Startup modes, 26
STARTUP OPEN command, 341–42, 345,
    356–57, 360
Statement-level read consistency, 273
Statements, defined, 296
Statements vs. transactions, 296–97
STMT_AUDIT_OPTION_MAP data
    dictionary view, 259
svrmgrl, 26
Synonyms, for objects, 233
SYS, 28, 50
SYSTEM, 28, 50
System Change Number (SCN), 271
System Global Area (SGA), 25
System privileges, 218
    granting, 221
    revoking, 227
SYSTEM tablespace, 86

T

Table directory, data block, 135, 141
Table export mode, 314
Table locks, 300
Table segments, 104, 105–6, 108–9
Tablespaces, 83–102
    active, 89
    compared to a datafile, 88
    CREATE TABLESPACE command, 92–93,
        96–98
        DATAFILE keyword, 96
        INITIAL keyword, 98
        MAXEXTENTS/MAXEXTENTS
            UNLIMITED option, 98
        MINEXTENTS option, 98
        PCTINCREASE parameter, 98
        PERMANENT keyword, 93, 99
        TEMPORARY keyword, 93, 99
    creating, 92–95
    defined, 85–86
    deleting, 93, 95–96
    dropping, 93
    grouped data in, 87
    how data relates to, 86
    INDX tablespace, 88, 89
    as logical areas of storage, 85–90
    names, examples of, 88
    new, reasons for creating, 89
    offline, 89
    online/active, 89

RBS tablespace, 88
    relationship to physical files, 91–92, 96
    SYSTEM tablespace, 86
    TEMP tablespace, 88
    use of, 86–87
    USERS tablespace, 88, 89
Tail, 274
Technet, 6
Technical Assistance Request (TAR), 6–7, 9,
    10–11
TEMP tablespace, 88
TKPROF utility, 366, 369, 377–79, 394–98
    optional parameters, 395
    and trace binary file, 396
TNS_ADMIN directory, 60
    location of, 60–62, 64
tnsnames.ora file, 60
    manually configuring, 58–62
tnsping command, 72
TNS service names, 60–61
Transaction directory, 273
Transactions:
    concurrent, 297
    defined, 297
    statements vs., 296–97
    understanding, 272–73
Transaction table, 273
TRUE value, AUDIT_TRAIL parameter,
    253

U

Undo entries, 273
Undoing transactions, 272
UPDATE operation, auditing, 256
UPDATE statement, 305
user_dump_dest parameter, 50, 377, 379,
    392
User export mode, 314
Users:
    CONNECT privilege, 204
    CREATE SESSION privilege, 204
    creating/manipulating, 202–15
    DBA privilege, 204
    Default Tablespace option, 203
    Identified By option, 203
    options for creating, 203
    privileges, 203–4
    Profile option, 203
    Quota option, 203
    RESOURCE privilege, 204
    roles, 203–4

Temporary Tablespace option, 203
User option, 203
USERS tablespace, 88, 89, 196–97
UTLESTAT.SQL, 406–7, 414–15, 423

V

V$CONTROLFILE view, 332
V$DATABASE view, 332
V$DISPATCHER view, 79
V$LIBRARYCACHE, 407, 418
V$LOGFILE view, 332

V$ROLLNAME, 286–87
V$ROLLSTAT, 286–87
V$ROWCACHE, 407, 418
V$SESSION dynamic performance view, 304
V$SHARED_SERVER view, 80
V$SYSSTAT, 407

W

WITH GRANT OPTION clause, GRANT statement, 220

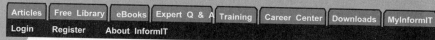